MW00586032

Recovering the Love Feast

Recovering the Love Feast

Broadening Our Eucharistic Celebrations

PAUL FIKE STUTZMAN

For Ruthann:
Thank you so much for your
kind words on the back cover.
I pray that these words will
benefit the Brethren and the
broader church in our celebrations
of the Love Feast.
      God's blessings,
       Paul Stutzman
             11/13/10

WIPF & STOCK · Eugene, Oregon

RECOVERING THE LOVE FEAST
Broadening Our Eucharistic Celebrations

Wipf & Stock
An Imprint of Wipf and Stock Publishers
199 W. 8th Ave., Suite 3
Eugene, OR 97401
www.wipfandstock.com

ISBN 13: 978-1-60899-456-4

Manufactured in the U.S.A.

For Karen

My best friend and loving wife

Contents

Foreword

Today many Christians are engaged in a recovery of worship in the context of table hospitality. More and more, people have become discontented with what seems like formula or performance in the place of spiritual depth in public worship. They long for worship in which they can freely express praise to God and at the same time know truthful intimacy and gracious, respectful love with other worshippers. In emerging small churches as well as in traditional "inherited" churches, people are drawing on a New Testament form of worship which takes place at table. It is a pleasure to welcome Paul Stutzman's fascinating work to this growing movement of recovery. Believing that his work has relevance for a wide spectrum of Christian traditions, he states his intention at both the start and the close of his book:

- the task is to explore the past in order to understand the present and chart the way forward.

- the goal of Christian worship is both to glorify God and edify the church.

Stutzman examines the Love Feast form of worship in the New Testament and proposes five disciplines, each of which has an attendant practice: submission/feetwashing, love/fellowship meal, confession/preparation for communion, reconciliation/kiss, thanksgiving/communion. Each discipline is a gift of God; each looks back and forward; each moves us toward the goal of holistic worship—the loving, reconciled body responding in thanksgiving and praise to God. I am convinced that the full-orbed Love Feast which draws the five themes together carries potential for genuine renewal.

Ranging across the New Testament Stutzman charts values present in the various Christian communities—love, reconciliation, confession, fellowship. mutual submission, thanksgiving. The young communities possess memories, tensions, and hopes, all of which they express in the disciplines and practices of their worship. No early Christian community practiced all the disciplines Stutzman outlines, but all of his five disciplines are vital to healthy New Testament Christian communal life and worship. Stutzman hopes that Christians in all traditions today will reclaim at least some of these disciplines as they attempt to embody the values of wholesome Christian communal life.

Each of the five disciplines has both an inward and an outward expression. Love within the church spills out into love for neighbor. Reconciliation and service within the fellowship flower into care for the needy and love for the enemy. Christ-motivated subordination of private desires or preferences to brothers and sisters in the church translates into respectful listening and willing mutuality among co-workers in the workplace. As John H. Yoder pointed out, the church can do first what the world will learn to do (from the Christian way) later. A healthy worship life embodies good news for the watching world.

I sense that a church which practices these five disciplines will be a community which will attract people to the gospel of Christ. It will practice vulnerable truth telling, forgiveness in grace, hard-won reconciliation, and an overall grateful and joyful spirit. All this will issue in a compelling ethos of sincerity of belief and vision, offered with laughter, shared food, conversation, hope and joy. As this church gives praise and thanks to God, the watching outsider will say, "God is truly here." Who could resist being drawn into such a house of God's love?

Stutzman's is an authentic voice from within the Church of the Brethren, a tradition which has cherished and practiced the Love Feast for three centuries. In this book he now offers the charism of Love Feast worship to the wider church.

Of course, the task is not simply to revive old ways. The church now has to discover fresh ways to embody the gospel—to live out the good news. And that requires revitalized worship, worship that both glorifies God and edifies the church. The old but made-new Love Feast has the potential to renew and reenergize worship in churches of all Christian traditions.

Eleanor Kreider

Preface

HYBRIDS ARE ALL THE rage these days. From cars to flowers to vegetables, different forms are being merged to create new products that combine the best characteristics of their original components. This book is a hybrid. It contains two parts, the first of which provides an overview of the Love Feast and its related practices throughout Christian history. The second part reflects upon this history and names five ways that celebrating the Love Feast today can help to form the church and its members. It is my belief that one part, without the other, is incomplete. Hence this hybrid. There may be some who would prefer to read a book that simply focuses on the history of the Love Feast, and others who do not care much about Love Feast history but who are passionate about celebrating the Love Feast today. Hopefully this hybrid will engage individuals in both camps. Overall, however, this book is geared toward those like me who enjoy the interplay between historical analysis and contemporary practice. I pray that these words will inform and inspire.

Many groups and individuals have contributed to the formation of this book. First, I am deeply grateful for the people in my church communities who have taught me the meaning of the Love Feast over the years. I wish to thank the members of the Dranesville Church of the Brethren (Herndon, VA), the Mill Creek Church of the Brethren (Port Republic, VA), and the Germantown Brick Church of the Brethren (Rocky Mount, VA), who have shared their food, their service, and their lives with me. I am also thankful for the library staffs at Eastern Mennonite University and Regent University who have helped to secure and deliver many resources through Interlibrary Loan. Additionally, I have benefitted greatly from the many ancient resources available online from the Christian Classics Ethereal Library (www.ccel.org). Without the contributions of these groups of people, this book could not have come together.

There are also several individuals whose assistance is appreciated greatly. Mark Thiessen Nation, my thesis advisor at Eastern Mennonite

Seminary, helped to point me toward helpful resources and gave me important feedback during the initial writing process. Nate Yoder, Director of the M.A. in Religion program at EMS, gave me helpful advice concerning both content and style. Sara Wenger Shenk and Dorothy Jean Weaver, the final two members of my thesis committee, caught several errors and highlighted some sections that needed clarification. Jeff Bach, of Elizabethtown College, directed me to several crucial texts and gave me feedback on the entire manuscript. Frank Ramirez and Reggie Mervine also read the manuscript and offered helpful suggestions. I am thankful to Eleanor Kreider for her willingness to write the foreword and for several helpful resources that she sent to me. My editor, Duncan Burns of Forthcoming Publications, has spent many hours improving the readability of the text. Jim Tedrick, Christian Amondson, and Diane Farley and Tina Campbell Owens of Wipf and Stock Publishers have been professional and helpful. These individuals have strengthened this book.

Finally, my family has been tremendously supportive to me during the writing process. My memory is fuzzy, but I believe that it was a conversation in the home of my grandparents, Emerson and Elaine Fike, that led me to choose to write my thesis on the Love Feast. I am also grateful for the conversations on the Love Feast that I have had with my cousin, Nathan Myers, who was at seminary with me. My aunt, Marcia Troyer, and my friend from church, Angela Corn, have helped me many times by watching our daughter, Kaylee, so that I could work. My wife's parents, Barry and Debbie Altice, have supported us in many ways and have helped me many times by caring for Kaylee. I thank my parents, Craig and Rhonda Stutzman, who have read over and edited the manuscript and have been generous in their financial support during the process leading to publication. There are no words that can convey my deep gratitude for my wife, Karen, and her loving patience with me as I have worked to bring this project to completion. I love you, Karen. And finally, I give thanks to God the Father, who created all things; God the Son, who redeems us and who established the Love Feast; and to God the Spirit, who empowers the church to embody submission, love, confession, reconciliation, and thanksgiving.

Paul Stutzman
Maundy Thursday
April 1, 2010
Rocky Mount, VA

1

Introduction

If I speak in the tongues of mortals and of angels, but do not
have love, I am a noisy gong or a clanging cymbal. And if I
have prophetic powers, and understand all mysteries and
all knowledge, and if I have all faith, so as to remove moun-
tains, but do not have love, I am nothing. If I give away all
my possessions, and if I hand over my body so that I may
boast, but do not have love, I gain nothing. Love is patient;
love is kind; love is not envious or boastful or arrogant or
rude. It does not insist on its own way; it is not irritable or
resentful; it does not rejoice in wrongdoing, but rejoices in
the truth. It bears all things, believes all things, hopes all
things, endures all things. . . . And now faith, hope, and love
abide, these three; and the greatest of these is love.

—1 COR 13:1–7, 13[1]

IN THE VERSES ABOVE, some of the most beautiful and powerful in
the New Testament, the Apostle Paul explains that love is a verb, and
not merely a feeling. Love is more than an emotion; it requires action!
Throughout the centuries this passage has grown in prominence in
Christian communities, although it has often taken on a context far from
its original one. Today it is frequently read during wedding ceremonies.
It has been commercialized, and is found on posters and bookmarks and
T-shirts. Since we often read only ch. 13 (or a portion of the chapter) in
public worship services, there are many people who have no clue that
the original context is the weekly evening meal and worship service of
the Corinthian church. What is needed is for this text to be presented in

---

1. Unless otherwise noted, all quotations from the Bible are from the NRSV.

the context of chs. 11–14, which make clear that love is to motivate and characterize Christian worship, which occurred in the context of a fellowship meal. In essence, although Paul does not use this specific term, he wants their meal to be a Love Feast.

What exactly was the Christian Love Feast? What role did it play in the worship of the early church? If it was important, why do many Christian groups not celebrate it today? Should we try to recover the Love Feast? How does celebrating the Love Feast help to form Christian character, both for the individual and for the church? This book attempts to answer these questions. In the following pages we explore the banqueting practices of the Greco-Roman world, the practice of the Love Feast in the early church, problems that emerged and led to the decline of the Love Feast, and the attempts made by various Christian groups to recover the Love Feast. In addition to looking at the history of the Love Feast, the second part of the book focuses on ways celebrating the Love Feast might help to broaden our eucharistic worship.

The central argument of the present book is that the Love Feast is a valuable Christian practice that should be recovered in the broader church. Recovering the Love Feast will help to broaden our eucharistic worship as it helps us to practice the disciplines of submission, love, confession, reconciliation, and thanksgiving. In other words, I believe that celebrating the Love Feast will help us to broaden our understanding of what Christian worship entails. Celebrating the Love Feast should give church members the opportunity to practice submission, love, confession, reconciliation, and thanksgiving. These five disciplines do not appear randomly, but emerge as the core disciplines of practices that were at the heart of the Love Feast in the early church: feetwashing (submission), *agape*/fellowship meal (love), examination/preparation (confession), holy kiss (reconciliation), and Eucharist/Communion (thanksgiving). Focusing on the core disciplines of the Love Feast allows for variations in practice among a wide range of Christian denominations. Thus, I articulate a broad view of the Love Feast that is not restricted to a particular set of practices, but rather incorporates a variety of practices that embody submission, love, confession, reconciliation, and thanksgiving.

Before proceeding further, let me share a few details about who I am so that you can understand my personal context and what it is that I bring to the Love Feast table. I am a white, young adult male who has grown up in the Church of the Brethren. When I was twelve I committed my life to Christ and was baptized. As a member of the Church of the Brethren, I have had many experiences celebrating the Love Feast, as the Brethren are one of a few Christian groups who celebrate the Love Feast today. In high school and college I was involved in Young Life, a non-denominational Christian ministry that helped to energize my faith and to broaden my experiences with a variety of Christians from different backgrounds. After college I worked as a youth pastor for several years and began my studies at Eastern Mennonite Seminary in Harrisonburg, Virginia. The present work is largely based on my Master's thesis, written to fulfill the graduation requirements at EMS. I am married to my wonderful spouse, Karen, and together we have a young daughter, Kaylee. I am currently a licensed minister in the Church of the Brethren and am considering several ministry options.

Having shared these few details, let me briefly chart the course of this book before we begin the journey together. Part I is focused on the history of the Love Feast in the church. Chapter 2 begins by describing the basics of banqueting in the Greco-Roman world. By learning about the general banqueting practices, as well as club banquets and Jewish banquets, we are better able to understand the context in which the Christian banquet—the Love Feast—emerged. Chapter 3 explores the New Testament scriptures that relate to and bear witness to the celebration of the Love Feast in the early church. We will focus on the scriptures that point to the fellowship meal of the church, the bread and the cup of Communion, the holy kiss, examination, and feetwashing. Chapter 4 continues by tracing these Love Feast practices into the second and third centuries and by pointing out developments in eucharistic worship. In chapter 5 we explore the decline of the Love Feast, which occurred over several centuries as a result of socioeconomic and ascetic challenges within the church, licentious practices among Gnostic groups that claimed to be Christian, and the significant changes brought about by the Constantinian shift in the fourth century. Chapter 6, the final chapter of Part I, explores the various groups that have sought to recover the Love Feast over the past several centuries, with a particular focus on the Brethren.

In Part II we shift to thinking about ways that churches today can recover aspects of the Love Feast in their worship. In particular, I believe that the celebration of the Love Feast today helps to form Christians, both individually and as communities, in five specific disciplines.[2] Chapter 7 examines the discipline of submission and the practice of feetwashing. Chapter 8 focuses on the fellowship meal as a powerful opportunity to demonstrate love to members within the church and even to strangers and enemies outside the church. Chapter 9 explores the discipline of confession and the ways that we prepare to celebrate the Eucharist. Chapter 10 explores ways that reconciliation can be an integral part of eucharistic worship today. In chapter 11 we discuss the discipline of thanksgiving and its relationship to the bread and the cup. The last chapter provides a brief summary of the importance of recovering the Love Feast for the church today.

Without further delay, let us commence the exploration of the history of the Love Feast.

---

2. For a helpful description of how our eucharistic practices form our character, see Kreider, *Communion Shapes Character*. In many ways, this current book builds upon Kreider's previous work.

PART I

The History of the Love Feast

THE HISTORY OF THE Love Feast has vital importance for how Christians celebrate it today. Too often, contemporary Christians have a poor understanding of the habits and practices that have shaped the church throughout history. In the opening essays of the *Blackwell Companion to Christian Ethics*, Stanley Hauerwas and Samuel Wells observe that with the rise of modernity came a corresponding loss of Christian habits in society at large. They argue that a primary task of the church today is to reclaim these lost communal habits:

> Protestantism, whether established or radical, "worked" because it could continue to rely on habits—habits as basic as the assumption that marriage means life-long monogamous fidelity—developed over the centuries. Once those habits are lost—and modernity names the time of the loss of Christian habits—Protestantism has often found it lacks even the resources to know how to form those that wish to be Christian.
>
> So we are brought back to the beginning, to the development of Christian ethics. Desperate to find a substitute for the habits that make us Christians, Protestants as well as many Catholics have assumed that they can think their way out of the challenges that face being Christian in modernity. Thus there has been the creation of the discipline of Christian ethics. *Yet no ethics, philosophical or theological, can ever be a substitute for what only communal habits can provide.* To be sure, some people trained in ethics may help communities see the connections between the habits that constitute their lives . . . [b]ut such connections cannot be made if the habits are no longer in place. What can be done, however, is . . . *to use the past to help us see what has been lost, in the hope that our imaginations will be renewed and begin to see what we must now do.*[1]

---

1. Hauerwas and Wells, "How the Church Managed Before There Was Ethics,"

It is important for the church to focus on communal habits rather than on the articulation of Christian ethics, per se. The aim of Part One is thus "to use the past to help us see what has been lost, in the hope that our imaginations will be renewed and begin to see what we must now do."

It should be observed at the outset that I interpret Love Feast in a broad manner. This means that our historical examination of the Love Feast not only explores the practices of the fellowship meal in the early church, but also looks at the elements associated with that meal: the ceremonial eating and drinking of the bread and the cup, the holy kiss greeting, the washing of feet patterned after Christ's example, and the examination practices that emerged in connection with the bread and the cup. Although nowhere do we have a *complete* description of an early church Love Feast, by combining the New Testament evidence and the earliest non-biblical writings it seems fairly clear that most, if not all, of these elements were a part of the earliest Love Feasts. Of course, variations in the elements of the Love Feast and the interpretation of those elements existed between churches across the Mediterranean. Finally, so as not to bore the reader with all of the minute details of Love Feast practices throughout history, the following chapters only contain the most prominent examples. For those who are inclined to study further, the two best resources remain those published in the beginning of the nineteenth century: J. F. Keating's *The Agape and the Eucharist in the Early Church* and R. Lee Cole's *Love-Feasts*.[2]

Our historical examination begins with a look at the general banqueting practices in the Greco-Roman world.

48–49 (emphasis added).

2. Keating's book is currently available to purchase from several print-on-demand publishers. To download a copy of Cole's book, which is now in public domain, or to read it online go to http://www.archive.org/details/lovefeastshistor00colerich.

2

Setting the Table

The Banquet in Antiquity

A T THE BEGINNING OF his valuable book *From Symposium to Eucharist*, Dennis Smith states, "[I]f we are to understand properly any individual instance of formalized meals in the Greco-Roman world, such as Greek philosophical banquets, or Jewish festival meals, or early Christian community meals [i.e., the Love Feast], we must first understand the larger phenomenon of the banquet as a social institution."[1] This claim is significant for our present study of the Love Feast. Smith argues persuasively that accurate knowledge of any one mealtime practice must be informed by the broader understanding of banqueting practices in Greco-Roman society. Therefore, it is important to begin this current analysis with a brief overview of the banqueting practices of the first-century Mediterranean world. The Love Feast did not just fall from heaven into the laps of the early Christians; rather, the Love Feast began as a combination of mealtime practices from the Greco-Roman world, the Jewish community, and those based on the teachings and example of Jesus Christ.

The last two decades have seen several significant advances in the scholarship on the mealtime practices of the Greco-Roman world and their relationship to the worship meals of the early church. It is crucial to note the formation in 2002 of the Seminar on Meals in the Greco-Roman World, a group of scholars within the Society of Biblical Literature.[2] Four of the members of the Seminar's Steering Committee have written ma-

1. Smith, *From Symposium to Eucharist*, 2.

2. See the seminar's web site at www.philipharland.com/meals/GrecoRomanMeals Seminar.htm.

7

jor books that are worth mentioning here briefly. Matthias Klinghardt published a substantial work in 1996 titled *Gemeinschaftsmahl und Mahlgemeinschaft: Soziologie und Liturgie Frühchristlicher Mahlfeiern* (*Communal Meal and Table Fellowship: Sociology and Liturgy of the Early Christian Eucharist*). Although I personally have not read this German work, scholars such as Smith and Taussig (see below) attest to its excellence in describing the mealtime context of the early Christian Eucharist. In 1999, Andrew McGowan published *Ascetic Eucharists: Food and Drink in Early Christian Ritual Meals*, a work which demonstrated the prevalence of bread-and-water Eucharists (as opposed to bread-and-wine Eucharists) in churches in Asia and Syria. McGowan's work helps us to understand some of the diversity of early Christian worship, and especially that the use of water in the Eucharist served not only as a rejection of wine's effect on an individual body but also a rejection of the entire Greco-Roman sacrificial system that wine represented.[3] In 2003, Dennis Smith released *From Symposium to Eucharist: The Banquet in the Early Christian World*. In this extremely informative book, Smith outlines the practices of the Greco-Roman banquet, the philosophical banquet, the sacrificial banquet, the club banquet, the Jewish banquet, and the banquet in the Christian scriptures. In 2009 Hal Taussig published *In the Beginning was the Meal: Social Experimentation and Early Christian Identity*. Taussig builds on the research of Klinghardt and Smith and proposes ways in which the early Christian meals were occasions for social experimentation and shaping Christian identity. In addition to these four important works, there are several other books and essays that have helped to broaden our knowledge of the Greco-Roman banquet context, in general, and Christian mealtime practices, in particular.[4]

The purpose of the present chapter, then, is to summarize the banqueting context of the Greco-Roman world, taking into consideration the most recent scholarship. If we fail to understand the context in which the Love Feast emerged, then our assumptions about the meaning and purpose of the Love Feast will be off-base. This chapter begins with an examination of general banqueting practices in the Greco-Roman

---

3. Penn, "Review of *Ascetic Eucharists*," 404.

4. Some works that come to mind are Harland, *Associations, Synagogues, and Congregations*; Joncas, "Tasting the Kingdom of God"; Koenig, *Feast of the World's Redemption*; Witherington III, "Making a Meal of It"; Corley, *Private Women, Public Meals*.

world. The focus then shifts to the banquets of clubs/associations in the Mediterranean. We will end our analysis with a look at banqueting in a Jewish context.[5]

A. GRECO-ROMAN BANQUETS

In his work *Table Talk*, the ancient historian Plutarch (46–120 CE) wrote: "The Romans . . . are fond of quoting a witty and sociable person who said, after a solitary meal, 'I have eaten, but not dined today,' implying that a dinner always requires friendly sociability for seasoning."[6] This differentiation between "eating" and "dining" was common in the ancient world. Thus, although people in this context ate several meals each day for sustenance, we are most concerned here with the evening meal, the banquet, which involved formalities in terms of dress, placement of guests, order of the meal, types of food offered, and expected behavior. In general, the evidence for banqueting practices reflects the customs of the upper, cultured classes, though some generalizations can be made from the data as to the practices of the lower classes. This brief summary answers the basic questions of when people ate banquets, how they ate and how they prepared to eat, where they ate, what they ate, who was present at meals, and the overall order of the banquet.

1. When Did Banquets Occur?

People in the first-century-Greco-Roman context generally ate three meals a day, although the poor and the working class likely ate less frequently. In the Homeric Greek era, breakfast was called *ariston*, the main meal eaten at midday was called *deipnon*, and the light evening meal was called *dorpos*. However, by the Classical Greek era (the sixth through fourth centuries BCE) the main meal (*deipnon*) had become the evening meal, the *ariston* had become the midday meal, and breakfast proper was called *akratisma*. Following the *deipnon* was a time of drinking and entertainment called the *symposion*. Roman meals were largely adopted and adapted from Greek culture. In early Roman practice, breakfast was called *ientaculum*, the main meal at midday called a *cena*, and the light

---

5. Those who have read extensively on the dining customs of this period may wish to jump ahead to chapter 3, where we explore the Love Feast in the New Testament scriptures. I say this as a courtesy and an acknowledgment that what I am presenting in this chapter does not add significantly to recent scholarship.

6. Quoted in Smith, *From Symposium to Eucharist*, 13.

evening meal called *vesperna*. Over time, the *cena* too was repositioned as an evening meal and a new term—*prandium*—was used to name the lunch meal. In Roman circles, the drinking party following the *cena* was a *convivium*—a term that could also be used to describe the combination of the meal and entertainment.[7]

While the breakfast and lunch meals were occasions for eating, in general, it can be understood that *banqueting* occurred in the evening during the *deipnon/symposion*. This was the occasion when participants reclined on couches to eat and talk (see below). On certain occasions, such as religious holidays, weddings, birthdays of family members or patrons, etc., the evening meal and entertainment would have been more distinguished than on ordinary occasions. In addition, banqueting was also a central part of the gatherings of various associations (*collegia*) in the Greco-Roman world (see section B).

2. Who Was Present at Banquets?

The general practice was that banqueting was reserved for men, especially when guests from outside the home were present. In fact, the dining room in Greek homes was called the *andron*, which translates to mean "men's room."[8] The main exception to this rule was for wedding banquets, in which the bride and her attendants were allowed to recline at the banquet.[9] It appears that when the *deipnon* was eaten only by members of the household, women were present at table, although they sat and did not recline.[10] By the first century BCE, however, it appears that in Roman contexts women were beginning to be allowed to participate in banquets. The Roman biographer Cornelius Nepos writes: "Many actions are seemly according to our code which the Greeks look upon as shameful. For instance, what Roman would hesitate to take his wife to a dinner party? What matron does not frequent the front rooms of her dwelling and show herself in public? But it is very different in Greece; for there a woman is not admitted to a dinner party, unless relatives only are present, and she keeps to the more retired part of the house called 'the

---

7. Ibid., 20–22. Also, see Joncas, "Tasting the Kingdom of God," 335.

8. Smith, *From Symposium to Eucharist*, 25.

9. Ibid., 40. See Lucian's *Symposium* 8.

10. Ibid., 43.

woman's apartment."[11] Larger and wealthier households had servants to prepare and serve the food. These servants may have been able to sit and eat in the dining room during a family meal, but they most often ate at a different time and in a different place than the banquet participants. It was common for a host to extend invitations, either written or oral, for guests and clients to join him for a dinner party, especially on holidays and other festive occasions. If the guest was a client to the patron host, their attendance at the meal was (almost) obligatory. There were entertainers present at banquets; musicians, dancers, actors, singers, teachers, and so on. These individuals were called upon to perform or lead discussion during the *symposion*. The most common form of entertainment was provided by a flute girl. Smith writes that since "flute girls and other entertainers were traditionally the only women allowed at a Greek symposium in the Classical period, they tended to be considered as little more than harlots, and it is likely that many [though not all] of them were."[12] Dogs were also commonly present during meals; they cleaned up the scraps that fell from the table. Uninvited guests—friends of invitees, wandering sages, latecomers, troublemakers—were also present at many meals.[13]

3. How Did People Eat and How Did People Prepare to Eat?

It was customary for men to eat while reclining on couches. A man would lie on his left side with his elbow resting on a pillow, and he would eat using his right hand.[14] In family contexts where men were reclining to eat, women, children, and servants generally sat on a mat on the floor to eat. Of course, many people of modest means did not have money to buy couches to eat on, nor the space to accommodate them in their dwelling places. Thus, these people would have regularly eaten while sitting on floor mats. Diners may have occasionally used spoons, but forks and knives had not come into use yet during meals, so diners mainly ate with

---

11. *De viris illustribus, praef.*, as quoted in Ibid.

12. Ibid., 35.

13. Taussig, *In the Beginning Was the Meal*, 82–84.

14. Since people ate with their right hands, the reference in Gal 2:9 to James and Cephas giving the right hand of fellowship (*koinonia*) to Paul and Barnabas likely refers to sharing a meal together—especially considering the chapter's mealtime context—and not a handshake. See ibid., 50.

their hands, tearing food with their fingers.[15] Because of this, before the meal began and at its conclusion, servants would bring around basins of water and towels so that diners could wash and dry their hands. During the meal, participants would wipe their hands on pieces of bread, which were thrown to the floor for the dogs to eat. Another cleansing ritual connected with the meal was feetwashing. It was customary that guests would wash their own feet, or have them washed by a servant, when they entered a house for a banquet.[16]

4. Where Did People Eat Banquets?

In general, banquets were held in larger homes or in a public dining room in a temple or inn. For those who were wealthy enough to have a larger home (*domus*), banquets were held in the *triclinium*, literally the "three couch place." The room receives its name from the typical occurrence of three dining couches, which were arranged in the shape of a "U."

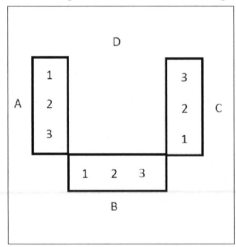

Each couch could hold three male diners, so a classic *triclinium* could hold nine male diners. Each diner would lay on his left side, freeing his right hand for eating and drinking. The feet of the diner at A1 would lay behind the diner at A2, and so on. Food was either placed on a large square table that all diners could reach, or on smaller, portable tables placed in front of individual couches. The fourth side (position D) was left open for serving food and drink and to give diners visual access to the entertainment.[17] We should recall, however, that small homes or apartments of working class and

---

15. Ramsay, *A Manual of Roman Antiquities*, 496.

16. Within his broader examination of feetwashing, John Christopher Thomas has shown that in the Greco-Roman world the majority of all feetwashing references are found in contexts where the washing occurs before a meal or banquet; see Thomas, *Footwashing in John 13*, 47–50.

17. Joncas, "Tasting the Kingdom of God," 335.

poor people did not have dining rooms.[18] In Roman cities and colonies, people who lived in the upper portions of the four- and five-story tenement buildings (*insulae*) often shared a single room, no larger than ten meters square, in which they would cook, eat, and sleep.[19] Cooking in *insulae* was often discouraged because of the risk of fire, however, so it was common for these residents to buy bread from a local baker and to eat a cold meal. People of lower class background would have had opportunities to banquet if they belonged to a trade guild or association. These clubs often held their (monthly) banquets in the dining rooms connected to almost all Hellenistic temples, or in rented space in a local inn or temple, or in a building owned by the club.[20]

5. How Were Guests Arranged in the Banquet?

In both Greek and Roman settings, where diners sat in the *triclinium* communicated social status and importance. Table A (*lectus summus*) and table B (*lectus medius*) were generally reserved for guests, while the host and his family sat at table C (*lectus imus*). Traditionally the most honored position was A1, with relative importance decreasing counter-clockwise around the table. A later custom arose for position B3 to be considered the place of highest honor. This position was called the *locus consularis* ("the place of the consul"), and would be occupied by a consul, if present.[21] On some occasions when the number of participants grew too large to fit in the *triclinium*, less honorable guests would eat in the adjoining *atrium* (courtyard).[22]

6. What Did People Eat and Drink?

Following Jan Michael Joncas's description, it is helpful to categorize nourishment as "staples," "relishes," and "drinks." Staples consisted of cereal grains, primarily wheat and barley:

18. Taussig, *In the Beginning was the Meal*, 43.

19. Jewett, "Tenement Churches and Pauline Love Feasts," 49. For a more detailed examination of *insulae*, see Packer, "Housing and Population in Imperial Ostia and Rome," 80–95.

20. Smith, *From Symposium to Eucharist*, 92, 102–4.

21. A consul may have had to sign official documents during the course of a meal and *symposion*, thus his being seated at position B3 allowed servants and messengers to approach from the right side to obtain a signature.

22. Ramsay, *A Manual of Roman Antiquities*, 518; Hays, *First Corinthians*, 196.

Wheat was the preferred staple, ground into flour and formed
into leavened or unleavened loaves, but it also appeared as a paste
("pasta"). Barley was less preferred, usually formed into biscuits
or wafers. Legumes such as lentils, chick peas, and fava beans
were sometimes ground to make flour and were sometimes dried
and cooked like vegetables. Relishes provided flavoring for the
staples. Fresh and dried fruits marked the cuisine of various
regions. Figs, dates, grapes, apples, plums, pears, quinces, and
pomegranates were known in varying proportions throughout
the Mediterranean basin. Of the vegetables, olives were probably the most important, eaten fresh, pickled, or made into oil
which served both as a cooking medium and a sauce. Other fresh
and dried vegetables included brassicas like cabbage, root vegetables like carrots, leafy greens like lettuces, and cucurbits such
as squash. Onions and garlic were probably the most common
vegetable relishes.[23]

There were several distinctions between the victuals of the wealthy and
others. First, the rich often served "soft" food that had to be delivered
quickly to the banquet and consumed immediately before it putrefied,
while the common people ate only "hard" foods, i.e., food that did not
spoil quickly.[24] Second, and related to the first, fish and meat were not
considered staples; they were rarely accessible to the poorer classes and
only occasionally eaten by the middle classes. While meat may have been
eaten more regularly by those in the upper class, because of its expense
and the difficulties associated with its preservation, it was most likely
to be eaten when many people could consume the entire animal on one
occasion (i.e., at a wedding or club banquet).

Concerning beverages, the most common drinks in the ancient
Greco-Roman culture were water and wine. Water was the normal drink
for most people, especially those living in Roman cities where aqueducts
provided access to fresh water. Basic wine was affordable for all but the
most destitute in society. Wine was almost always mixed with water,
with the president of the *symposion* (the *symposiarch*) choosing the ratio
(common proportions were five parts water to two parts wine, or three
parts water to one part wine).[25] Joncas states that

23. Joncas, "Tasting the Kingdom of God," 336–37.

24. Dupont, *Daily Life in Ancient Rome*, 276, quoted in Snyder, *Inculturation of the Jesus Tradition*, 146.

25. Joncas, "Tasting the Kingdom of God," 338. Ancient sources record a range from 20:1 water to wine all the way down to a 1:1 ratio. Margaret Visser, *The Rituals of*

the best wine (*vinum*) was reserved for the wealthy; it could be
flavored with herbs and honey. The middle classes frequently
drank an "afterwine" (*lora*) made by mixing the residue remaining after the first pressing of the grapes with water. The poorer
classes drank "wines" notable for their sour character, concoc-
tions created by mixing grape pulp with vinegar and/or salt water
as preservatives. . . . Though liquids such as milk and beer were
known, they were culturally assigned to special groups: infants in
the case of milk and barbarians in the case of beer.[26]

Perhaps the best summary of this material is that a basic meal consisted
of bread and water. Meals were then amplified to varying degrees. Wine
was commonly drunk at meals. Various relishes were eaten with the
bread. Except for the wealthiest in society, *if* meat was eaten, it was *only*
on special occasions.

7. How Did the Evening Meal Progress?

Building on the previous descriptions, we can generalize a basic pattern for Greco-Roman festive meals in the first century CE. First, the
guests would have arrived. In the Middle East, taking off one's shoes was
customary upon entering a home. "Outside the house is dirt, and leaving shoes at the door not only respect[ed] cleanliness, but also ritually
recognize[d] the sacrality of 'inside'. . . . [G]uests had their feet washed
by the host or the host's servant on arrival. Water, the great purificatory
symbol, [brought] not only physical but also ceremonial cleanliness."[27]
The host would take care to arrange the guests around the *triclinium*
according to their social standing. Before the food was served, diners
washed their hands in a basin provided by a servant. After hands were
washed, "the food was brought in by the slaves on the tables, if they were
the normal portable kind, or on trays if the tables were permanent."[28]
The meal began with the *gustatio* (hors d'oeuvres), then moved on to
the *prima mensa* (main course), and ended with the *secunda mensa*

Dinner, 249, explains that "a mixture of half water, half wine was daring, while unmixed
wine was regarded as perilous." A good *symposiarch* would adjust the ratio throughout
the *symposion*, depending on the relative inebriation of the participants.

26. Joncas, "Tasting the Kingdom of God."

27. Visser, *The Rituals of Dinner*, 110.

28. Smith, *From Symposium to Eucharist*, 28.

(dessert).[29] At the end of the *deipnon/cena*, any women who were present would leave; the *symposion* was reserved for men only (excluding entertainers).[30]

Several things happened at the transition from *deipnon* to *symposion*. A *symposiarch* (the president/emcee of the *symposion*) was chosen, either by election or by lot.[31] The *symposion* officially began with the ceremonial libation of wine made by the *symposiarch*, who would pour undiluted wine from the storage vessel into the large mixing bowl (*krater*) in the center of the room. Water was then added, in varying proportions, to dilute the wine. Hal Taussig explains that the "action of a libation generally included the *symposiarch* pouring a small bit of wine into a cup, dedicating the cup to a god, pouring some of the wine on the ground or into a fire, taking a sip of the wine, and passing the cup around to all those reclining, who also took a sip . . . [The libation was] almost always accompanied by a paean (a unison song of hymn or chantlike quality)."[32] Another variant of the libation involved individual meal participants spilling a small amount of wine from their cups onto the ground before them to signify communion with the god or hero honored by the *symposiarch*. It was common for several gods or heroes to be "toasted" by the president of the banquet. After Caesar Augustus's military victory in Egypt (30 BCE), it was ordered that all *symposia* were to include a libation to honor the emperor. This decree was impossible to

---

29. Joncas, "Tasting the Kingdom of God," 337.

30. While wives and daughters might attend the beginning of a feast in their home, they would retire when it was time for the symposium to begin. *Symposia* and *convivia* were notorious for being occasions to taste the pleasures of the palate and the pillow. Kathleen Corley, "Women Around Jesus," 513, writes: "It is clear that women who were associated with banquet settings were seen in the popular imagination as prostitutes. Certain Greco-Roman women did in fact attend dinners with their husbands, but the practice may not have been all that common, even in the associations, and its pervasiveness outside the upper classes is difficult to determine. Areas still influenced by Greek ideals and practices would also still adhere to a certain extent to the exclusion of women from some meals, and certainly from those meals characterized as *symposia*. Women who did attend such parties would have engendered a great deal of social criticism."

31. The symposiarch was not always the same at each meal, and was sometimes disputed.

32. Taussig, *In the Beginning was the Meal*, 74. In the original, the last sentence precedes the earlier sentence.

enforce, and various groups that resisted Roman occupation (including Christians) experimented with ways of omitting this libation.[33]

Following the libation, the dessert course of the meal was served (*tragēmata*). Typical desserts included cakes (sesame cakes were often served at wedding banquets), fruit, nuts (heavily salted to encourage drinking), eggs, and of course, wine.[34] After dessert was cleared, some hosts would provide perfume or scented oil for guests, as well as wreaths to wear.[35] The entertainment during the symposium could include flute-playing and other musical offerings, hymn-singing, philosophical discussions, dramatic presentations, jokes and riddles, and the playing of (drinking) games. Some *symposia* devolved into erotic and orgiastic behavior. "The conclusion of the symposium might involve burning incense for ritual purification, further prayers, and a concluding libation accompanied by a traditional hymn to the goddess of health. . . . Hand washings, shared wishes, and fond embraces marked the guests' departure at the conclusion of the symposium."[36]

Having covered the basics of the Greco-Roman banquet, let us now focus on two specific examples of banqueting: club banquets and Jewish banquets.

B. CLUB/ASSOCIATION BANQUETS

A variety of clubs/associations existed in the Greco-Roman world.[37] These clubs were organized to bring together people for several different purposes, including trade guilds, religious societies, political associations, or funerary societies.[38] Philip Harland has proposed an alternative way

---

33. See Ibid., 131–35.

34. Smith, *From Symposium to Eucharist*, 30, 40.

35. Ibid., 30.

36. Joncas, "Tasting the Kingdom of God," 339.

37. There were many terms used to name clubs in the ancient world; they can be divided by language into Greek terms (*koinon, koinonia, thiasos, orgeones, ekklesia, synogoge, eranos*); Latin terms (*collegium, secta, factio*); and Hebrew terms (*marzeach, havurah*). See Taussig, *In the Beginning was the Meal*, 219 n. 5. Often the term *collegia* was used as a broad description of associations. I will use the descriptive terms club and association interchangeably.

38. For a helpful and concise description of club banquets in the Greco-Roman world, see the chapter "The Club Banquet" in Smith, *From Symposium to Eucharist*, 87–131. Also see Harland, *Associations, Synagogues, and Congregations*; Kloppenborg and Wilson, eds., *Voluntary Associations in the Graeco-Roman World*.

of understanding the composition of associations based on "network connections associated with the household, common ethnic or geographic origins, the neighborhood, common occupational activities, and common cult (regular attendance at the temple of a given deity)."[39] Regardless of the formal purpose of the club, Dennis Smith has observed that "in virtually every case where we have documented records of club activities, we find that the banquet emerges as one of their primary reasons for gathering."[40]

Greco-Roman clubs met regularly (often monthly), and their numbers ranged from as small as ten to as large as 150. On average, their size tended to be between fifteen and fifty members.[41] Association banquets were sometimes held in the vicinity of a local temple, where dining rooms could be rented and meat could be obtained from sacrifices. Or perhaps a wealthier member of the club would host the banquet in his home.[42] Sometimes the group rented a public dining space, and some clubs grew strong enough to purchase a building for their meetings. A large number of clubs were primarily comprised of working-class members. Slaves could be leaders in such groups, as long as they had obtained permission from their master.[43] In fact, club banquets allowed for such otherwise rare social occasions as slaves and free people, men and women, dining together. Many clubs, even those not specifically organized as funerary associations, provided for the burial of their members, "since—with the weakening of family and ethnic ties and a growing impoverishment in urban settings—many people lacked the means, land, or connections for a proper burial."[44]

The associations made various arrangements for how the food for the banquet was to be provided. Wealthy patrons often provided much of the food, especially when hosting a banquet in their home. Most associations had monthly dues, which could consist of money and/or wine, and some clubs had appointed members who would pool the resources and make arrangements for the banquet food and wine.[45] We also know that

39. Harland, *Associations, Synagogues, and Congregations*, 25.
40. Smith, *From Symposium to Eucharist*, 87.
41. Taussig, *In the Beginning was the Meal*, 88–89.
42. Taussig and Nerney, *Re-Imagining Life Together in America*, 12.
43. Smith, *From Symposium to Eucharist*, 98.
44. Taussig, *In the Beginning was the Meal*, 90.
45. Smith, *From Symposium to Eucharist*, 100.

some club banquets were "pot luck" meals in which members brought food to the meal. The Greek author Xenophon, writing in the fourth century BCE, states:

> Whenever some of those who came together for supper brought a small portion of food, and others brought much, Socrates used to bid the attendant boy to put the small portion before the whole company, or to divide a part to each. They, then, who brought much could not for shame refuse to partake of that which was set before them, and, in return, to put their own food before the whole company; and since they had nothing more (to eat) than they who brought little, they ceased bringing much food.[46]

It seems likely that the banqueting problems that the Apostle Paul addresses in 1 Cor 11, over three centuries later, were problems connected with a pot luck meal, that is, some members of the church having much more to eat and drink than other members.

Dennis Smith argues persuasively that the banquet was often the central activity of clubs, regardless of their specific focus as an organization. He describes their banquets as follows:

> The meal was a symposium, a typical formal meal and drinking party, in which an emphasis was placed on luxurious dining and copious drinking. Yet *symposia* had their own rules as well. Thus the conversation accompanying them was to be proper and orderly, conducted at the direction of the *symposiarch*, and perhaps even directed to topics appropriated to community life and self-identity. The symposium included a libation at the beginning; the club banquet adapted the libation to fit its own religious piety. The symposium traditionally included entertainment, such as poetic reading or pantomimic dances. . . . The custom of assigning positions by rank at the table was a standard accompaniment of the banquet. It served as a useful function in the clubs by identifying individuals who were especially honored by the club. Yet it also was a continual source of friction among members, so that [club rules] had to be passed to keep members from trying to usurp the [higher] position of another. . . . Another way in which the meal and its customs contributed to this aspect of community life was by the awarding of different sizes of portions to members on the basis of their rank in the community. . . . So also the clubs forbade taking community disputes to public courts, but the *Iobakchoi* [club] in particular provided an opportunity to air

46. *Memorabilia*, Book 3, quoted in Cole, *Love-Feasts*, 19–20.

grievances before the community itself. Other clubs with similar references to inter-community [*sic*, intra-community?] disputes probably had similar systems for handling them.[47]

It should be noted that these clubs had similar difficulties to those that, as we see shall later, occurred in the early church, namely, the need for a leader to maintain order among participants and to guide the conversation of the symposium, the difficulties of organizing a group composed of members from many social classes, disputes over how much food and drink individuals received (or did not receive), and the challenge of dealing with group grievances in-house, rather than in the public courts.

Finally, it should be mentioned that there is strong evidence that the Roman government saw association banquets as suspicious, particularly because of the possibility that they could become occasions for organizing or carrying out sedition.[48] In 64 BCE, during the Roman civil war, the Roman Senate dissolved *collegia* they deemed to be suspicious; that is, those that "appeared to be in conflict with the public interest."[49] In the next fifteen years, two further decrees against associations were issued.[50] As Hal Taussig observes,

> [M]any associations, and even more Jewish and Christian associations in particular, experienced tension with Rome. When they gathered for a meal, they did so with a range of implicit challenges from Rome to their gathering. These challenges included— depending on the time and place—explicit bans from the emperor himself, explicit bans from the senate or provincial authorities, a range of Roman laws and edicts on who could and could not belong to associations, insistence that every meal gathering include a libation to the emperor, decisions on whether one should eat the meat at the meal in case it had been part of a sacrifice honoring the emperor or imperially connected god (for example, Apollo, Aphrodite, and Zeus), and the porous boundaries of the meal allowing imperial spies to inform on the meal activities.[51]

The restrictions on clubs in the Roman Empire continued into the reign of Emperor Trajan (98–117 CE). In 112 CE, after a fire had

47. Smith, *From Symposium to Eucharist*, 124–25.
48. See the discussion in Taussig, *In the Beginning was the Meal*, 118–25.
49. Cotter, "Collegia and Roman Law," 76.
50. Ibid.
51. Taussig, *In the Beginning was the Meal*, 122.

devastated the city of Nicomedia in Bithynia, Governor Pliny requested permission from Trajan to form an association of firefighters (*collegium fabrorum*) in order to protect the city better. The emperor was so wary of *collegia* that he rejected Pliny's request, stating:

> we must remember that it is societies like these which have been responsible for political disturbances in your province, particularly in its cities. If people assemble for a common purpose, whatever name we give them and for whatever reason, they soon turn into a political club (*hetaeria*). It is a better policy to provide the equipment necessary for dealing with fires, and to instruct property owners to make use of it, calling on the help of the crowds which collect if they find it necessary.[52]

This word *hetaeria* is the same word used by Pliny a short while later when he wrote to the emperor concerning a group of Christians that he had interrogated: "After [their pre-dawn meeting was] done, it was their custom to depart and meet together again to take food; but ordinary and harmless food [a Love Feast?]; and they said that even this had ceased after my edict was issued, by which, according to your commands, I had forbidden the existence of clubs (*hetaerias*)."[53] For our current discussion, it suffices to say that the Roman government was often wary of associations, and that it appears that the Christians brought before Pliny were understood as a religious club/association.

Having given brief attention to banquets in Greco-Roman clubs, let us now turn our focus to banquets in the Jewish context.

C. JEWISH BANQUETS

Banquets in the Jewish world shared much in common with general banqueting practices in the Greco-Roman world, although there are several noteworthy distinctions. A central element of Jewish worship and living was the holiness code, which entailed dietary restrictions that distinguished the menu of Jewish banquets from those in the wider context. In addition, the cultural practice of making sacrifices of meat and/or wine to Greco-Roman gods placed further restrictions on observant Jews, that is, foodstuffs that normally would have been ritually clean could become

---

52. Pliny *Epistulae* 10.34 (LCL), quoted in Wilken, *The Christians as the Romans Saw Them*, 12–13.

53. Fremantle, ed. *Treasury of Early Christianity*, 254.

unclean due to their connection to pagan cultic practices. Another aspect of Jewish banqueting relevant to our current topic is the celebration of the Passover Feast, since the synoptic Gospels all record that the Last Supper was a Passover meal. Finally, the custom of the messianic or eschatological banquet developed within Judaism, which also is significant to the current study of the Christian Love Feast.

1. The Festive Banquet

The overall structure of the Jewish banquet mirrored the banqueting form of the broader culture. This is evident as early as the eighth century BCE in the writings of the prophet Amos, who condemns self-indulgence among the Israelites:

> Alas for those who lie on beds of ivory,
> and lounge on their couches,
> and eat lambs from the flock,
> and calves from the stall;
> who sing idle songs to the sound of the harp,
> and like David improvise on instruments of music;
> who drink wine from bowls,
> and anoint themselves with the finest oils,
> but are not grieved over the ruin of Joseph!
> Therefore they shall now be the first to go into exile,
> and the revelry of the loungers shall pass away. (Amos 6:4–7)

Notice that the diners are on couches, that they sing songs during the banquet, that they drink wine from bowls, and that they anoint themselves with (scented) oils—all of which were elements of the Greco-Roman banquet. Even though the point of the passage is that the Israelites should avoid such extravagance, nevertheless it seems to be the case that some people in their midst were dining in such fashion.

Further evidence of Jewish banquets having similar characteristics to the broader societal practices is found in the book of Sirach, which was written by the sage Jesus son of Sirach (Ben Sira) in Jerusalem sometime between 200 and 180 BCE.[54] The book is chiefly an instruction in the rules of ethical living written by one who trained young men in upper-class Jewish society. In Sir 32:1–2 we read: "If they make you master of the feast (*symposiarch*), do not exalt yourself; be among them as one of their number. Take care of them first and then sit down; when

---

54. Smith, *From Symposium to Eucharist*, 134–35.

you have fulfilled all your duties, take your place [on the couch], so that you may be merry along with them and receive a wreath for your excellent leadership." Here we see that the Jews of the day were accustomed to picking a *symposiarch* to lead the banquet. Ben Sira gives the instruction that a good *symposiarch* does not act with pride, but rather is meticulous in taking care of the needs of the diners before he reclines in the place of honor. In the preceding chapter Ben Sira writes: "Wine drunk at the proper time and in moderation is rejoicing of heart and gladness of soul. Wine drunk to excess leads to bitterness of spirit, to quarrels and stumbling" (Sir 31:28–29). Here the sage instructs his reader (and listeners) that drinking wine, in moderation, during the symposium is appropriate and joyful, but that excessive drinking leads to problems for the individual and the community. These are but two examples in Sirach that reveal the similarities between Jewish banqueting and the banquets in the surrounding culture.[55]

There were, of course, unique aspects of Jewish banqueting. Jewish meals opened and closed with particular prayers of blessing called *berakoth*. Each individual *berakah* began with the phrase: *Barukh atah Adonai Elohenu melek ha-olam* ("Blessed are you, Lord our God, Sovereign of the Universe"). The blessing at the beginning of the meal was called the *birkat ha-motzi*, and the standard prayer is translated "Blessed are you, O Lord our God, King of the universe, who brings forth bread from the earth." The series of three prayers at the end of the meal was called the *birkat ha-mazon*. The first *berakah* in the series praises God for providing food for all created things; the second thanks God for his unique relationship with the people of Israel, forged through history, covenant, and Torah; the third *berakah* petitions God to fulfill the covenant promises made to his people, being merciful to Israel and Jerusalem. "Thus at every main daily meal observant Jews would yoke the present (blessing for what sustains life), the past (thanksgiving for covenant promises), and the future (petition for restoration and fulfillment) into the ongoing story of their relationship with the God who 'spreads the table before them in the sight of their foes.' [Ps 23:5]"[56]

55. For a list of eleven rules of etiquette that correspond to rules in the non-Jewish society, see ibid., 139.

56. Joncas, "Tasting the Kingdom of God," 344. The previous paragraph borrows much from Joncas, 343–44.

There were three courses in a Jewish banquet: the appetizer course, the main course, and the dessert course. The following description of a general festive banquet is given in the Talmud:

> What is the order of the meal? The guests enter [the house] and sit on benches, and on chairs until all have entered. They all enter and they [servants] give them water for their hands. Each one washes one hand. They [servants] mix for them the cup; each one says the benediction for himself. They [servants] bring them the appetizers; each one says the benediction for himself. They [guests] go up [to the dining room] and they recline, and they [servants] give them [water] for their hands; although they have [already] washed one hand, they [now] wash both hands. They [servants] mix for them the cup; although they have said a benediction over the first [cup], they say a benediction [also] over the second. They [servants] bring them the dessert; although they said a benediction over the first one, they [now] say a benediction over the second, and one says the benediction for all of them. He who comes after the third course has no right to enter [the symposium].[57]

Apparently some Jews had a custom of sitting on benches at the beginning of the meal before later moving to couches to recline. Also, at the beginning of the meal they would only wash one hand, which they used to eat the appetizers; only later would they wash both hands for the meal proper. Other passages in the Talmud clarify that "the benediction over the second cup was said by one of the diners for the entire group, and the other diners responded with "*amen*." It was no longer necessary for each diner to say the benediction for himself, as in the case of the first cup, because the diners now constituted a unified group, rather than a collection of individuals."[58] The traditional wine benediction was "Blessed art Thou, O Lord, our God, King of the universe, Creator of the fruit of the vine."[59] In the next chapters we will see that the "fruit of the vine" language appears in the Last Supper narratives and that the early church adopted the Jewish tradition of responding to the benediction with "*amen*."

57. *T. Ber.* 4, 8, 98, from the translation by Bahr, "Seder of Passover," 182, quoted in Smith, *From Symposium to Eucharist*, 145.

58. Bahr, "Seder of Passover," 193.

59. Ibid., 189.

The Jewish banquet—and Jewish meals in general—were also characterized by the absence of certain foods. Jews were known throughout the Mediterranean world as those who abstained from eating pork (as well as those who observed the Sabbath and practiced circumcision). Also a part of Jewish dietary restrictions was the eating of blood, which meant that meat had to be prepared in certain ways to be eaten by observant Jews.[60] Another component of the dietary laws was abstaining from meat sacrificed to idols or wine offered to pagan gods (see 1 Cor 8:1–13; 10:14–33). One example is found in the book of Daniel, when Daniel "resolved that he would not defile himself with the royal rations of food and wine" (Dan 1:8) while in captivity in Babylon. It should be stated that an observant Jew could dine with Gentiles and simply watch what they ate, an option that is often mentioned in literature of the day.[61] Thus, Jewish dietary restrictions did not forbid interacting with or even reclining at table with Gentiles. Let us now turn to examine the banqueting tradition of the festival of the Unleavened Bread.

2. The Passover Banquet[62]

The Jewish celebration of Passover (*Pesach, Pasch*) is the commemoration of the escape from slavery in Egypt. The celebration is a high point in the Jewish year. It was primarily a sacrificial meal prior to the destruction of the Temple in 70 CE; thus pilgrims would travel to Jerusalem to make the sacrifice and celebrate the Passover. The Passover sacrificial ritual was different from other sacrifices because the layperson performed the sacrifice himself, although it may have been the case that priests officiated in certain parts, such as handling the sacred blood of the animal. For our purposes, it is important to note that no fixed Seder ("order") existed before the end of the second century CE.[63] Thus, we can at best make generalizations about how the Passover was celebrated by Jesus and his disciples.

The Passover Seder was characterized by four ceremonial cups of wine that were blessed and drunk by participants. The Seder began with

60. Smith, *From Symposium to Eucharist*, 160, writes that it is not clear how widespread this restriction against consuming blood was, particularly in diaspora Judaism

61. Smith, *From Symposium to Eucharist*, 161.

62. The information in this section is primarily drawn from Bahr, "Seder of Passover," 181–99.

63. Smith, *From Symposium to Eucharist*, 147.

a *berakah* offered over the first cup of wine, which was offered by each person individually. Then the food for the meal was brought before the head of the household, and a bowl of water was passed among diners, who washed one hand. Next the appetizer course was served, which likely consisted of some combination of lettuce, radishes, cucumbers, fruit, cheese, eggs, and so on. No bread was served in the first course. At the conclusion of the first course, Gordon Bahr states that diners moved from the anteroom to the dining room, where they reclined to take their dinner.[64] After the guests had reclined, each in his proper place, the second cup of wine was mixed and served. Water was again provided for diners to wash both hands, and then the host broke the unleavened bread and offered a blessing for the meal, to which all responded with "*amen*."

The main course of the Passover meal consisted of unleavened bread, lettuce, fruit puree, bitter herbs, and two cooked dishes. Prior to the destruction of the Jerusalem Temple in 70 CE, the paschal lamb was a part of the main course and was eaten last, so as to be that food which satiates.[65] During the main course, the events of the exodus were recounted through a dialogue initiated by a son, who asks his father: "Why is this night different from all other nights?" The father explained, "A wandering Aramean was my father . . ." (Deut 26:5), and continued to tell the story of the exodus from Egypt. Bahr notes that "the 'telling' (*haggadah*) had no fixed form. . . . [The different forms found in the Mishnah] all fulfill the two requirements for the narration, that one should begin with disgrace and conclude with praise, and that one is obliged to see himself as though *he* had gone out of Egypt."[66] The first portion of the Hallel psalms (Pss 113–118) was recited at the end of the discussion. The meal proper concluded with a third cup of wine followed by a benediction (*birkat ha-mazon*) closing the meal and opening the symposium. When lamb was not served in the meal, salted desserts were served during the symposium, accompanied with the fourth cup of wine. The Passover Seder ended with the singing of the remaining Hallel psalms and a benediction.[67]

---

64. Bahr, "Seder of Passover," 190.

65. Ibid., 195.

66. Ibid., 196–97 (emphasis in original).

67. For the actual Talmudic texts that describe the Passover Seder, see ibid., 183–86.

3. The Messianic Banquet

Up to this point we have been talking about actual dining practices of the Jews, but it is also important to note the emergence of metaphorical language describing the banquet of the future messiah ("anointed one"). After the Israelite kings were defeated and the leaders and people exiled to Babylon, various groups began to imagine a time in the future when God would redeem his people, restore a king to the throne, and judge the nations. This eschatological vision was often imagined as a messianic banquet. Two passages from Isaiah illustrate this banquet:

> On this mountain the Lord of hosts will make for all peoples
> a feast of rich food, a feast of well-aged wines,
> of rich food filled with marrow, of well-aged wines strained clear.
> And he will destroy on this mountain
> the shroud that is cast over all peoples,
> the sheet that is spread over all nations;
> he will swallow up death forever.
> Then the Lord God will wipe away the tears from all faces,
> and the disgrace of his people he will take away from all the earth,
> for the Lord has spoken. (Isa 25:6–8)

> Ho, everyone who thirsts, come to the waters;
> and you that have no money, come, buy and eat!
> Come, buy wine and milk without money and without price.
> Why do you spend your money for that which is not bread,
> and your labor for that which does not satisfy?
> Listen carefully to me, and eat what is good,
> and delight yourselves in rich food. Incline your ear,
> and come to me; listen, so that you may live.
> I will make with you an everlasting covenant,
> my steadfast, sure love for David. . . .
> See, you shall call nations that you do not know,
> and nations that do not know you shall run to you,
> because of the Lord your God, the Holy One of Israel,
> for he has glorified you. (Isa 55:1–3, 5)

This theme of the messianic banquet was important in certain groups within Judaism, and especially found resonance in the thinking of the early church. In particular, Rev 19:7–9 describes the feast as a wedding banquet celebrating the union of Christ and the church.

One theme connected to the eschatological banquet is the numinous nature of certain foods. In Greek literature, the food of the gods was ambrosia and the drink of the gods was nectar, and mortals who partook of these supposedly became immortal.[68] In Isa 55 (quoted above), the Lord offers "rich food" that brings satisfaction beyond that of normal food. A similar motif is also present in the Jewish work *Joseph and Aseneth*, which was written in Egypt between the first century BCE and the first century CE.[69] In this narrative, an angel from the Lord appears to Aseneth, the virgin daughter of Pharaoh's priest, after she has confessed her sins to God, including the offense of eating food sacrificed to Egyptian idols (12:5–6). As a result of her confession, the angel tells her: "Your name was written in the book of the living in heaven. . . . For behold, from today you will be renewed and formed anew and made alive again. And you will eat blessed bread of life, and drink a blessed cup of immortality, and anoint yourself with blessed ointment of incorruptibility" (15:4–5).[70] In the following chapter, Aseneth and the angel share a meal that includes honeycomb, which has mysteriously appeared and which is described as giving immortality to those who eat it (16:8–9). It is helpful to note these instances of eating bread/honeycomb and drinking from the cup that are connected with immortality in Jewish apocalyptic literature, for, as we shall see later, Christian communities will begin to connect the Eucharistic bread and cup to the immortality of those who partake of it.

D. SUMMARY

In this chapter we have explored the basics of banqueting in the Greco-Roman world. Although there were certain elements that were characteristic of particular groups, in general it is the case that banqueting practices were remarkably similar in the ancient Mediterranean world. Feetwashing and handwashing were parts of the banquet. The evening banquet had two primary parts: the *deipnon* and the *symposion*. Diners ate while reclining on couches. The location of diners in the *triclinium* communicated something of their social status. Higher-class members of Greco-Roman clubs received better food and larger portions than lower-class members. A ceremonial libation was made at the transition from meal to entertainment. Women were largely absent from the sym-

68. Smith, *From Symposium to Eucharist*, 167. See Homer's *Odyssey* 5.93 and *Iliad* 5.335–42, 19.38–39.

69. Burchard, "Joseph and Aseneth," 94.

70. Ibid., 101–2.

posium, and those who were present were often thought to be courtesans. Entertainment for the evening could include hymn-singing and reading poetry or sacred writings. In Jewish contexts, it was important that the banquet food did not contain elements that had been part of sacrifices in pagan temples. All of these are important for our understanding of the celebration of the Love Feast in the early church. Now that we have set the table, let us share the supper with those first followers of Jesus.

3

Sharing the Supper

The Love Feast in the New Testament

H AVING EXPLORED THE GENERAL banquet practices of the Greco-Roman world, we now turn to examine the banquet in the early church. More specifically, in the current chapter we will focus on the New Testament and the passages therein that relate to the Love Feast. The Love Feast, or *agape*, was a practice that began in the earliest stages of Christianity. Although there is only one specific text that names the Christian banquet as "Love Feast" (Jude 12), many other texts bear witness to the importance of sharing a fellowship meal remembering and celebrating Jesus Christ. Most important among these texts are the Gospel accounts of the Last Supper and the Apostle Paul's teaching on the Lord's Supper.[1] Several other New Testament passages concerning eating, mealtime worship, and breaking bread together also inform our understanding of early eucharistic practices.[2] This chapter begins by exploring the textual diversity regarding the name of the banquet and the practices associated with it. Then the focus shifts to the fellowship meal, the bread and the cup, the holy kiss, feetwashing, and eucharistic examination.

A. DIVERSITY IN NAME AND PRACTICE OF THE BANQUET

The New Testament contains several names for the Christian banquet: the Lord's Supper (1 Cor 11:20), communion/fellowship (1 Cor 10:16,

1. Matt 26:17–30; Mark 14:12–26; Luke 22:7–34; John 13; 1 Cor 11:17–34.

2. John 6:22–59; Acts 2:42, 46; 10–11; 20:7–12; Rom 14; 1 Cor 5:6–8; 8–11; Gal 2:11–14; 2 Pet 2:12–13; Jude 12; Rev 3:20; 19:7–9.

Acts 2:42), the breaking of bread (Acts 2:42), and the Love Feast (*aga-pais*, Jude 12). Although the term does not appear in the New Testament, by the early second century the word "Eucharist" (lit. "thanksgiving") was also being used to name the meal in general, and the bread and cup, in particular.[3] I will not attempt here to provide a thorough analysis of Communion in the New Testament. This has already been done by many notable scholars.[4] It must suffice for our current endeavor to state briefly that in the first decades, a variety of terms were used to name the Christian meal.

In the texts mentioned above, along with the accounts of the Last Supper found in the four Gospels, several different themes are emphasized, including: the breaking of bread, thanksgiving, remembrance, fellowship, covenant, discernment, and love. The challenge has been to determine how these different themes relate to one another. Were the earliest eucharistic celebrations of the church a combination of a fellowship meal and commemorative remembrance of Christ through the bread and cup, or were these elements separate from the beginning? Or perhaps some communities combined the two while others kept them separate? Moreover, how does feetwashing relate to the celebration of the Eucharist? In the Gospel of John feetwashing is a part of the Last Supper, and Jesus states: "If I, your Lord and Teacher, have washed your feet, *you also ought to wash one another's feet*" (13:14, emphasis added). The synoptic Gospels, however, mention nothing of this shocking and intimate action. These are simply a few examples of the difficulty in understanding the earliest eucharistic practices of the church.

Although a plurality of themes in the early eucharistic texts does exist, several strong themes do emerge. Most scholars agree that there are two primary traditions present in the texts: (1) the communal fellowship meal (*koinonia*), represented in the Gospels as the feeding miracles and evident in the meals of 1 Cor 11, Acts 2, Jude and 2 Peter,[5] and (2) the remembrance (*anamnesis*) tradition commemorating Jesus' death through sharing the bread and cup, found in the Synoptic Gospel ac-

---

3. For a helpful analysis of the various names for the Christian meal, see the chapter "Naming the Meal" in Finger, *Of Widows and Meals*, 48–79.

4. For general analysis of the Eucharist in the New Testament, see Koenig, *Feast of the World's Redemption*; Moloney, *A Body Broken for a Broken People*; Chilton, *A Feast of Meanings*; Leon-Dufour, *Sharing the Eucharistic Bread*; WCC, "Baptism, Eucharist and Ministry"; Wainwright, *Eucharist and Eschatology*; Jeremias, *Eucharistic Words*.

5. Bach, "Agape in the Brethren Tradition," 162.

counts of the Last Supper and in Paul's words of institution in 1 Cor 11. Scholarly debate has focused on whether these two traditions were separate from the beginning, whether they were integrated, or whether one can distinguish either way.

German scholar Hans Lietzmann, in his seminal work on this topic, *Messe und Herrenmahl* (1926 [English translation, *Mass and the Lord's Supper*, 1979]), argues that the two eucharistic traditions were distinct from the very beginning.[6] His work has strongly influenced the opinions of many international scholars regarding the early practice of the Lord's Supper.[7] Brethren theologian Graydon Snyder summarizes this two-part approach as follows:

> The first eucharist, spoken of as the breaking of bread in Acts 2:42, 46, celebrated the unity of the faith congregation (*koinonia*, being in common or communion). The cup was drunk first (1 Cor. 10:16) and then the one bread shared (1 Cor. 10:17). The meal celebrated the unity of the community in the present and in the age to come. Once we understand this form of the eucharist, we can see its rich history in Christian tradition. We can suspect it became the *agape* or love feast we have seen in 1 Corinthians 11:17–22 [and also Jude 12]. We also suspect it coalesced with the popular meal for the dead. Whatever happened, the only eucharist portrayed in early Christian art shows about seven people sitting at a table with fish, seven or twelve baskets of bread and a cup of wine. According to the art we possess, the common meal of the early Christians through, perhaps, seven centuries was a breaking of the one loaf as a sign of unity. The meal is described in the gospel stories of the feeding of the five thousand. . . .
>
> There was a second form of the eucharist. As the Passover redramatized the exodus from Egypt, so the eucharist redramatized the death and resurrection of Jesus. The primary event of liberation for the Jews was the escape from Egypt and the entrance into the promised land. Every year, to this day, they reenact that saving event. According to the synoptic Gospels, Jesus took the celebration of the Passover and shifted it to his own death and resurrection. That death and resurrection liberated a person from the old age and brought them to the edge of the new. Consequently a eucharist developed which reenacted the cross and the resurrection

6. Lietzmann, *Mass and the Lord's Supper*.

7. Others who build on Lietzmann's work include Keating, *Agape and Eucharist in the Early Church*; Cole, *Love-Feasts*; Mack, *Myth of Innocence*; Smith, *Drudgery Divine*, 116–43; Chilton, *A Feast of Meanings*.

of the new body of Christ. That reenactment began, as it should, with the breaking of the bread, the body. After the believers re-enact the cross by breaking the bread, they then drink of the cup. In that way they reenact the spilling of the blood which marks the beginning of the new covenant. . . . In Paul's tradition of the Last Supper this reenacting of the redemptive event is called the *anamnesis*. In 1 Corinthians 11:24 he said to do (act out) this breaking of bread (the body on cross) in remembrance of me (the *anamnesis*). The "remembrance" tradition can be found in the accounts of the Last Supper in the synoptics, in 1 Corinthians 11:23–26, and in Justin Martyr, *Apologia* 65–66.[8]

According to Snyder, celebrating Eucharist in the early church consisted of both *koinonia/agape* and *anamnesis*—both loving fellowship (in the context of a meal) and remembrance of Jesus, whose death and resurrection bring salvation and inaugurate the Kingdom of God. However, recent scholarship has begun to challenge the notion that there are *clear* distinctions between these two forms of the Eucharist in the New Testament.

While Lietzmann's view was prominent until the mid-twentieth century, in more recent decades scholars have disputed the claim that the early church had two distinct forms of eucharistic worship. Michael Townsend has argued that the bread and cup were part of a full meal from the very beginning.[9] Similarly, Ben Witherington III argues that the bread/cup Eucharist would have occurred in the context of a normal meal, with the breaking and sharing of bread and the cup occurring at the beginning of the meal, and the sharing of a final cup of wine following the meal. This final cup of blessing would correspond to the libation that joined the *deipnon* to the symposion and its worship activities, which included hymn singing, the reading of the Scriptures and epistles, and ethical teaching.[10] Dennis Smith and Hal Taussig, whose work we examined in the previous chapter, also argue that the remembrance of Jesus using bread and the cup was firmly located in the midst of a fellowship meal. Lastly, Luke Timothy Johnson, in a chapter titled "Meals are Where the

8. Snyder, *First Corinthians*, 239–40.

9. Townsend, "Exit the Agape?," 360.

10. Witherington III, "Making a Meal of It," 85, 98–99. These after-supper worship activities were essentially Christian modifications to the *symposium*. For instance, excessive drinking should not be a part of Christian practice, but was a normal part of a Greco-Roman *symposium*.

Magic Is," criticizes the dualistic approach made by Lietzmann, Burton Mack, Bruce Chilton, and Graydon Snyder.[11] He writes: "My complaint about the dissections of Lietzmann, Mack, and Chilton [and Snyder] is not the premise of a plurality of practice—which makes good sense, given the circumstances of Christianity's expansion—but the pretense that (1) these strands can now adequately be distinguished, and that (2) the diversity represented fundamental disagreement among the parties. There is simply no basis in the sources for either premise."[12] Johnson's argument is persuasive. The scriptural diversity does not clearly evidence two separate traditions, but instead is representative of several vibrant communities remembering the life, death, and resurrection of Jesus Christ.

It is evident, then, that the New Testament contains a variety of eucharistic traditions—the most prominent being the fellowship meal and the remembering of Christ in that meal through the sharing of the bread and the cup. Other traditions connected to the Christian banquet included feetwashing, examination/preparation, and the holy kiss. There is no single text that authoritatively outlines the celebration of the Lord's Supper; rather, each individual text contributes to the broader picture of the celebration of the Love Feast in the early church. Recent scholarship has demonstrated the shortcomings of the earlier approach, which argued that there were clear distinctions between the various eucharistic traditions from the beginning. Indeed, it will be shown below that there is strong textual evidence that the fellowship meal and the bread/cup commemoration of Jesus were connected from the very beginning. We begin our analysis of the Love Feast in the New Testament by looking at the fellowship meal.

B. THE FELLOWSHIP MEAL IN THE NEW TESTAMENT

The New Testament contains several passages indicating that a fellowship meal was a fundamental part of early church gatherings. This meal is called different names in different texts—the Lord's Supper, "the breaking of bread," the *agapais* (Love Feast).[13] While some passages in

11. Johnson, *Religious Experience in Earliest Christianity*, 137–79.

12. Ibid., 171 n. 127.

13. I prefer to use the English words "Love Feast" to translate *agapais* and to name the worship meal of the early church. When other forms appear in this book, they reflect denominational tradition (e.g., the Moravian lovefeast, the Methodist love-feast)

Acts indicate that fellowship meals may have occurred throughout the week, Sunday, the first day of the week and the day of Jesus' resurrection, became the most prominent occasion for Christians to gather and break bread together.[14] When practiced faithfully, the fellowship meal was the most conspicuous example of the way in which followers of "the Way" of Jesus were radically transformed: Jewish Christians ate with Gentile Christians, masters and slaves dined together, women and men shared a meal, and the rich and the poor gathered in one place to break bread. Or at least disciples of Jesus were supposed to behave in such a way. The record indicates that there were occasions when social and religious barriers were not broken down and subjected to Christ, thus causing divisions in the meal gatherings of the early church. When the New Testament addresses these concerns, however, it is clear that followers of Jesus are not to accept human-made divisions; rather, through obedience to Jesus and his gospel of love and reconciliation, they are to strive to overcome these divisions in their fellowship meals.

1. The Lord's Supper in Corinth

The first letter from Paul to the church in Corinth, written between 53 and 56 CE, likely contains the earliest references to the Lord's Supper in Christian literature. First Corinthians 11:17–34a contains the broadest description of eucharistic practice in the New Testament record.[15] In

---

or indicate a sacrilegious celebration (e.g., the Carpocratian love feast, see chapter 4).

14. For a thorough look at the meals of the first Christians, see the chapter "Feasts of the Church's Founding" in Koenig, *Feast of the World's Redemption*, 45–85. Also see Witherington III, "Making a Meal of It."

15. Paul writes, "Now in the following instructions I do not commend you, because when you come together it is not for the better but for the worse. For, to begin with, when you come together as a church, I hear that there are divisions among you; and to some extent I believe it. Indeed, there have to be factions among you, for only so will it become clear who among you are genuine. When you come together, it is not really to eat the Lord's supper. For when the time comes to eat, each of you goes ahead with your own supper, and one goes hungry and another becomes drunk. What! Do you not have homes to eat and drink in? Or do you show contempt for the church of God and humiliate those who have nothing? What should I say to you? Should I commend you? In this matter I do not commend you!

For I received from the Lord what I also handed on to you, that the Lord Jesus on the night when he was betrayed took a loaf of bread, and when he had given thanks, he broke it and said, 'This is my body that is for you. Do this in remembrance of me.' In the same way he took the cup also, after supper, saying, 'This cup is the new covenant in my blood. Do this, as often as you drink it, in remembrance of me.' For as often as you eat

these verses Paul is concerned with how the church in Corinth comes together to eat their fellowship meal, which he calls the "Lord's Supper" (*kuriakon deipnon*, 11:20). He is upset with them because they are experiencing divisions and factions during the Lord's Supper (11:18–20).[16] At the heart of the matter is the disparity between members at the meal: "For when the time comes to eat, each of you goes ahead with your own supper, and one goes hungry and another becomes drunk" (11:21). To

this bread and drink the cup, you proclaim the Lord's death until he comes.

Whoever, therefore, eats the bread or drinks the cup of the Lord in an unworthy manner will be answerable for the body and blood of the Lord. Examine yourselves, and only then eat of the bread and drink of the cup. For all who eat and drink without discerning the body, eat and drink judgment against themselves. For this reason many of you are weak and ill, and some have died. But if we judged ourselves, we would not be judged. But when we are judged by the Lord, we are disciplined so that we may not be condemned along with the world. So then, my brothers and sisters, when you come together to eat, wait for one another. If you are hungry, eat at home, so that when you come together, it will not be for your condemnation" (1 Cor 11:17–34a).

16. We should also note that immediately before our passage Paul addresses the role of women in worship (11:2–16). The inclusion of women in the Christian gatherings appears to have caused some difficulties (cf. also 14:33b–36). In order to understand these passages concerning women and worship we must remember that Corinthian worship appears to have occurred after a shared meal, much like the *symposia* and *convivia* in Greco-Roman culture. Women were generally not participants in *symposia*; those who were present were often considered to be harlots (see the discussion on Greco-Roman banquets in chapter 2). In this context, the simple fact that women were *present* at Christian worship gatherings at all, especially after the meal had finished, indicates that the Jesus community was radically inclusive of women. Moreover, the record implies that women are *praying* and *prophesying* (11:5, 13), to which Paul responds by instructing the church about head coverings (11:2–16). Since women present in symposia were often thought of as courtesans, it makes perfect sense for Paul to write about head coverings/hair bindings, for "loose" women of the day were recognized by their loosed/unbound hair. Thus, if women are to be present at these post-meal gatherings, Paul wants them to take authority over their own head/hair (11:10) by covering/binding it so that they do not appear to be prostitutes. Even the passage instructing women to be silent in worship (14:33b–36, which many scholars believe to be a later addition to the epistle) makes sense if we consider the following logic: since the very inclusion of women in the post-meal worship gathering was already a remarkable adaptation, perhaps their vocal participation pushed the already fragile social order beyond its tipping point. The instruction for women to be silent in worship could therefore have been a temporary tactic aimed at maintaining some sense of decency and order (14:40), while giving the church time to grow up into the teachings of Christ, who calls his disciples to preach the good news of freedom to those who are oppressed. A failure to understand the cultural norms concerning female participation in mealtime and post-mealtime activities makes it easier to misread these passages, seeing them as restrictive rather than revealing the revolutionary involvement of women in the early church.

Paul, this severely undermines the purpose of the fellowship meal, which is meant to develop and give witness to the unity of the church.[17]

We should recall the previous chapter's discussion about the general Greco-Roman banquet in order to make sense of these difficulties in Corinth. It appears that some members are treating the Christian worship meal like a normal *symposion*, rather than as the Lord's Supper; they are getting drunk and causing divisions instead of remembering the sacrificial love of Jesus. Although the text does not overtly state that the divisions are being caused by problems between the rich and the poor, most scholars agree that differences in wealth are at the heart of this dilemma. The church in Corinth would likely have met in a member's home, and only the wealthier members would have had homes that were large enough to accommodate church gatherings. The divisions may simply have occurred because the church was too large to meet in the dining room of one house (a typical dining room was designed to accommodate nine people), thus forcing the host to divide the church into two groups: a smaller group to eat in the dining room and a larger group to eat in the adjoining atrium. It is likely that the host would have invited the more prominent members to join him in the dining room while the rest of the group ate in the atrium/courtyard. It was also normal for the higher-status members to have more food, and of better quality, than lower-class diners.[18] The logistical difficulty of inadequate space for Christians to eat together was therefore likely addressed by dividing the group according to social customs, which Paul finds offensive to the gospel of peace.

This logistical separation impacted the church's ability to share food with one another. Paul writes that some are going hungry, while others are getting drunk (11:21). Some translations (including the NIV) suggest that the problem was simply bad manners, that is, people were not waiting for others and thus the food was gone by the time the latecomers had arrived. Richard Hays explains: "Although the Greek verb *prolambanein*—[which the NIV translates] 'go ahead without waiting'— might carry such a temporal sense ('to take beforehand'), it does not necessarily have this meaning. A simpler translation would be 'For,

---

17. For more on vv. 23–26, see section C below; for more on vv. 27–34, see section E below.

18. Smith, *From Symposium to Eucharist*, 124; Hays, *First Corinthians*, 196.

when you eat, each one *consumes* his own supper."[19] The problem was probably not that people were failing to wait for others to show up, but rather that they were eating their own individual food without sharing it. This does not make for a very good potluck meal, especially considering that wealthy members could afford to contribute meat and other costly foods, which the poor rarely, if ever, ate.[20] By allowing these injustices, the Corinthians "show contempt for the church of God and humiliate those who have nothing" (11:22). It is clear that an evening fellowship meal was central to the Lord's Supper in Corinth.

2. Fellowship Meal Problems in Antioch

While the problems with the Lord's Supper in Corinth seem to have been between the wealthy and the poor, Paul's letter to the Galatians (52–56 CE) indicates that the Christian common meal was also challenged by divisions between members from Gentile and Jewish backgrounds. In Gal 2:11–14 Paul confronts Cephas (Peter) for his hypocrisy. In 2:12–13 we read: "[F]or until certain people came from James, [Peter] used to eat with the Gentiles. But after they came, he drew back and kept himself separate for fear of the circumcision faction. And the other Jews joined him in this hypocrisy, so that even Barnabas was led astray." Again we see that Paul is primarily focused on the unity of the church, especially when they came together to eat. The Galatians were embroiled in conflict over following the Jewish Law. Although his letter mainly argues that circumcision is not necessary for Gentiles to become Christians, Paul also includes this story about his experience with Peter in Antioch to demonstrate that the Jewish practice of not eating with Gentiles was contrary to "the truth of the gospel" (2:14). For Paul, the unity of the body of Christ was to be powerfully evident when the church came together to eat, and there were to be no divisions caused by social status or racial/religious heritage.

---

19. Hays, *First Corinthians*, 197.

20. For the Lord's Supper as a potluck meal, see Snyder, *First Corinthians*, 156–57. For more on the diet of early Christians, see Neyrey, "Meals, Food and Table Fellowship," 164–68.

3. "The Breaking of Bread" in Luke and Acts

In Luke and Acts the Christian meal is referred to as "the breaking of bread." The origin of this term apparently goes back to Jesus and the way in which he broke bread before meals. There must have been something unique about the way that Jesus blessed and broke bread before a meal; his disciples had witnessed this act countless times during his ministry, and it was this feature that identified him at the table with the two journeying to Emmaus.[21] After the Holy Spirit descends on the disciples at Pentecost, Luke writes the following description of the church:

> They devoted themselves to the apostles' teaching and fellowship (*koinonia*), to the breaking of bread (*he klasis tou artou*) and the prayers. . . . Day by day, as they spent much time together in the temple, they broke bread at home and ate their food with glad and generous hearts. (Acts 2:42, 46)

Additionally, we see the phrase later in Acts when Paul visits Troas:

> On the first day of the week, when we met to break bread (*klasai arton*), Paul was holding a discussion with them; since he intended to leave the next day, he continued speaking until midnight. There were many lamps in the room upstairs where we were meeting. . . . Then Paul went upstairs, and after he had broken bread and eaten, he continued to converse with them until dawn; then he left. (Acts 20:7–8, 11)

Although these texts were written decades after 1 Corinthians (where Paul uses the term "Lord's Supper"), C. K. Barrett argues: "*he klasis tou artou* is probably an old traditional Christian term, antedating the Pauline development [of the Lord's Supper terminology]."[22]

What do the scriptures tell us about "the breaking of bread?" In Acts 20 we see that the breaking of bread occurred on the first day of the week

---

21. After the resurrection, Jesus appeared to two disciples on the road to Emmaus, who convinced Jesus to stay and eat supper with them: "When he was at the table with them, he took bread, blessed and broke it, and gave it to them. Then their eyes were opened, and they recognized him; and he vanished from their sight. . . . [They returned to Jerusalem and told the other disciples] what had happened on the road, and how he had been made known to them in the breaking of the bread (*te klasei tou artou*)" (Luke 24:30–31, 35).

22. Barrett, *Commentary on Acts*, 165, quoted in Koenig, *Feast of the World's Redemption*, 91–92.

(Sunday), the day of Jesus' resurrection.[23] It was a supper meal which was followed by discussion that, on this occasion, lasted until dawn. John Koenig explains that "a Sunday supper, according to the usual Jewish reckoning of time, could take place anytime after sundown on Saturday, thus making possible what a number of scholars have termed an 'extended Sabbath.'"[24] He writes later, "Sabbath sundowns presented the perfect liturgical time for such blendings of old and new [covenants]. In these weekly commemorations of the Last Supper, Israel's past, present and future could manifest themselves as a holy and seamless garment."[25] A fair conclusion is that the early church met weekly for "the breaking of bread," an "extended Sabbath" celebration that began Saturday evening and lasted into the Sunday morning hours, according to the Jewish reckoning of time.

It is difficult to know whether "the breaking of bread" refers to the common supper meal, a specific element of such a meal (bread/cup) remembering Jesus, or both. Koenig writes, "'breaking of bread' was not a standard Jewish designation for a full meal, but only for the ritual act that initiated it. What seems to have happened is that the early believers took up this typical description of a meal's commencement and applied it to their entire liturgy of eating and drinking."[26] After his resurrection, Jesus was recognized by the two disciples "in the breaking of bread" (Luke 24:35), and he disappeared immediately afterward, apparently not staying to share the rest of the meal with them. Perhaps, then, the breaking of bread should be understood as the ritual remembrance of Jesus using bread (and a cup?), not as sharing a full meal.

In contrast, John Howard Yoder understands the breaking of bread to refer to the early church practice of sharing a common meal together.[27] We see in Acts 2:46 that believers break bread together *daily* in their homes. This seems to indicate simply sharing meals together, rather than a bread/cup remembrance of Jesus.[28] Yoder writes, "What the New

---

23. All four Gospels report that Jesus' resurrection occurred on the first day of the week (Matt 28:1; Mark 16:2; Luke 24:1; John 20:1). In 1 Cor 16:2 we also find that the collection for the saints occurred on the first day of the week.

24. Koenig, *Feast of the World's Redemption*, 69.

25. Ibid., 74.

26. Ibid., 91.

27. See chapter 2, "Disciples Break Bread Together," of Yoder, *Body Politics*, 14–27.

28. Koenig, *Feast of the World's Redemption*, 73, writes, "we have no data to suggest

Testament is talking about wherever the theme is 'breaking bread' is that people actually were sharing with one another their ordinary day-to-day material sustenance. . . . Bread eaten together *is* economic sharing. Not merely symbolically, but also in fact, eating together extends to a wider circle the economic solidarity normally obtained in the family."[29] Brethren scholar Dale Brown also observes, "the emphasis is not as much on eating bread as on breaking it. Bread already broken in many places constitutes a privatized symbol of chewing and swallowing, of individual possession. The breaking of bread signifies the intention to share it, to give it to others, thus portraying the character of Christ's body."[30] Yoder and Brown help us to see that the breaking of bread has profound implications on the social and economic ethics of the church; that breaking bread together necessarily engages the church in the economic newness of the Kingdom of God while also reminding the church of the cruciform love of Jesus. Therefore, while acknowledging that "the breaking of bread" may have referred to a ritual element of the common meal, we must not overlook its broader sense as sharing a fellowship meal together—a meal uniting people who might never normally dine together in society.

4. The Love Feast in Jude (and 2 Peter?)

The epistles of Jude and 2 Peter also help us to understand more fully the origins of the Love Feast. Scholars are divided on the dating of the letter of Jude; it was written either between 60 and 100 CE or between 100 and 125 CE, depending upon whether the author was actually Jude, Jesus' brother, or a later disciple writing pseudonymously.[31] There are remarkable similarities between Jude and 2 Peter, leading most schol-

that the *daily* meals of the Jerusalem congregation were ever shaped, liturgically, by the bread and cup words found in our New Testament accounts of the last supper. A priori, the daily use of wine by believers with limited resources is highly improbable."

29. Yoder, *Body Politics*, 20. Yoder continues, "By interpreting the early Christian meals as set-apart religious rituals, as Christians have been doing since the early Middle Ages, or by trying to interpret them through the narrow focus of a single annual Passover model, we have been enabled to duck their impact for social ethics, first in the church and also in the world" (p. 21).

30. Brown, "An Anabaptist Theology of the Sacraments," 17.

31. Duane Watson favors the earlier dating, while Edwin Freed argues for a later date of authorship; cf. Watson, "The Letter of Jude," 474; Freed, *The New Testament*, 395.

ars to conclude that the author of 2 Peter borrowed material from Jude. Following this logic, 2 Peter would be dated a decade or two later than the dates listed above for Jude. The similarities between Jude and 2 Peter are clear in the two passages that relate to the Love Feast.

The only undisputed example of the term "Love Feast" in the New Testament is found in Jude 12. The author of Jude is deeply concerned about persons who are corrupting the Christian community: "These [intruders] are blemishes (*spilades*) on your love-feasts (*agapais*), while they feast with you (*suneuochoumenoi*) without fear" (Jude 12). Second Peter echoes Jude's concern that intruders are defiling the purity of Christian feasts: "They are blots and blemishes (*spiloi*), reveling in their dissipation (*apatais*) while they feast with you (*suneuochoumenoi*)" (2 Pet 2:13). The two passages are very similar, both talking about blemishes on the church that are evident during times of feasting. In fact, these two passages are the only two examples in the New Testament where we find the word *suneuochoumenoi*, "feast with you." Reta Finger explains that the writer of 2 Peter uses *apatais* as a deliberate pun on Jude's *agapais*, since the same word (*suneuochoumenoi*) is used for feasting.[32] The most authoritative ancient texts of 2 Pet 2:13 contain the word *apatais* (dissipation), although some sources do contain *agapais* (Love Feasts).[33] Bruce Metzger attributes these later appearances of *agapais* to scribal attempts to assimilate the text to Jude 12 (and thus to remove the pun between *apatais/agapais*).[34] The word *agapais* is a plural form of the word *agape* (love), and thus could literally be translated "loves," although this does not make sense. Because of the feasting context, the word *agapais* is best translated into English as Love Feasts. Thus, in Jude (and redacted copies of 2 Peter) we see that "Love Feast" appears to be an inclusive term for the common meal of the early church, which apparently has been experiencing challenges brought on by intruders who "pervert the grace of our God into licentiousness and deny our only Master and Lord, Jesus Christ" (Jude 4).

---

32. Finger, *Of Widows and Meals*, 62.

33. The textual evidence favors *apatais* (25 ancient sources, earlier texts). However more than a few sources, largely later redactions, contain the *agapais* variant (16 sources); see Aland et al., eds., *The Greek New Testament*, 803 n. 7.

34. Metzger, *A Textual Commentary on the Greek New Testament*, 704. See Finger, *Of Widows and Meals*, 62.

5. *The Feeding Miracles and the Meal in John 21*

It is also important to mention several meals of abundance found in the Gospels. First, all four Gospels contain the story of Jesus feeding the five thousand.[35] In this miracle, which occurred on the shores of the Sea of Tiberias, Jesus multiplied five loaves of bread and two fish into enough food to feed the multitudes. In a separate but similar story, in John 21 the resurrected Jesus returns to Galilee and appears to seven disciples, who have been fishing overnight on the Sea of Tiberias. After failing to catch even a single fish all night, a man on the shore (Jesus) tells them to try their nets on the right-hand side of the boat, and their nets become swamped with fish. They rush to shore to see Jesus, who has prepared a breakfast meal of bread and fish for them. After the meal, Jesus asks Peter three times if Peter loves him (21:15–17, two times he asks using the verb *agape*, the last time he asks using the verb *phileo*). Peter responds three times that he loves (*phileo*) the Lord. Thus, this meal can be called a "meal of love."

R. Lee Cole is convinced that this post-resurrection lakeside meal gave the name to the Love Feast. He writes:

> That this lakeside meal gave the name to the Agape there cannot be much doubt. We shall see that in the catacomb pictures the words "Eirene" and "Agape" are at times connected with the common meal, but the preponderance is given to the word "Agape"; we shall see, too, that in many of the pictures the number of figures is not twelve, as at the Last Supper, nor ten, nor eleven, as at the post-resurrection suppers, but seven, in evident remembrance of the "come and dine" incident recorded by St. John in his last chapter.
>
> It is a little extraordinary how the writers on the Agape have overlooked this pertinent incident and have sought elsewhere for the source of the name "Agape." The fact that the Agape and the Eucharist were joined in one ceremony for over a century has turned attention almost exclusively to the Last Supper; but the significance of this last meal (at Tiberias) of our Lord on earth is very great. It was a meal deliberately arranged and prepared by Himself, probably the only one ever so arranged by Him. It was introduced by a striking miracle, the miraculous draught of fishes; and that it became in later days a much-discussed incident is evidenced by the fact that St. John found it necessary, after he had finished his Gospel and perhaps published it, to add a

35. Matt 14:13–21; Mark 6:32–44; Luke 9:10b–17; John 6:1–15.

> supplement describing accurately what had taken place on that important occasion. Surely, then, one may conclude that we have in it the incident which of all others eventually decided the title which the common meal of the Christians was to bear.[36]

Although it may not be as clear-cut as Cole makes it out to be, several of his points are valid. As we shall see in the following chapter, the earliest archaeological evidence does overwhelmingly depict seven disciples eating bread and fish at a common meal. This does appear to point back to the meal at Tiberias. And these pictures do often contain the word *agape*. Yet, as we shall see later in this chapter, the Johannine Last Supper also prominently features *agape*, with Jesus giving his disciples a new command to "love one another" (*agapate*, 13:34). Thus, I would counter Cole's strong claim that the Love Feast is based primarily on the meal at Tiberias by saying that the Love Feast appears to have received its name from two meals in the Gospel of John: the Last Supper and the meal on the shores of the Sea of Tiberias.

C. COMMUNION/EUCHARIST IN THE NEW TESTAMENT

It is clear in the New Testament that the bread and the cup are powerfully linked to remembering and participating in the life, death and resurrection of Jesus. We have already seen that Paul must remind the Corinthian church that they are partaking in the *Lord's Supper*, not their own dinner party, and that the bread and cup are a common union/communion in the body and blood of Christ (1 Cor 10:16).[37] In the synoptic Gospels, Jesus adapts the Passover tradition by teaching his disciples that, from this point forward, they should understand the ceremonial bread and cup as the body and blood of Jesus.[38] The title "Eucharist" later

---

36. Cole, *Love-Feasts*, 62–63.

37. Paul writes, "The cup of blessing that we bless, is it not a sharing in (*koinonia*) the blood of Christ? The bread that we break, is it not a sharing in (*koinonia*) the body of Christ? Because there is one bread, we who are many are one body, for we all partake of the one bread. . . . You cannot drink the cup of the Lord and the cup of demons. You cannot partake of the table of the Lord and the table of demons" (1 Cor 10:16–17, 21). The title "Communion" comes from *koinonia*, which is translated *communio* in Latin and in English is translated "to share in," "to fellowship with," or "to have communion/common union with."

38. It is anachronistic to read these texts through the lens of the philosophical debates of the Middle Ages and Reformation era on the "real presence" of Christ in the elements. John Koenig, *Feast of the World's Redemption*, 38, writes, "That Paul and the

emerges from the prayer of thanksgiving (*eucharisteo*, "to give thanks") that Jesus offers at the Last Supper prior to distributing the elements of the bread and cup.[39] And although John's account of the Last Supper is not a Passover meal and does not have Jesus teaching the disciples about the bread and cup, John 6 clearly contains eucharistic teaching, beginning with Jesus giving thanks (*eucharistesas*, 6:11; cf. 6:23) over bread before feeding the multitudes, and ending with Jesus saying: "my flesh is true food and my blood is true drink" (John 6:55). Hence, the New Testament authors bear witness that the earliest Christians gave thanks to God for the gift of Jesus and remembered his broken body and spilt blood through the sharing of the bread and cup.

1. Challenges Regarding the Last Supper

In recent years, scholars in the Jesus Seminar have challenged the historicity of the Last Supper accounts, arguing in various ways that the words concerning the bread and cup are products of the early church, not authentic words of Christ.[40] These scholars point to the variations in the four different eucharistic texts as evidence that they could not have emerged from one historical meal. For ease of comparison, the passages are shown below:

---

synoptic gospels, still in a Jewish orbit, would be able to show Jesus connecting bread and wine with his body and blood in such a direct manner must mean that the verb 'is' ['This *is* my body'] (absent in Aramaic but present in the Greek) meant something other than simplistic identification. Jewish sensibilities, including those of Jewish believers, would not have allowed for a medieval doctrine of transubstantiation. At the last supper, Jesus' disciples almost certainly avoided a cannibalistic interpretation of their actions."

39. Matt 26:27; Mark 14:23; Luke 22:19; 1 Cor 11:24.

40. John Dominic Crossan is the most skeptical of these scholars in his interpretation of the historicity of the Last Supper. Crossan writes, "What Jesus created and left behind was the tradition of open commensality [Crossan's term for Jesus' unusual practice of eating with marginal people and social outcasts] . . . [W]hat happened was that, after his death, certain Christian groups created the Last Supper ritual that combined commensality from his life with a commemoration of his death. It spread to other Christian groups only slowly. It cannot be used as a historical event to explain anything about Jesus' own death," Crossan, *Jesus*, 130, quoted in Koenig, *Feast of the World's Redemption*, 6. Koenig addresses the historical questions raised by Crossan and the other Jesus Seminar scholars, demonstrating that while there are variations between the respective texts, there are significant similarities that support the claim that the accounts stem from a common historical meal (see pp. 3–44).

Variations in the Institution of the Bread

This is my body that is for you. Do this in remembrance of me. (1 Cor 11:24)

This is my body, which is given for you. Do this in remembrance of me. (Luke 22:19)

Take; this is my body. (Mark 14:22)

Take, eat; this is my body. (Matt 26:26)

Variations in the Institution of the Cup

This cup is the new covenant in my blood. Do this, as often as you drink it, in remembrance of me. (1 Cor 11:25)

This cup that is poured out for you is the new covenant in my blood. (Luke 22:20)

This is my blood of the covenant, which is poured out for many. (Mark 14:24)

Drink from it, all of you; for this is my blood of the covenant, which is poured out for many for the forgiveness of sins. (Matt 26:27–28)

Variations in Jesus' Words Concerning the Cup

Truly I tell you, I will never again drink of the fruit of the vine until that day when I drink it new in the Kingdom of God. (Mark 14:25)

I tell you, I will never again drink of this fruit of the vine until that day when I drink it new with you in my Father's kingdom. (Matt 26:29)

I tell you that from now on I will not drink of the fruit of the vine until the Kingdom of God comes. (Luke 22:18)

For as often as you eat this bread and drink the cup, you proclaim the Lord's death until he comes. (1 Cor 11:26)

When one compares the various texts, several things become evident. First, there are noticeable similarities between 1 Corinthians and Luke (i.e., "Do this in remembrance of me"). Joseph Fitzmyer posits that 1 Corinthians/Luke may reflect the liturgical practice at Antioch, while Mark/Matthew may reflect the practices of the church in Jerusalem.[41] Second, the synoptic Gospels all contain an eschatological section where Jesus reflects on the cup, telling his disciples that he will not drink the fruit of the vine until the day God's kingdom comes. This eschatological

41. Fitzmyer, *Luke X–XXIV*, 1392–93.

motif is present in a different form in 1 Corinthians, where Paul writes that the celebration of the bread and cup "proclaim the Lord's death *until he comes*" (11:26). Third, even though there are differences among the texts, it is still possible to see several key components shared among the four texts. John Koenig argues that the historical Jesus said something similar to this to his disciples during the Last Supper:

1. This [bread] *is* my body.

2. [The wine in] this cup *is* the covenant in my blood.

3. Truly I tell you, I will never again drink of the fruit of the vine until that day when I drink it new in the Kingdom of God.[42]

Even though some argue that the historical veracity of the Last Supper is doubtful, based on the commonalities among the different words of institution, a strong case can be made that the various eucharistic texts do in fact point back to an actual evening meal where Jesus used bread and a cup to redefine the Passover ceremony for his disciples.

2. The Synoptic Last Supper: Echoes of the Passover

The three synoptic Gospels all record that the Last Supper was a Passover meal.[43] In the Jewish Passover meal there were four occasions where the *paterfamilias* blessed and shared a cup of wine with all who were present.[44] The meal also featured unleavened bread, reminding the participants of the swift departure their ancestors made from Egypt. Although most eucharistic passages address the bread before the cup, in 1 Cor 10:16–21 and Luke 22:17–20 the cup precedes the bread, which could correspond to the first ceremonial cup of the Passover meal. In the 1 Corinthians passage, however, Richard Hays observes that Paul places the cup before the bread in 1 Cor 10:16 so that he can end by emphasizing that partaking in the one bread effects communion with Christ and all the members of the church (10:17), not somehow to confuse the Corinthians about the order of celebrating the elements.[45] In the following chapter, when

---

42. Koenig, *Feast of the World's Redemption*, 36. "Is" would not have been present in Aramaic.

43. Matt 26:19; Mark 14:16; Luke 22:13.

44. See the discussion of the Passover Banquet in chapter 2 above.

45. Hays, *First Corinthians*, 167.

Paul "hands over" his instruction concerning the Eucharist in the next chapter, the bread clearly precedes the cup.

Although the reversal of the cup and bread in 1 Corinthians may serve to emphasize more strongly that the church is "one bread," the cup-first passage in Luke 22 still remains:

> Then [Jesus] took a cup, and after giving thanks he said, "Take this and divide it among yourselves; for I tell you that from now on I will not drink of the fruit of the vine until the Kingdom of God comes." Then he took a loaf of bread, and when he had given thanks, he broke it and gave it to them, saying, "This is my body, which is given for you. Do this in remembrance of me." And he did the same with the cup after supper, saying, "This cup that is poured out for you is the new covenant in my blood." (22:17–20)

This is the only eucharistic passage in the New Testament where two cups are mentioned. Having previously noted that the Passover meal involved four cups, it is best to understand the cup in v. 17 as one of the early Passover cups (perhaps the second cup, which immediately precedes the meal). The breaking of bread in v. 19 then initiates the meal. The cup in v. 20 would likely correspond to the fourth cup of the Passover meal, which was drunk during the symposium after the meal. We should also recall that this last cup was connected with the singing of the final Hallel Psalms. Although Luke does not record that the meal ended with singing, Matthew and Mark do (Matt 26:30; Mark 14:26).

A. REMEMBRANCE IN THE PASSOVER AND THE EUCHARIST.

The theme of remembrance is important to both the Passover and the Eucharist. The Passover is a memorial meal celebrating Israel's liberation from slavery in Egypt: "This day shall be a day of remembrance for you. You shall celebrate it as a festival to the Lord; throughout your generations you shall observe it as a perpetual ordinance" (Exod 12:14). Similarly, in 1 Corinthians and Luke the bread and cup are celebrated "in remembrance" (*anamnesin*)" of Jesus, who liberates disciples from the law of sin and death (Rom 8:2; 1 Cor 15:56–57). Just as the lamb was slaughtered so that the angel of death might pass over the homes of the Israelites (Exod 12), "our paschal lamb, Christ, has been sacrificed" (1 Cor 5:7) and—more importantly—has been "raised from the dead, the first fruits of those who have died" (1 Cor 15:20). The theme of remembrance in both meals emphasizes that both traditions are rooted in historical events: the Passover celebrates the salvation of the Hebrews from the angel of death and Egyptian bondage, while the Eucharist celebrates the salvation and eternal life made available to *everyone* through the death of Jesus of Nazareth, crucified on a Roman cross in Jerusalem during the rule of Pontius Pilate.

B. THE EMPHASIS ON THE BREAKING OF BREAD IN THE EUCHARIST.

One significant difference between the Eucharist and the Passover is the meaning and placement of the breaking of bread. Regarding its placement, although Luke clearly places the sharing of the cup before the breaking of the bread (like the Passover ceremony), in Matthew, Mark, John 6 and 1 Cor 11 the breaking of bread comes before the sharing of the cup. This adaptation indicates that the Christian ceremony soon began to be differentiated from its Passover heritage. Regarding its meaning, the breaking of unleavened bread in the Passover meal recalls the shared meals of the Israelites, whose hasty flight from Egypt prevented them from adequately preparing bread with yeast. In contrast, the eucharistic breaking of bread emphasizes the death of Christ, when his body was broken on a Roman cross, resulting in the shedding of his blood. By breaking bread before drinking the cup, participants more precisely remember the horrible death of Jesus on the cross.[46]

3. The Last Supper in John: A Pre-Passover Meal

Eucharist in the Gospel of John is distinctly separate from the Passover tradition. In John, the Last Supper occurs on the *day before* the Passover meal (John 13:1) and does not contain the bread and cup narrative found in the synoptic Gospels. This means that in John, Jesus is crucified on the same day that the Passover lambs are slaughtered.[47] John does not com-

---

46. Graydon Snyder, *First Corinthians*, 157–58, writes, "The breaking of the bread first indicates an important faith shift. Historically, the breaking of the body of Jesus occurred before the shedding of the blood. But more important, the death of the body is a preliminary work of the Spirit. That is, the body of Christ must continually be broken (contrite) so that the Spirit of God can be effective. The *anamnesis* or remembrance style . . . always has the bread first, because it recalls the faith paradigm of the death and resurrection. The celebration takes its name from the opening prayer of thanksgiving (*eucharisteo*)."

47. Thus only John refers to Jesus as the "Lamb of God who takes away the sin of the world" (1:29; cf. 1:36).

pletely omit Jesus' instruction concerning the bread and cup; rather, he places this eucharistic teaching earlier in Jesus' ministry at the feeding the five thousand (John 6), not during the Last Supper.[48] By the time the Gospel of John was written, Christians had been put out of Jewish synagogues (John 9:22; 12:42; 16:2). This split between Jews and Christians may relate to the non-Passover Last Supper, for John may want clearly to distinguish between Jewish and Christian celebrations. There is a difference in the frequency of the celebrations as well: Christians met weekly for the Lord's Supper, while Passover is celebrated just once a year. John also includes the feetwashing account and the command for the disciples to wash each other's feet, the practice of which would have clearly distinguished the Christian celebration from the Passover tradition.

4. The Eschatological Focus of the Eucharist

There is a strong eschatological focus in the eucharistic texts that is often overlooked.[49] In the Synoptics, Jesus tells the disciples that he will not drink the fruit of the vine again until he drinks it new in his Father's kingdom. To his Jewish disciples, this talk of a coming kingdom characterized by feasting and drinking would have likely recalled the eschatological texts in Isaiah and Zechariah, which describe the end times as a heavenly feast (Isa 25:6–8; Zech 8:7–8, 19–23).[50] John Koenig comments:

> Jesus' presence at the last supper was shaped both by his vision of God's abundance and his willingness to sacrifice himself. We tend to accentuate the latter because Jesus' "institutional" words point to it and because his death followed so rapidly upon the meal's completion. But it is God's abundance, foreseen in Mark 14:25 and implied in the use of the word "covenant," that provides the real basis for Jesus' self-giving, both in the supper itself and in the events that followed soon afterward. Jesus knew and treasured the prophecy transmitted in Isa 25:6–8, where God's final purpose for Israel and for the world is depicted in terms of a feast: "On [Mount Zion] the Lord of hosts will make for all peoples a feast of rich food, a feast of well-aged wines, of rich food with

---

48. For a sacramental interpretation of John, see Moloney, *A Body Broken for a Broken People*, 113–50; Moloney, "A Sacramental Reading of John 13:1–38."

49. Perhaps the best resource examining eucharistic eschatology is Wainwright, *Eucharist and Eschatology*.

50. See the discussion of the messianic banquet in the previous chapter.

marrow, of well-aged wines strained clear. And he will destroy on this mountain the shroud that is cast over all peoples . . . ; he will swallow up death forever."

This hope had guided Jesus' behavior during the whole course of his ministry, especially in his practice of eating with sinners and outcasts. Now, at the Last Supper, a sharpened vision of God's cosmic feast in the perfected kingdom empowered him to complete his self-offering. Only by means of this personal act, Jesus believed, could God's messiah open the doors of the banquet hall to Israel and the nations. But the feast itself was already there. Jesus could see it, and it drew him forward.[51]

Jesus was drawn forward, anticipating the eschatological feast that accompanies the coming of God's kingdom in its fullness. The cup of Christ's blood should remind us of his return, the time when he will joyfully share its contents with Israel and the nations in the kingdom banquet.

Paul also highlights the eschatological importance of the Eucharist in 1 Corinthians. The bread and cup both look *back* to the death of Christ and are to be *recurring practices* reminding the Corinthians to look *forward* to the return of the resurrected Jesus: "For *as often as* you eat this bread and drink the cup, you proclaim the Lord's death *until he comes*" (11:26, emphasis added). First Corinthians 11 is the only institution narrative that contains the phrase "as often as" attached to the bread and cup (11:25–26). The Apostle is clear that the *continued* celebration of the bread and cup proclaim the Lord's death until he comes. Paul later explains in ch. 15 that the return of Jesus will be the occasion for the resurrection of those who belong to Christ: "For as all die in Adam, so all will be made alive in Christ. But each in his own order: Christ the first fruits, then *at his coming* those who belong to Christ" (15:22–23, emphasis added). Hence the broader picture painted here by Paul is one in which the church meets together to share a meal, remembering the death of Jesus and anticipating the return of their resurrected Lord, at which time his followers will also be "raised imperishable" (15:52).[52]

51. Koenig, *Feast of the World's Redemption*, 42.

52. The eschatological dimensions of the Eucharist are also reflected in the parables comparing the Kingdom of Heaven/God to a banquet (Matt 22:1–14; 25:1–13; Luke 12:35–40; 14:7–24) and in the allusion to the "marriage supper of the Lamb" in Rev 19:9.

D. THE HOLY KISS IN THE NEW TESTAMENT

The holy kiss (or kiss of love) was a common mealtime worship practice in the early church.[53] There are five instances at the conclusion of various New Testament epistles where listeners are instructed to greet one another with a holy kiss: "Greet one another with a holy kiss" (Rom 16:16; 1 Cor 16:20; 2 Cor 13:12); "Greet all the brothers and sisters with a holy kiss" (1 Thess 5:26); "Greet one another with a kiss of love (*agapes*). Peace to all of you who are in Christ" (1 Pet 5:14). Because worship in the early church almost always occurred in the context of a meal, and because epistles were read during the worship service, we can place the holy kiss in the general context of the Love Feast.[54] When the command to "greet one another with a holy kiss" was read, the meal participants likely followed through by sharing the greeting. Since epistles were read during the *symposion* element of the Love Feast, and the commands to greet one another with a holy kiss occur at the end of the epistles, it appears that in early practice, the holy kiss was one of the final elements of the Love Feast. Some argue that no church ordinance is stated in the New Testament in plainer terms or with more authority than the holy kiss.[55]

It is possible that the holy kiss originated from the ministry of Jesus. At the end of John's Gospel, Jesus appears to the disciples on the evening of his resurrection and says "'Peace be with you. As the Father has sent me, so I send you.' When he had said this, he breathed on them and said to them, 'Receive the Holy Spirit. If you forgive the sins of any,

53. Helpful sources on the kiss, in general, and the holy kiss in the early church include Perella, *The Kiss Sacred and Profane*; Benko, "The Kiss."; Kreider, "Kiss of Peace."; Frijhoff, "Kiss Sacred and Profane."; Phillips, *Ritual Kiss in Early Worship*; Penn, "Performing Family."

54. Hal Taussig, *In the Beginning was the Meal*, 36–37, writes, "[M]eals provided a primary location for the reading of the early Christian documents. Again, there is little dispute in scholarship that the writings of the first hundred years were read primarily at the meals of these communities. It is just that scholarship has not noticed that this location for reading the early Christian literature both confirms the social significance of the meals and frames in an important way the meanings of the writings themselves. / The most obvious kind of document read at the meals was the letter. This most frequent genre of early Christian writing was explicitly written for the meals. The letters of Paul were written to communities of mostly illiterate persons. These people gathered in the name of Christ almost exclusively at meals. It is very clear from Paul's letters that he is not writing to a small, exclusively educated or representative subset of the communities in Corinth, Galatia, Philippi, Rome, or Thessalonica. Rather, he means his letters to be heard by all of the members of the communities."

55. Shuman, "Kiss, Holy," 698.

they are forgiven them; if you retain the sins of any, they are retained'"
(20:21–23). Stephen Benko ponders:

> [H]ow did he breathe on them? Simply by blowing air in their
> direction, or holding out his palm and blowing on it? Although
> we have no information on this particular point, the answer that
> comes most readily to mind is that Jesus kissed the disciples. As
> [previously] mentioned, an early animistic belief may have as-
> sociated the kiss with transmission of the spirit (breath of life)
> [see Gen 2:7]; these verses from the gospel of John may reflect the
> same belief. At any rate the practice of the holy kiss in the early
> church involved communication with the Holy Spirit (pneuma-
> breath), and it may have been based on the [implied] kiss of Jesus
> mentioned in John.[56]

This is certainly an intriguing possibility, although one wonders why
John would not have mentioned a kiss if it actually did occur. This hypothesis is strengthened by the fact that the implied kiss is connected to
the peace that Christ gives and Christ's teaching on forgiveness, for the
early church soon shifts to call the kiss the "kiss of peace," or simply *pax*
(peace), and the kiss came to represent reconciliation with God and one
another.

Apart from this implied kiss in John, when the holy kiss is mentioned in the epistles, it often occurs with two other benedictions: "The
grace of our Lord Jesus Christ be with you," and "The God of peace be
with you all." Eleanor Kreider writes:

> The ideas expressed in the three phrases are highly significant.
> And at the core of them, according to G.J. Cuming, was the
> kiss, which expressed the reconciliation which had taken place
> among the members. The phrase "God of peace," which had not
> occurred in the Old Testament, now indicated that God himself
> was the source of the peace which the church was experiencing.
> Peace was from God and grace was the "grace of our Lord Jesus
> Christ." . . . .
>
> Grace and peace—these became a reality in the life of the early
> believers through the activity of the Spirit who energized their
> worship. Through the Spirit they gave thanks to God for his pro-
> vision of salvation in Jesus Christ; through the Spirit they looked
> forward to the coming in fullness of God's reign. And day by day
> they acknowledged the presence of the Spirit in their life and

56. Benko, "The Kiss," 82.

worship as the fulfillment of Jesus' promise to them. The Spirit
was the source of all gifts; it was in the Spirit that they offered
their prayers. And just as they recognized Jesus as they partook
of the bread and cup of the ceremonial meal, so also they symbolized and dramatized the reality of the Holy Spirit among them
by a ritual observance—the holy kiss.[57]

Thus we see from the context of the holy kiss in the epistles that it symbolized and expressed outwardly the grace of Christ and the peace of
God.

The holy kiss served practically to redefine the members of the
church as brothers and sisters in Christ. Because kisses most often occurred between family members in antiquity, the holy kiss shared by
early followers of Jesus served to emphasize the church as the family of
God. Michael Penn writes, "[T]he adoption and modification of a typical
familial gesture into a decidedly Christian ritual helped early Christians
to redefine the concept of family."[58] Let us consider the command to
greet one another with a holy kiss found at the end of Romans. Recent
scholarship has tended to support the idea that Romans was written to
help Gentile Christians to respect Jewish Christians and to help the two
communities live together in Christian community.[59] In Rom 4:16–17,
Paul argues that Abraham was both the spiritual and the fleshly father
of Jewish and Gentile believers. This assertion "was especially significant to people in antiquity, for it meant that the two groups were now
closely related. In ancient culture, people had a deep corporate sense
of identity. To be was to be part of a group, and the primary group was
one's kin, both immediate and extended. To be related to another person
was to be responsible for and committed to the well being of that person or group."[60] Throughout Romans Paul emphasizes the importance
of Gentile and Jewish believers putting aside judgment and learning to
live and worship together in love. When he concludes the letter with the
command to "greet one another with a holy kiss" (16:16), it is not an
afterthought, but a final action embodying the familial relationship that
now exists between believers of Jewish and Gentile backgrounds. Thus,

57. Kreider, "Kiss of Peace," 30–31. Her reference to Cuming is from Cuming,
"Service-Endings in the Epistles."

58. Penn, "Performing Family," 154.

59. See for example, Gager, *Reinventing Paul*; Stowers, *A Rereading of Romans.*

60. Allen, *Wholly Scripture*, 56.

greeting one another with a holy kiss was a way of "performing" family, although the family was much broader than one's family of birth.

In a related manner to the family kiss, it should be stated that in its earliest practice, the holy kiss was shared between men and women in the church. This is no doubt a key reason that the scriptures clearly define that it is to be a *holy* kiss. When the author of 1 Peter describes it as a "kiss of love" (5:14), it is the kiss of *agape* love, not erotic love. It is similar to the kiss between family members who love one another, even to the point of death, not the kiss of lovers who find passion in each other's embrace. "The attribute *holy* lifts it above mere human friendship or fellowship; it links it to that which is sacred and divine. It lifts it to the realm of eternal love and fellowship. As the kiss is a binding pledge in earthly ties, so the holy kiss is a binding pledge in heavenly ties, binding believers in Christ together with the cords of sweet and holy union, making them strong in brotherly and sisterly love and Christian affection."[61] In sum, we have seen from a few powerful examples in New Testament epistles that the holy kiss was a greeting of Christian love shared in the context of mealtime worship.

E. FEETWASHING IN THE NEW TESTAMENT

Feetwashing was a common practice in antiquity that was commonly associated with personal hygiene/comfort, hospitality, servitude, and cultic practices.[62] In his doctoral dissertation, John Christopher Thomas notes many examples of feetwashing in the Greco-Roman world which inform our understanding of the practice found in the Bible.[63] His research highlights that feetwashing most frequently is recorded before a meal or banquet. Additional ancient sources indicate that feetwashing was closely related to preparation; to be inadequately prepared was likened to doing a task "with unwashed feet."[64] In the Old Testament, feetwashing is named in connection with worship, personal hygiene/comfort, hospitality, and servitude.[65] In Judg 19:21, feetwashing immediately precedes

61. Shuman, "Kiss, Holy," 698.

62. See chapter 3, "Footwashing in the Jewish and Graeco-Roman Environment," in Thomas, *Footwashing in John 13*, 26–60; Allison, "Foot Washing," 322.

63. Thomas, *Footwashing in John 13*, 42–56.

64. Lucian says of Demonax: "You must not conceive, however, that he rushed into these matters with unwashed feet, as the saying goes," *Demonax*, 145.

65. For worship examples, see Exod 30:17–21; 40:30–32; 1 Kgs 7:38; 2 Chr 4:6. For

a meal. Of the four examples of feetwashing in the New Testament, in three cases the action occurs during a meal (Luke 7:36–50; John 12:1–8; 13:1–20). Although the fourth reference in 1 Tim 5:9–10, which speaks of widows washing the feet of the saints, does not specifically mention a meal, it is plausible that the action was connected to Christian mealtime worship. Thomas observes seven prominent Christian interpretations of feetwashing: an example of humility, a symbol of the Eucharist, a symbol of Baptism, cleansing/forgiveness from sin, a sacrament separate from Baptism and the Eucharist, a soteriological sign, and a polemical tool.[66]

1. Feetwashing in John 13

The most prominent feetwashing narrative in the New Testament is the account in John 13, where Jesus washes his disciples' feet during the Last Supper.[67] There are two general aspects of this narrative that are

---

personal hygiene/comfort references, see 2 Sam 11:6–13; 19:24; Song 5:3. For hospitality connections, see Gen 18:4; 19:2; 24:32; 43:24; Judg 19:21 (immediately preceding a meal!); 1 Sam 25:41. For servitude/slavery associations, see 1 Sam 25:41; Pss 60:8; 108:9.

66. Thomas, *Footwashing in John 13*, 11–17.

67. John writes, "Now before the festival of the Passover, Jesus knew that his hour had come to depart from this world and go to the Father. Having loved his own who were in the world, he loved them to the end. The devil had already put it into the heart of Judas son of Simon Iscariot to betray him. And during supper Jesus, knowing that the Father had given all things into his hands, and that he had come from God and was going to God, got up from the table, took off his outer robe, and tied a towel around himself. Then he poured water into a basin and began to wash the disciples' feet and to wipe them with the towel that was tied around him. He came to Simon Peter, who said to him, 'Lord, are you going to wash my feet?' Jesus answered, 'You do not know now what I am doing, but later you will understand.' Peter said to him, 'You will never wash my feet.' Jesus answered, 'Unless I wash you, you have no share with me.' Simon Peter said to him, 'Lord, not my feet only but also my hands and my head!' Jesus said to him, 'One who has bathed does not need to wash, except for the feet, but is entirely clean. And you are clean, though not all of you.' For he knew who was to betray him; for this reason he said, 'Not all of you are clean.'

After he had washed their feet, had put on his robe, and had returned to the table, he said to them, 'Do you know what I have done to you? You call me Teacher and Lord—and you are right, for that is what I am. So if I, your Lord and Teacher, have washed your feet, you also ought to wash one another's feet. For I have set you an example, that you also should do as I have done to you. Very truly, I tell you, servants are not greater than their master, nor are messengers greater than the one who sent them. If you know these things, you are blessed if you do them. I am not speaking of all of you; I know whom I have chosen. But it is to fulfill the scripture, 'The one who ate my bread has lifted his heel against me.' I tell you this now, before it occurs, so that when it does occur, you may

noteworthy. First, this story is unique in ancient literature, "for no other person of superior status is described as voluntarily washing the feet of a subordinate."[68] This distinctiveness serves to emphasize the point that Jesus' action was motivated by *agape* love (13:1, 34). Second, as we have already observed, the idiomatic use of "with unwashed feet" comes to mean "without adequate preparation."[69] It is not surprising, then, that John 13:1–20 tells of Jesus washing his disciples' feet, for the whole section of John 13–17 is dedicated to Jesus' preparation of the disciples for his departure and their subsequent role in continuing his ministry.

A. The Unity of John 13:1–20.

A crucial element in the interpretation of John 13 is whether the first twenty verses of the chapter should be understood as describing one tradition (Jesus' action and his subsequent commands to repeat feet-washing) or two events (a radical action and a separate teaching concerning service in general). More than a few scholars argue that John 13:1–20 should be divided into two sections (vv. 1–11 and 12–20).[70] In general, they believe that vv. 6–11 are original material, while vv. 7–20 are general ethical teachings which were added later. Since Jesus equates the feetwashing in vv. 6–11 with cleansing/forgiveness of sin, which is clearly a divine prerogative, scholars in this camp have sought to inter-

---

believe that I am he. Very truly, I tell you, whoever receives one whom I send receives me; and whoever receives me receives him who sent me.' . . . [Jesus identifies Judas as his betrayer by giving him a piece of bread, Judas leaves] . . . When [Judas] had gone out, Jesus said, 'Now the Son of Man has been glorified, and God has been glorified in him. If God has been glorified in him, God will also glorify him in himself and will glorify him at once. Little children, I am with you only a little longer. You will look for me; and as I said to the Jews so now I say to you, "Where I am going, you cannot come." I give you a new commandment, that you love (*agapate*) one another. Just as I have loved you, you also should love (*agapate*) one another. By this everyone will know that you are my disciples, if you have love (*agapen*) for one another' " (John 13:1–20; 31–35).

68. Thomas, *Footwashing in John 13*, 59.

69. Thomas, ibid., 34, writes, "In the first century CE footwashing came to be such an expected part of personal hygiene that to approach a task without adequate preparation could be described as acting 'with unwashed feet,' i.e. impromptu."

70. Ibid., 116–19. Scholars distinguish the two sections in vv. 6–11 and 12–20 in three basic ways: Boismard, "Le lavement des pieds (Jn XIII, 1–17)," contrasts sacramental and moral interpretations. Richter, *Die Fusswaschung im Johannesevangelium*, 252–78, distinguishes between christological and sacramental interpretations. Bultmann, *Gospel of John*, 467, differentiates between a cleansing by hearing the revealer's word and a gesture of humility. Also see Segovia, "John 13:1–20."

pret Jesus' command to wash feet "as a moral example of humility to be imitated by others."[71]

However, other scholars make a convincing argument that John 13:1–20 should be understood as a literary unit.[72] First, at face value, the attempt to divide the story into original material and subsequent moral teaching comes across as trying to explain away a difficult text.[73] Second, David Daube observes that John 13:1–20 contains a tripartite structure (a mystifying gesture, a question, and an interpretation) that is common in many ancient sources, especially rabbinic literature.[74] Daube's analysis leads one to the position that John clearly intends that Jesus' command for imitation be linked to the act of feetwashing. Third, Catholic scholar Francis Moloney treats John 13:1–17 as a literary unit and argues that it is better to divide John 13 into three sections (vv. 1–17, 18–20, and 21–38) based on the presence of several double-*amen* statements in the chapter (*amen amen lego humin*, "Amen, Amen, I say to you," vv. 16, 20, 21, 38).[75] Fourth, Baptist pastor Paul Duke also interprets vv. 1–17 as a literary unit and draws significant connections between these verses and the new commandment to love one another at the end of the chapter.[76] Finally, Ralph P. Martin argues for the literary unity of John 13 and criticizes Richter, a chief proponent of the two-section hypothesis, writing:

> [H]is arguments are not conclusive, since it is always problematical to call in a redactor to smooth out alleged stylistic differ-

71. Brown, *The Gospel According to John (XIII–XXI)*, 562.

72. John Christopher Thomas and others; see Thomas, *Footwashing in John 13*, 120–25.

73. A. Weiser writes, "Does not there exist the danger that we approach the Gospel too much with our own understanding and determine ourselves why it should have been and why it should not have been written? As long as the text allows a meaningful explanation, and statements of other passages contribute to a non-contradictory understanding, one has no right to interpret the text in a mutually exclusive sense and to draw out of it a conclusion for the literary critical judgment," Weiser, "Joh 13:12–20," 256, quoted in Thomas, *Footwashing in John 13*, 124.

74. Daube, *The New Testament and Rabbinic Judaism*, 182–83, notes, "John is an accomplished writer—the tripartite framework and the setting we have ascribed to it are quite plain. A master is surrounded by his circle. The former deliberately acts in a way for the moment unintelligible to the latter, in a way that must seem paradoxical, though its significance will ultimately be made clear . . . and once the significance is revealed, the master's practice turns out to have been right and worth imitating."

75. Moloney, *A Body Broken for a Broken People*, 122–27.

76. Duke, "John 13:1–17, 31b–35."

ences. Nor is there any compulsion to see verses 12–20 as saying something different from the earlier section. Rather, Jesus' words to the disciples as a group reinforce what has just taken place. There is little force in Richter's argument that the christological-soteriological significance of verses 6–11 cannot be harmonized with the ethical connotation of verses 12–20.[77]

Let us examine vv. 6–11 and the way in which feetwashing is related to cleansing from sin.

B. Feetwashing and Cleansing.

The conversation between Jesus and Peter in vv. 6–11 reveals that in addition to removing dirt from the disciples' feet and demonstrating radical humility, the feetwashing also effects the spiritual cleansing of the disciples.[78] When Peter refuses to allow Jesus to wash his feet, Jesus responds: "Unless I wash you, you have no share with me" (13:8b). Peter relents, but wants Jesus to wash him all over, to which Jesus replies: "One who has bathed does not need to wash, except for the feet, but is entirely clean. And you (plural) are clean, though not all of you [i.e., Judas]" (13:10). By definition, bathing and feetwashing are acts of physical cleansing. It was common for first-century individuals to bathe before a journey, and upon arriving at their destination they would only wash their feet, not rebathe their entire body.

Yet Jesus is talking about more than physical cleansing in these verses. By washing his disciples' feet, Jesus offers them a form of spiritual cleansing, building upon the complete cleansing of baptism. John Christopher Thomas argues that the feetwashing is a ceremony focused on the cleansing of post-baptismal sin, an issue the Johannine community struggled to comprehend.[79] John Colwell comments:

---

77. Martin, *New Testament Foundations*, 308.

78. It is not feasible to address fully this complex topic here. John Christopher Thomas has written at length about the connection between the feetwashing and cleansing; see Thomas, *Footwashing in John 13*, 89–107, 155–72, and "Footwashing and the Lord's Supper," 178–82. Other helpful sources include the chapter "The Sacrament of Cleansing" in Colwell, *Promise and Presence*, 179–96; Nation, "Washing Feet"; Duke, "John 13:1–17, 31b–35."

79. Thomas, *Footwashing in John 13*, 155–71. Post-baptismal sin was an issue the Johannine community wrestled with. See 1 John 1:5–10; 2:1–6, and also Heb 6:4–6; 10:26–29.

> The problem of post-baptismal sin is inherently sacramental and it is therefore appropriate for the Church to identify a sacramental resolution [feetwashing]. The problem of post-baptismal sin is inherently sacramental since through baptism we are included in Christ, we receive a new nature, we receive a "sacramental character" which is indelible. Post-baptismal sin therefore . . . is deeply incongruous with this sacramentally mediated character; it is a denial of sacramental identity.[80]

That the disciples receive spiritual cleansing from Jesus is a central reason that some scholars have sought to differentiate between 13:6–11 and 13:12–20. Can it be that Jesus wants his disciples to imitate him in washing feet *and* in effecting spiritual cleansing?

Although it seems preposterous, the New Testament does indicate that Jesus gives the church authority to forgive sins. In a post-resurrection appearance in John, Jesus tells his disciples, "If you forgive the sins of any, they are forgiven them; if you retain the sins of any, they are retained" (John 20:23). Similarly, in Matt 18:18–20, Jesus instructs the disciples in dealing with communal conflict, saying: "Truly I tell you, whatever you bind on earth will be bound in heaven, and whatever you loose on earth will be loosed in heaven. Again, truly I tell you, if two of you agree on earth about anything you ask, it will be done for you by my Father in heaven. For where two or three are gathered in my name, I am there among them."[81] The phrase "Truly I tell you" (*amen lego humin*) in both v. 18 and v. 19 indicates that these statements are authoritative and deeply meaningful. The "you" in both John and Matthew is plural, and it is clear from Matthew that the "you all" Jesus refers to is the church.[82]

80. Colwell, *Promise and Presence*, 182. Earlier (pp. 3–4) Colwell, a Baptist, explains his use of the term sacramental: "The tentative (and perhaps non-sustainable) distinction between the sacraments and the sacramental will recur throughout this book as a means of avoiding unnecessary and unhelpful semantic squabbles. . . . Ultimately I really do not care too much whether we refer to something as a sacrament or as a sacramental act. I am far more concerned to recognize and to affirm an underlying dynamic as it is rooted in the nature of God and of God's relatedness to the world."

81. For an in-depth analysis of binding and loosing, see Yoder, "Binding and Loosing (1998)."

82. In 18:17, immediately prior to the quoted verses, we find one of the two places in the New Testament where Jesus uses the word church (*ekklesia*). The other instance is Matt 16:18, another "binding and loosing" passage that follows after Peter's confession of Jesus as Messiah. Yoder writes, "It is no accident that in Matthew 16 the assignment by Jesus of the power to bind and loose follows directly upon Peter's first confession of Christ as Messiah. The confession is the basis of the authority; the authorization given

Thus, in both Matthew and John, Jesus wants the church to be involved in the process of forgiving sins.

But how can this be? Only God has the authority to forgive sins! In his chapter "The Sacrament of Cleansing," John Colwell draws the connection between binding and loosing and the feetwashing passage in John 13:

> [T]his is a mediated responsibility and authority, mediated by the Spirit, mediated through the Church, mediated through the ministers given to the Church by the ascended Christ. Only Christ has the authority to forgive sin, *only Christ has the authority to wash our dirty feet and to pronounce us clean—but Christ mediates this authority, by his Spirit, through those he has so called.* In Christ's name and in the power of the Spirit the [follower of Christ] has the authority . . . to pronounce forgiveness, to enact restoration.[83]

Members of the church, the body of Christ on earth, are given the mediated authority to wash feet, and in so doing, to participate in cleansing and forgiving one another in Jesus' name. The example of Judas is a reminder, however, that one cannot simply equate feetwashing with spiritual cleansing. Merely participating in feetwashing does not make one clean, for Judas received the feetwashing from Jesus and yet is declared to be unclean. As Gail O'Day observes: "Cleanliness has to do with one's relationship to Jesus and acceptance of the foot washing, not with the cleansing power of the water itself. To be unclean is not to be unwashed, for Judas belongs to the circle of those whose feet Jesus washed. Rather, to be unclean is to turn away from union and intimacy with Jesus."[84] Judas's uncleanness stems from his rejection of Jesus and his redefinition of Messianic prophecy, which led Judas to betray Jesus to the religious authorities. Jesus' relationship with the other eleven disciples was much more intimate, even though they fled when he was arrested. Christ con-

---

is the seal upon the confession. The church is where, because there Jesus is confessed as Christ, men and women are empowered to speak to one another in God's name," ibid., 332.

83. Colwell, *Promise and Presence*, 187 (emphasis added). I have adapted the last sentence to be more egalitarian. Colwell's original sentence reads, "In Christ's name and in the power of the Spirit the Christian minister has the authority (and the responsibility) to say 'I absolve you' (*ego te absolvo*), to pronounce forgiveness, to enact restoration."

84. O'Day, "The Gospel of John," 724.

tinues to cleanse his followers today from the sin that they have accumulated in their lives, and this cleansing is wonderfully demonstrated when the church continues the practice of feetwashing.

c. Feetwashing and Intimacy.

John tells us that Jesus was motivated by love to wash his disciples' feet (13:1). Feetwashing revealed Christ's desire for a personal and intimate relationship with his disciples, for when he stooped to wash their feet he crossed normal boundaries for the rabbi-disciple relationship. It was truly shocking for the disciples when Jesus reached out and touched their feet—the dirtiest parts of their bodies. Paul Duke comments:

> We can feel [the disciples] squirming. Their embarrassment is palpable, as enacted by Peter. But the dread is not so much centered in how menial an act Jesus has undertaken for them, as in how painfully intimate it is. It is often noted that Jewish slaves could not be required to wash feet, as if it were merely too servile a function. Overlooked is the fact that a man's feet were often washed by his wife or his children or by a welcoming host. An issue of intimate acquaintance seems to apply. The indignity for the disciples resides in their teacher's disarming initiative to touch them in this way, to bring himself so near and naked to their need, to apply himself to their private rankness, to cleanse for them what they would prefer almost anyone else to cleanse.[85]

Being a disciple of Jesus is radically different than following after any other leader or practicing any other religion. True Christian discipleship brings followers of Jesus to a place of intimacy that is uncomfortable. To confess Christ as Lord means that he is Lord of every part of our lives. When Jesus "moves in" to our lives, he is not content to occupy the presentable areas of our bodily house (i.e., the guest room, living room, and dining room). He wants to be Lord in the bedrooms, closets, and basements of our lives as well. Feetwashing demonstrates Jesus' desire for intimate fellowship with his followers.

d. Feetwashing and Servanthood.

The account in John 13 makes it clear that feetwashing is connected to servanthood. Jesus

---

85. Duke, "John 13:1–17, 31b–35," 399.

got up from the supper (*deipnon*), took off his outer robe, and tied a towel around himself. Then he poured water into a basin and began to wash the disciples' feet and to wipe them with the towel that was tied around him. . . . [He said to them] "If I, your Lord and Teacher, have washed your feet, you also ought to wash one another's feet. For I have set you an example (*hypodeigma*), that you also should do as I have done to you. Very truly, I tell you, servants are not greater than their master, nor are messengers greater than the one who sent them. If you know these things, you are blessed if you do them." (13:4–5, 14–17)

We have seen above that it is best to interpret 13:1–20 as a single unit, so that Jesus' words in vv. 14–17 are instruction concerning the action of feetwashing. This is the only instance in the New Testament where Jesus tells the disciples that he has given them an example (*hypodeigma*) that they should follow.[86] In case they have trouble understanding him, he tells them three times (vv. 14, 15, and 17) that they should wash one another's feet! The message was clear. If he, their Lord and Teacher, could humble himself and do the task of a servant, then they have no excuse for demurring (other than their own pride). And this servanthood, this feetwashing, is not to be undertaken reluctantly, but rather should flow from the disciples' love for one another (13:34). A central theme of the feetwashing narrative in John is the voluntary servanthood of Jesus and Jesus' instruction for his disciples likewise voluntarily to serve one another in love.

2. An Allusion to Feetwashing in Luke?

While John is the only Gospel to tell explicitly of Jesus washing his disciples' feet, Luke does place a pericope on servanthood in his Last Supper narrative, which may be an indirect reference to feetwashing (Luke 22:24–27).[87] We should note two things that are unique in Luke's narrative. First, only Luke places this pericope in the midst of the Last Supper

---

86. Coloe, "Sources in the Shadows," 78.

87. After Jesus institutes the bread and cup remembrance we read: "A dispute also arose among them as to which one of them was to be regarded as the greatest. But he said to them, 'The kings of the Gentiles lord it over them; and those in authority over them are called benefactors. But not so with you; rather the greatest among you must become like the youngest, and the leader like one who serves. For who is greater, the one who is at the table or the one who serves? Is it not the one at the table? But I am among you as one who serves'" (Luke 22:24–27).

(in Matthew and Mark this teaching on servanthood emerges from an argument that occurred earlier on the road to Jerusalem[88]). Assuming the primacy of Mark, the reader is left wondering: Why does Luke move the pericope and merge it into his account of the Last Supper? Second, Luke adds v. 27 to the material found in Mark: "For who is greater, the one who is at the table or the one who serves? Is it not the one at the table? But I am among you as one who serves" (Luke 22:27). Since this teaching in Luke occurs during the Last Supper, it makes sense for Luke to mention the table. Notice that it would fit perfectly for us to move from Jesus' words "I am among you as one who serves" into the John 13 narrative where Jesus washes the disciples' feet. Also notice the parallels between Jesus' discussion of the master/servant relation in Luke and his words in John:

> You call me Teacher and Lord—and you are right, for that is what I am. So if I, your Lord and Teacher, have washed your feet, you also ought to wash one another's feet. For I have set you an example, that you also should do as I have done to you. Very truly, I tell you, servants are not greater than their master, nor are messengers greater than the one who sent them. If you know these things, you are blessed if you do them. (John 13:13–17)

Without the feetwashing narrative in John 13, it would be foolish to infer that the servanthood pericope in Luke somehow communicates that Jesus stooped to serve his disciples by washing their feet. However, when considering the parallels mentioned above, it is plausible that Luke knew of the feetwashing tradition and subsequently chose to convey Jesus' teaching on servanthood in the context of the Last Supper rather than on the road into Jerusalem.

3. Feetwashing in First Timothy

There is one final passage in 1 Timothy that mentions feetwashing: "Let a widow be put on the list if she is not less than sixty years old and has been married only once; she must be well attested for her good works, as one who has brought up children, shown hospitality, washed the saints'

---

88. Matt 20:20–28; Mark 10:35–45. In these passages, James and John—likely assuming that Jesus' intention in going to Jerusalem was to overthrow the government and establish a new kingdom—ask to be seated at the right and left of Jesus in his kingdom. This petition infuriates the other disciples, and Jesus uses the conflict to teach them that "whoever wishes to be great among you must be your servant" (Matt 20:26).

(*hagion*) feet, helped the afflicted, and devoted herself to doing good in every way" (1 Tim 5:9–10). In Paul's writings it is clear that *hagion* refers to believers, so for widows to wash the believers' feet implies that this action was a distinctively Christian practice. It follows that this practice was most likely based upon the feetwashing tradition conveyed in the Gospel of John. John Christopher Thomas has shown that there is little evidence in ancient writings that women who were not slaves washed the feet of guests. He concludes, "Since few would want to argue that the widows were the slaves of the community, what accounts for their action unless it has been prompted by Jesus' own example? For there is no reason for the widows to perform this function for the community unless it has been redefined in the light of Jesus' action."[89] Thus, it is probable that the feetwashing in First Timothy is based on Jesus' washing of the disciples' feet during the Last Supper.

4. Was Feetwashing a Part of the Love Feast?

It seems likely that mutual feetwashing was a part of some Christian Love Feasts, particularly in those churches (in Asia Minor?) where the Gospel of John was circulating. However, it may not have been the case that mutual feetwashing patterned after the example of Christ was practiced in all Love Feasts. Nevertheless, it appears probable that some type of feetwashing occurred as guests arrived to celebrate the Love Feast; after all, this was a normal custom of hospitality. And it seems most likely that those Christians who were familiar with the tradition of Jesus' feetwashing likely would have imitated Christ's example before the meal began, when feetwashing was normally practiced, rather than after the meal during the symposion, which was when Jesus first taught the lesson on servanthood. Two additional points indicate that feetwashing occurred during the Love Feast. First, Jesus *commanded* his disciples to wash each other's feet, just as he has washed their feet. To be obedient followers, his disciples would have continued the practice of washing one another's feet, and this would have logically occurred during their weekly meal/ worship gatherings. Second, John 13 begins and ends with *agape* love (13:1, 34–35). At the conclusion of the chapter (vv. 34–35) Jesus gives his disciples a new command to love one another just as he has loved

89. Thomas, *Footwashing in John 13*, 136.

them (recently and powerfully demonstrated by the feetwashing).[90] The feetwashing scene is thus framed by love. If John accurately records that Jesus gave his disciples a new command to love one another during the Last Supper, it would make sense that "Love Feast" would become a primary name for the church's subsequent fellowship meals. In the same way that the Eucharist looks back to Synoptic accounts of the Last Supper when Jesus gave thanks and gave the disciples the bread and cup, so too the Love Feast looks back to the Johannine Last Supper when Jesus washed his disciples' feet and commanded them to love one another.[91] While one cannot definitively demonstrate from the scriptures that feetwashing was a regular (or even an occasional) part of the earliest Love Feasts, if the Love Feasts were based on John 13 it would be reasonable for feetwashing to accompany the fellowship meal.

One can make a strong argument that the term Love Feast (*agapais*) largely developed from the Johannine Last Supper, where Jesus commands his disciples to love one another (*agapate*). In John's account, Jesus demonstrates his love for his disciples by humbly washing their feet, which he also connects to cleansing. By washing their feet, Jesus has cleansed and prepared them, physically and spiritually, to love one another. Paul Duke writes:

> Clean for what? For the New Mandate, at last. To his friends with the freshly scrubbed ankles and toes, Jesus, back in his place and reclothed, says, "Do as I have done to you . . ." (v. 15). "I give you a new commandment, that you love one another. Just as I have loved you, you also should love one another" (v. 34). It is worth noticing that in John's Gospel, this is the first positive use of the verb *agapao* [love] for anyone but God and Jesus. In fact, the verb applied to humans has been used three times negatively (3:19; 8:42; 12:43) and the only use of the noun *agape* has been negative

---

90. Koenig, *Feast of the World's Redemption*, 94, writes, "In context, this command probably refers back to the footwashing. Such humble service would embody the manner in which Jesus loves his followers and in which they are to love one another. By the time the fourth gospel was composed (about 90 CE), footwashing might well have comprised part of an agape feast that the Johannine churches associated with Jesus' last supper."

91. We should also note that Paul's popular passage on love, 1 Cor 13, occurs in the context of his discussion of the Lord's Supper, gifts in the body of Christ, and appropriate behavior during post-meal worship services (chs. 11–14). Paul does not call the meal a Love Feast, but it is clear that he wants the Corinthians to share their food with one another, feasting together in unity and love.

(5:42). It is as if human love had been impossible until now. Only after receiving the cleansing sign of Jesus' love for them are the disciples in position to love each other. In more ways than one, this commandment is "new."[92]

Only after the disciples have their soles (and souls) washed are they fully prepared to love one another. They receive the gift of love from Jesus and, in turn, are called both to wash one another's feet (v. 14) and to love one another (vv. 34–35). When the disciples washed one another's feet, they must have remembered their continual need for cleansing. Having given and received this act of cleansing and service, the disciples were prepared truly to share the Love Feast with one another.

F. EUCHARISTIC PREPARATION/EXAMINATION IN THE NEW TESTAMENT

The New Testament actually gives us very little information on how church members prepared to eat the bread and drink the cup. It is likely the case that in the first decades the church had not developed the practices of eucharistic preparation and examination that became more prominent in the second and third centuries. Rather, the early church celebrated Jesus Christ in their common meal, which included a simple ceremonial remembrance that used the bread and the cup, which were part of the mealtime food and drink.

The only example of examination connected with the Lord's Supper is in 1 Cor 11:27–32.[93] In these verses Paul returns to his critique of the abuses of the Lord's Supper mentioned in 11:17–22. When church members gather to celebrate the Lord's Supper, they should do so as a community united by the gospel that proclaims: "There is no longer Jew or Greek, there is no longer slave or free, there is no longer male and female; for all of you are one in Christ Jesus" (Gal 3:28). Whatever divisions were present in the church must be negotiated out of love for the unity of the church, just as "Christ loved the church and gave himself up for her" (Eph 5:25). Paul tells the Corinthians: "Examine yourselves, and only then eat of the bread and drink of the cup. For all who eat and drink without discerning the body, eat and drink judgment against themselves" (11:28–29). Is Paul calling the Corinthians individually to

92. Duke, "John 13:1–17, 31b–35," 400.
93. See p. 49 above for the text.

examine their lives and actions (hence the tradition in many churches of observing a time of personal examination prior to taking communion), or is this examination something that occurs at the communal level?

The context of 11:17–34 indicates that Paul is primarily concerned with communal relations, not individual piety. Therefore his instruction concerning examination focuses on their interpersonal relationships, not their introspective consciences.[94] The key to this eucharistic examination is found in the phrase "discerning the body" in 11:29. Richard Hays writes:

> For Paul, "discerning the body" means recognizing the community of believers for what it really is: the one body of Christ. Paul has already used this image for the church in 10:16–17, *and he will develop it at greater length in 12:12–31a.* Those who are failing to "discern the body" are those who act selfishly, focusing on their own spirituality and exercising their own social privileges while remaining heedless of those who share with them in the new covenant inaugurated by the Lord's death.[95]

For the Corinthians, to discern the body means for them to evaluate the health of the church, the body of Christ ("Now you are the body of Christ and individually members of it," 12:27). When there are divisions at the Lord's Supper (like some going hungry and others getting drunk), the body of Christ is not healthy and faithful. Paul wants the members of the church to judge themselves and to change their behavior, rather than risk being judged by the Lord for their continued abuse of the Lord's Supper. When considering Paul's earlier recommendation for the church to remove the sexually immoral man from their gathering (5:1–13), it is entirely consistent to assume that if the abusers of the Lord's Supper failed to change their behavior for the good of the whole body, then they would be disciplined by the church.[96]

94. Krister Stendahl has masterfully demonstrated that the Apostle Paul did not focus on introspective matters like wrestling with guilt from sin—views which have emerged when reading Paul through Augustine and Luther—but rather on mediating between Jews and Gentiles as they argued over the importance of keeping the Law. See Stendahl, "Paul and the Introspective Conscience," 78–96.

95. Hays, *First Corinthians*, 200 (emphasis added).

96. Hays, ibid., 202, writes, "We should perhaps understand 11:31 not just as a summons to individual self-judgment but rather as a call for the *community* to exercise self-regulatory judgment to bring greater order to the Lord's Supper by disciplining those who treat it as their own private dinner party. Where the church exercises such

In 11:33 Paul wraps up his discussion of the Lord's Supper by instructing, "when you come together to eat, wait for [or receive] one another." Richard Hays observes that the verb *ekdechesthai* (here translated "to wait for") can also be translated "to receive."[97] This reading may correspond better with the problems mentioned in 11:21–22, namely that the Corinthians must work harder to receive one another as guests. The overall message is essentially the same, regardless which translation is used: when the Corinthians come together to eat they are to be mindful of one another so that their meal reflects the sacrificial love of Jesus. If their own personal hunger negatively impacts the fellowship meal, they should eat at home before the meal (11:34). In sum, in the only text that addresses preparation for the Lord's Supper in the New Testament (1 Cor 11:27–34), the instruction is primarily about the importance of communal examination/discernment and not about personal examination before taking the bread and cup.[98]

G. SUMMARY

In this chapter we have analyzed the relevant scriptural passages that inform our understanding of the Love Feast. It has been demonstrated that while there are two early forms of the Eucharist—the *koinonia/agape* and the *anamnesis*, (1) the textual evidence is not sufficient to distinguish reliably between the two, and (2) the differences in the two forms do not indicate a fundamental disagreement in practice or belief among various Christian communities. In 1 Corinthians and Acts we read that the church gathered on the first day of the week to break bread and celebrate the Lord's Supper. This evening meal was likely an "extended

---

disciplinary discernment, God's judgment is averted; where the church fails to exercise discernment, God's judgment intervenes to prevent them from falling under final condemnation."

97. Hays, ibid., 202–3, writes, "Paul is telling the Corinthians not just to wait for one another but to *receive* one another as guests (cf. Rom 15:7) when they come together. This meaning of *ekdechesthai*, though not found elsewhere in the New Testament, is well established in other Greek sources (e.g., 3 Macc. 5:26 and Josephus, *Antiquities* 7.351). On this reading, Paul is calling the more affluent Corinthians not merely to preserve a public appearance of unity in the celebration of the Supper but actually to break down the barriers of social status and to receive the poorer members as guests in their homes, sharing their food with those who have none."

98. Some, however, would want to emphasize that personal examination and confession are (necessary) precursors to successful communal examination.

Sabbath" celebration that began on Saturday evening and extended into Sunday morning (according to the Jewish calendar). The Christian meal was radically inclusive, bringing together the rich and the poor, women and men, Jews and Gentiles, masters and slaves, all of whom were equals at the Lord's table. There were, however, occasions when Christians fell back on the prevailing social customs and neglected to celebrate the Love Feast in love and unity.

One of the most important parts of the Love Feast was the celebration of Communion using the bread and cup. This special thanksgiving and remembrance occurred at some point during the evening meal, most likely at the junction between the *deipnon* and the *symposion*, when the ceremonial libation was customarily offered. Sharing the cup was an occasion to remember the once-for-all sacrifice of Christ on the cross and to watch expectantly for his return, when he will once again drink the fruit of the vine in the banquet of the Kingdom of God. We also saw that the early church had a fairly unusual greeting, a holy kiss, which served to emphasize the new familial bonds that were being formed between brothers and sisters in Christ. Another important practice in some church communities was feetwashing, which was redefined by Jesus during the Last Supper. The account in John reveals that feetwashing is connected to spiritual cleansing and to humble service. Lastly, we explored the origins of eucharistic examination in 1 Corinthians, which seems to have been primarily a task of communal examination rather than a call for the individual worshiper to look inside his or her conscience. Having examined the scriptural basis for the Love Feast, we now shift to examine its celebration in the first three centuries of the church.

4

Extending Hospitality

The Love Feast before Constantine

PAUL BRADSHAW HAS WRITTEN that "contemporary currents in New Testament scholarship . . . stress the essentially pluriform nature of primitive Christianity, and so render improbable the traditional idea that a single, uniform archetype ultimately underlies the later diversity in Christian worship practices."[1] In the previous chapter we saw some of this pluriform nature in the texts of the New Testament, noting different emphases and practices in the mealtime worship services of churches around the Mediterranean. The current chapter continues to explore the worship practices of the early church that are present in non-biblical witnesses and in archaeological evidence. We will limit the current analysis to those sources that can be dated to before the time of Constantine (i.e., 313 CE). Broadly speaking, in some places the evening Love Feast seems to have continued to function as the primary worship celebration for churches, while in other places the church began meeting for worship before dawn on Sunday morning. These Sunday morning services consisted of prayers and instruction and concluded with the celebration of the Eucharist, which was no longer a part of a broader meal but was now a token meal; the bread and the cup. In addition to exploring the practices of the fellowship meal and the Eucharist in the early church, we will continue to look at the developments of the holy kiss, feetwashing, and eucharistic examination. Of course, since worship in the early church was pluriform, there were variations in practice between churches in different locations. We begin by looking at the fellowship meal of the early Love Feast.

1. Bradshaw, *Origins of Christian Worship*, 52–53.

A. THE FELLOWSHIP MEAL

The fellowship meal was a central characteristic of the early Love Feast. The worship services of the early church almost always involved eating together. Christians gathered to share food in each other's homes or in rented spaces at the close of the day, most frequently on Sabbath evenings (although weekday meals may also have been shared too). It was common for most participants, if not all, to contribute food for the supper. At some point during the meal, likely at the transition between *deipnon* and *symposion*, bread and wine were consecrated and shared in thanksgiving and remembrance of Christ. The after-dinner worship service also included prayers, the singing of hymns, and the reading of epistles from other churches or bishops.[2] It was common for the worship service to last into the Sunday morning hours.[3] At the conclusion of their gathering believers passed the peace among each other, that is, they exchanged the holy kiss. In the first decades these communion services appear to have been celebratory occasions characterized more by joy and gratitude than by sorrow and repentance. Because of the radical nature of the Christian fellowship meal, however, it is not surprising that challenges began to develop in the celebration of the Love Feast.[4]

2. The earliest known Christian hymn, the *Phos hilaron* (Gladdening Light), indicates that worship services were held in the evening: "Hail Gladdening Light of His pure glory poured / Who is the Immortal Father, Heavenly, Blest / Holiest of Holies, Jesus Christ our Lord / Now we are come to the sun's hour of rest / The lights of evening 'round us shine / We hymn the Father, Son, and Holy Spirit Divine / Worthiest art Thou, at all times to be sung with undefiled tongue / Son of our God, Giver of life alone / Therefore, in all the world Thy glories, Lord, Thine own," Fremantle, ed., *Treasury of Early Christianity*, 579.

3. For Jews, the Saturday/Sunday transition occurred at sundown on Saturday evening. Romans marked the transition between Saturday and Sunday at midnight.

4. The *Dictionary of Christian Antiquities* describes the early Agape as such: "At the appointed hour they came, waited for each other (1 Cor 11:33), men and women seated at different tables, perhaps on opposite sides of the room, till the bishop or presbyter of the Church pronounced the blessing (*eulogia*). Then they ate and drank. Originally, at some time before or after the rest of the meal, one loaf was specially blessed and broken, one cup passed round specially as 'the cup of blessing.' When the meal was over, water was brought and they washed their hands. Then, if not before, according to the season of the year, lamps were placed (as at Troas, Acts 20:8) on their stands, and the more devotional part of the evening began. Those who had special gifts were called on to expound Scripture, or to speak a word of exhortation, or to sing a hymn to God, or to 'Christ as to a God' (Pliny). It was the natural time for intelligence to be communicated from other Churches, for epistles from them or their bishops to be read, for strangers who had come with [epistles] to be received. Collections were made for the relief of

The radical character of the fellowship meal, along with the winsome lifestyles of the earliest disciples, was elemental to the rapid growth of the early church. The revolutionary way in which the Christian worship meal brought together poor and rich, women and men, slave and master was powerfully attractive to an increasing number of outsiders. It is not surprising that as the number of participants increased, more difficulties developed in the celebration of the Love Feast; after all, the dynamics of the meal were radically different than the prevailing social norms, and old habits die hard! The increase in size also presented some logistical challenges. As the church grew, it became more difficult to find houses large enough to accommodate the Christian community, to say nothing of the challenge of serving a meal to feed fifty, seventy, or one hundred (or more) people! In addition, the rapid growth of the early church became a concern for local and regional government officials.

1. Imperial Challenges

There were several periods during the first three centuries of Christian practice where severe persecution and legal restriction made it difficult for Christians to worship publicly. Christians experienced sporadic persecution under Emperors Nero (64–68 CE) and Domitian (81–96 CE), and as they continued to grow in number, some officials became increasingly concerned about the practices of this new religion. Rumors had it that Christians practiced infanticide and incest at their evening love feasts.[5] Two policies of Emperor Trajan (98–117 CE) significantly

---

distressed churches at a distance, or for the poor of the district (1 Cor 16:1; Justin M. *Apol.* c.39). Then came the salutation, the kiss of love (1 Pet 5:14), the 'holy kiss' (Rom 16:16), which told of brotherhood, the final prayer, the quiet and orderly dispersion," Plumptre, "Agapae," 40.

5. Minucius Felix, a Christian apologist in the late second or early third century, conveys these rumors, writing: "Now the story about the initiation of young novices is as much to be detested as it is well known. An infant covered over with meal, that it may deceive the unwary, is placed before him who is to be stained with their rites: this infant is slain by the young pupil, who has been urged on as if to harmless blows on the surface of the meal, with dark and secret wounds. Thirstily—O horror!—they lick up its blood; eagerly they divide its limbs. . . . And of their banqueting it is well known all men speak of it everywhere . . . On a solemn day they assemble at the feast, with all their children, sisters, mothers, people of every sex and of every age. There, after much feasting, when the fellowship has grown warm, and the fervor of incestuous lust has grown hot with drunkenness, a dog that has been tied to the chandelier is provoked, by throwing a small piece of offal beyond the length of a line by which he is bound, to rush and spring; and thus the conscious light being overturned and extinguished in

impacted the nascent Christian communities. First, under Trajan, Christianity was declared to be an illicit religion. Christians were not to be specifically sought out to be punished, but if persons were accused of being Christian (i.e., confessing Jesus as Lord and not the Emperor), Roman officials were to investigate the matter. Those who refused to make sacrifices to the Roman gods and to recant their faith in Christ were to be executed.[6] Second, in an effort to maintain security and combat insurrection, Trajan reemphasized the harsh restrictions on *collegia* enacted previously by the Roman Senate, which had repercussions on the celebration of the Christian evening meal gatherings. According to Governor Pliny, Christians in Asia Minor ceased to gather for their evening supper after this decree and instead gathered before daylight to celebrate the Eucharist.[7] Thus, by the early second century some Christians were beginning to set aside the evening fellowship meal, either to quell rumors about orgiastic "love feasts" or to avoid persecution. In certain places the celebration of the Eucharist shifted from Saturday evening to early Sunday morning (ending in time for participants to go to work; Sunday was still a workday), and the bread and cup became a more symbolic meal, at least compared to the earlier supper practices.

2. *The Witness of the* Didache

The instructions in the *Didache* concerning the Eucharist clearly presuppose a mealtime celebration, although the text never uses the title "Love

---

the shameless darkness, the connections of abominable lust involve them in the uncertainty of fate. Although not all in fact, yet in consciousness all are alike incestuous, since by the desire of all of them everything is sought for which can happen in the act of each individual," Minucius Felix, "The Octavius of Minucius Felix," 177–78.

6. See the correspondence between Pliny the Younger, Governor of Bithynia (Asia Minor), and Trajan (c. 112 CE), in Fremantle, ed. *Treasury of Early Christianity*, 253–55.

7. Pliny writes of the Christians: "They asserted . . . that they had been accustomed to assemble on a fixed day before daylight and sing by turns [i.e., antiphonally] a hymn to Christ as a God; and that they bound themselves with an oath (*sacramentum*), not for any crime but to commit neither theft, nor robbery, nor adultery, not to break their word, and not to deny a deposit when demanded. After these things were done, it was their custom to depart and meet together again to take food; but ordinary and harmless food; and they said that even this had ceased after my edict was issued, by which, according to your commands, I had forbidden the existence of clubs," ibid., 254. We should note, however, that this testimony was obtained by torture, and that the evening meal may still have been held clandestinely, which would not have been reported to the governor.

Feast" (*agapais*) for this meal.[8] In 14:1 we find the following instruction: "On every Lord's Day—his special day—come together and break bread (*klasate arton*) and give thanks (*eucharistesate*)." Two things are important for Christians to do when they come together: sharing food with one another (breaking bread together) and offering prayers (giving thanks to God). These two practices meet most fully in the eucharistic prayers for the cup and bread. In the *Didache*, the celebration of the Eucharist begins with the cup (9:2).[9] Then, the church is to give thanks for "the piece" (9:3–4). Clearly, the reference is to a piece of bread, but strangely, the word bread is not used in the chapters (9–10) that discuss the Eucharist. Cyril Richardson explains that the piece "refers to the Jewish custom (taken over in the Christian Lord's Supper) of grace before meals. The head of the house would distribute to each of the guests a piece of bread broken off a loaf, after uttering the appropriate thanksgiving to God."[10] In the *Didache*, then, it appears that the thanksgiving for the cup and the piece of bread occur at the beginning of a common meal. Jewish tradition also included prayers at the end of a meal. Chapter 10 provides an example for the prayer to be said at the conclusion of the meal:

> After you have finished your meal, say grace [or give thanks, *eucharistesate*] in this way: "We thank you, holy Father, for your sacred name which you have lodged in our hearts, and for the knowledge and faith and immortality which you have revealed through Jesus, your child. To you be glory forever. Almighty Master, 'you have created everything' for the sake of your name, and have given men [and women] food and drink to enjoy that they may thank you. But to us you have given spiritual food and drink and eternal life through Jesus, your child. Above all, we thank you that you are mighty. To you be glory forever." (10:1–4)

The first sentence makes it clear that a fellowship meal is a key part of the worship described in the *Didache*. It is important to note that men and women receive food and drink *to enjoy*, that they may thank God, for some later Christians overemphasize ascetic principles that discourage the enjoyment of eating. There is, however, more to this meal

---

8. The *Didache* is the earliest known Christian church manual, likely written between 70 and 100 CE either in Syria or in Alexandria. All quotations from the *Didache* are from Richardson, *Early Christian Fathers*, 159–80.

9. This corresponds to the ordering in Luke (22:17–20) and may reflect the tradition of the Passover meal, which began with a blessing of the cup (see chapter 2).

10. Richardson, *Early Christian Fathers*, 175 n. 50.

than food and drink, because in this celebration the participants receive "spiritual food and drink and eternal life through Jesus." The comparison in the *Didache* is between good and better: physical food and drink are good, but spiritual food and drink and eternal life available through Jesus are much better.

3. The Witness of Ignatius of Antioch

The earliest non-biblical reference to the Love Feast appears in the letter Ignatius, Bishop of Antioch, wrote to the church in Smyrna. According to tradition, Ignatius wrote this passage en route to Rome (~107 CE), where he was to be executed for failing to reject his Christian faith: "You should regard that Eucharist as valid which is celebrated either by the bishop or by someone he authorizes. . . . Without the bishop's supervision, no baptisms or love feasts are permitted."[11] The fact that these two instructions appear in consecutive verses and relate to the bishop's supervision of the Christian worship meal leads most scholars to conclude that the Eucharist and the Love Feast are two parts of the same meal, not two separate services. Massey Shepherd writes: "It should not be supposed that Ignatius refers to two distinct types of assembly in the terms 'eucharist' and 'agape.' They are one and the same thing. Both terms are used to describe the entire service of worship, though strictly speaking they refer to only one specific characteristic of a Christian assembly."[12] Thus, the Love Feast referred to the common meal shared by the participants, and the Eucharist referred to the celebration of the bread and the cup, which was the climax of the mealtime service.[13] What is valuable about this text is that it demonstrates the strong relationship between the Eucharist and the Love Feast in the early second century and reveals that the Love Feast was an *officially sanctioned* practice of the church in Antioch.

4. The Easing of Government Restrictions

Although the policies of the Roman government had previously been restrictive of *collegia*, during the rule of Marcus Aurelius (161–180 CE) some of these restrictions were lifted. Marcus Aurelius greatly extended

---

11. *To the Smyrneans* 8.1–2, in Richardson, *Early Christian Fathers*, 115.

12. Shepherd, "Smyrna in the Ignatian Letters," 149.

13. Ibid., 149–51.

the privileges of *collegia tenuiorum*, those associations of lower class people that gave help to the poor and offered burial insurance. R. Lee Cole writes,

> Almost at once Christianity took advantage of the indulgence. The Agape had always taken account of the poor brethren—those in prison, those travelling, those deprived of goods and land, etc. From this time a new course of safety seemed to open up, if only the charity of the Agape were extended. We have seen that at this time a new emphasis on a charity meal took the place of the older idea of a brotherhood meal. We have now before us one of the causes of the change.[14]

From this point forward, most Christian churches were understood by the government to be *collegia tenuiorum*, that is, clubs that existed to help the poor. As such, the *agape* meal became a central way that the church helped the needy in the community. There were other benefits of the church finding a legal umbrella under the category of *collegia tenuiorum*; churches could now hold property, and they could form cemeteries (like the Roman catacombs) in which to bury their members and to meet to share meals in their memory. In sum, the Christian assemblies now had corporate rights.[15] With these developments in mind, let us now examine the *agape* in the writings of Tertullian, Clement of Alexandria, and the Apostolic Tradition.

5. *The Witness of Tertullian*

Tertullian is the most positive of all the ante-Nicene fathers in his description of the Love Feast.[16] In ch. 39 of his *Apology*, Tertullian refutes those who maliciously attack the worship practices of Christians (recall the rumors of infanticide and incest). He explains that the evening meals are not occasions of lust and violence, but rather of prayer and loving fellowship. Each month Christians offer to God a donation, which is used to meet the needs of the poor in the community, especially by providing

---

14. Cole, *Love-Feasts*, 162.

15. Ibid., 163.

16. Tertullian was born in Carthage around 160 CE to pagan parents (his father was a Roman centurion). He converted to Christianity in the early 190s in Rome. In 197 he returned to Carthage and began to write numerous treaties on the Christian faith in Latin.

food for them in the Love Feast. "Our feast explains itself by its name," he writes:

> The Greeks call it *agape* [love]. Whatever it costs, our outlay in the name of piety is gain, since with the good things of the feast we benefit the needy; not as it is with you, do parasites aspire to the glory of satisfying their licentious propensities, selling themselves for a belly-feast to all disgraceful treatment,—but as it is with God himself, a peculiar respect is shown to the lowly. If the object of our feast be good, in the light of that consider its further regulations. As it is an act of religious service, it permits no vileness or immodesty. The participants, before reclining, taste first of prayer to God. As much is eaten as satisfies the cravings of hunger; as much is drunk as befits the chaste. They say it is enough, as those who remember that even during the night they have to worship God; they talk as those who know that the Lord is one of their auditors. After manual ablution, and the bringing in of lights, each is asked to stand forth and sing, as he can, a hymn to God, either one from the holy Scriptures or one of his own composing,—a proof of the measure of our drinking. As the feast commenced with prayer, so with prayer it is closed. We go from it, not like troops of mischief-doers, nor bands of vagabonds, nor to break out into licentious acts, but to have as much care of our modesty and chastity as if we had been at a school of virtue rather than a banquet. . . . We are in our congregations just what we are when separated from each other; we are as a community what we are as individuals; we injure nobody, we trouble nobody. When the upright and the virtuous meet together, when the pious and the pure assemble . . . you ought not to call that a faction, but a *curia* (i.e., the court of God).[17]

Tertullian is quick to differentiate the Christian Love Feast from the banquets and "belly-feasts" held by pagans in Carthage. Immediately prior to the quoted text Tertullian wonders why such fuss is made over the Christian Love Feast, which is much more modest than feasts of other groups. Christians are to eat only enough to satisfy their hunger and drink only as much as befits the chaste, for drinking too much inhibits individuals in their primary task of worshiping God. In fact, each participant is asked to sing a hymn to God as a measure of his or her sobriety. Thus it is evident that Tertullian is a stout defender of the Love

17. Tertullian *Apology* 39. I have made some minor adaptations to enhance the readability of the text.

Feast, which he understands to be both an act of religious service and a modest supper supporting the poor.

6. *The Prison Agape*

In several places we see that the fellowship meal (*agape*) was a particular ministry to people in prison. Prior to the passage in *Apology* 39 quoted above, Tertullian writes that the voluntary gifts of money received by the church

> are not taken thence and spent on feasts, and drinking-bouts, and eating-houses, but [are used] to support and bury poor people, to supply the wants of boys and girls destitute of means and parents, and of old persons confined now to the house; such, too, as have suffered shipwreck; and if there happen to be any in the mines, or banished to the islands, *or shut up in the prisons*, for nothing but their fidelity to the cause of God's Church.[18]

While this passage reveals many of the ways that the meal was made available to the poor in the community, here we pay particular attention to the ministry given to those in prison. In 203 CE, less than a decade after Tertullian wrote the previous words in Carthage, we find an account of the martyrdom of Perpetua and Felicitas, who were killed in the gladiatorial ring of Carthage because of their Christian faith. On the day prior to their death, Christians were allowed to enter the prison to share an *agape* meal with Perpetua and Felicitas.[19] A century later the *agape* continued to function as a form of prison ministry, such that Pachomius, who was in prison as part of his conscription into the Roman army, converted to the Christian faith after receiving an *agape* meal in prison.[20] We can see, therefore, that the fellowship meal of the early church not only occurred in homes, but also in prisons, where it served as a ministry to persecuted Christians and as a witness to unbelievers.

18. Ibid. (emphasis added).

19. "[The] brethren and others [were permitted] to go in and be refreshed with them . . . On the day before, when in that last meal, which they call the free meal, they were partaking as far as they could, not of a free supper, but of an *agape* . . . ," *Passion of Perpetua and Felicitas* 5.3–4.

20. *Bohairic Life* 7–8. See Goehring, "Withdrawing from the Desert," 271.

7. The Witness of Clement of Alexandria[21]

Clement of Alexandria was not nearly as enthusiastic about the Love Feast as was his contemporary, Tertullian. Faced with the challenges of the luxurious and licentious banqueting practices of various groups in Alexandria, it is no surprise that Clement's writings concerning the Love Feast are fairly restrictive. Clement is frustrated that these so-called Love Feasts have become entertainment events featuring delicacies and sauces. "Such entertainments," he writes, "the Lord has not called *agapae*."[22] Clement is exasperated that people seem more interested in tasting luxurious sauces than dining in a modest and loving manner. These *"agapae"* are not only corrupt for their emphasis on lavish foods; Clement is also appalled at the paltry behavior of Christians who attend these suppers (apparently they are stuffing their faces with food and acting like dogs).[23]

21. Clement of Alexandria (~150–215 CE) was probably born in Athens. He was educated at the catechetical school in Alexandria, and later became a prominent Eastern theologian. He is regarded by many as the founder of the Alexandrian school which emphasized the divine nature of Christ.

22. "There is no limit to epicurism among men. For it has driven them to sweet-meats, and honey-cakes, and sugar-plums; inventing a multitude of desserts, hunting after all manner of dishes. A man like this seems to me to be all jaw, and nothing else. 'Desire not,' says the Scripture, 'rich men's dainties' [Prov 23:3]; for they belong to a false and base life. They partake of luxurious dishes, which a little after go to the dunghill. But we who seek the heavenly bread must rule the belly, which is beneath heaven, and much more the things which are agreeable to it, which 'God shall destroy,' says the apostle, justly execrating gluttonous desires. For 'meats are for the belly' [1 Cor 6:13], for on them depends this truly carnal and destructive life; whence some, speaking with un-bridled tongue, dare to apply the name *agape*, to pitiful suppers, redolent of savour and sauces. Dishonouring the good and saving work of the Word, the consecrated *agape*, with pots and pouring of sauce; and by drink and delicacies and smoke desecrating that name, they are deceived in their idea, having expected that the promise of God might be bought with suppers. Gatherings for the sake of mirth, and such entertainments as are called by ourselves, we name rightly suppers, dinners, and banquets, after the example of the Lord. But such entertainments the Lord has not called *agapae*," Clement of Alexandria, *Instructor* 2.1.

23. "[How] foolish for people to raise themselves on the couches, all but pitching their faces into the dishes, stretching out from the couch as from a nest . . . And how senseless, to besmear their hands with the condiments, and to be constantly reaching to the sauce, cramming themselves immoderately and shamelessly, not like people tasting, but ravenously seizing! For you may see such people, like swine or dogs for gluttony than men, in such a hurry to feed themselves full, that both jaws are stuffed out at once, the veins about the face raised, and besides, the perspiration running all over, as they are tightened with their insatiable greed, and panting with their excess; the food pushed with unsocial eagerness into their stomach, as if they were stowing away their victuals

Thus, in his writings Clement seeks to differentiate between the splendid banquets of the pagans and the humble Christian Love Feast.

Although it is obvious that Clement has a harsh attitude concerning the Love Feast, it is important to note that rival groups in Alexandria were celebrating "love feasts" that were extremely scandalous. Clement is concerned that the Christian Love Feast should not be confused with the "love feast" held by the Carpocratians.[24] In *Stromata* 3.2.10 he writes:

> These then are the doctrines of the excellent Carpocratians. These, so they say, and certain other enthusiasts for the same wickednesses, gather together for feasts (I would not call their meeting an *agape*), men and women together. After they have sated their appetites ("on repletion Cypris, the goddess of love, enters," as it is said), then they overturn the lamps and so extinguish the light that the shame of their adulterous "righteousness" is hidden, and they have intercourse where they will and with whom they will. After they have practiced community of use in this love-feast, they demand by daylight of whatever women they wish that they will be obedient to the law of Carpocrates—it would not be right to say the law of God. Such, I think, is the law that Carpocrates must have given for the copulations of dogs and pigs and goats.[25]

According to this passage, some of the orgiastic rumors surrounding the *agape* might have been accurate descriptions of the Carpocratian love feast, which was clearly not a Christian practice, although it apparently shared the same name. Clement later condemns Gnostic sects (like the Carpocratians) that celebrate a sham *agape* on the grounds that they have "diverged from the truth" by disregarding the Scriptures and basing their practices on "vain opinions" and pagan philosophy. According to

for provision for a journey, not for digestion," ibid., 2.1. Clement would clearly be opposed to the competitive eating tournaments that have become increasingly publicized in contemporary American culture (perhaps most obvious is the Nathan's hot dog eating competition every Fourth of July). Why has the church in America not been more vocal in opposing competitive eating and other activities that celebrate gluttony?

24. The Carpocratians were followers of Carpocrates, a second-century Gnostic teacher from Alexandria.

25. Oulton and Chadwick, eds., *Alexandrian Christianity: Selected Translations of Clement and Origen*, 45. (Book 3 of *Stromata* apparently contains Clement's most controversial writings, so much so that the editors of the *Ante-Nicene Fathers* do not translate it into English and only include the Latin text. Volume 2 of *The Library of Christian Classics*, thankfully, does contain an English translation.) Also see Irenaeus (*Against Heresies* 1.25), where he refutes the Carpocratians.

Clement, these heretics are more interested in occupying "the boasted first seat in their churches" and sitting in "the convivial couch of honour in the *Agape* (falsely so called)" than in practicing Christian faith based on the Scriptures.[26] In context, therefore, Clement's harsh treatment of the Love Feast is aimed at preserving the dignity and witness of the Christian church in Alexandria over against the immoral practices of groups like the Carpocratians.[27] Thus it is crucial to keep in mind the abuse by the Carpocratians when one examines what Clement wrote about the Love Feast.[28]

Even though Clement does harshly critique the Love Feast, he never advocates its abolition. He writes, "Do you imagine that I am thinking of a supper that is to be done away with?" From the context the answer is clearly, "No!" Rather, he aims to clarify what "love" is for Christians so that the Love Feast can be rescued from those who would abuse it:

> [T]he supper is made for love, but the supper is not love (*agape*); only a proof of mutual and reciprocal kindly feeling. "Let not, then, your good be evil spoken of; for the Kingdom of God is not meat and drink," says the apostle, in order that the meal spoken of may not be conceived as ephemeral, "but righteousness, and peace, and joy in the Holy Ghost." He who eats of this meal, the best of all, shall possess the Kingdom of God, fixing his regards here on the holy assembly of love, the heavenly Church. Love, then, is something pure and worthy of God, and its work is com-

26. "[For] while reading the books we have ready at hand, [the heretics] despise them as useless, but in their eagerness to surpass common faith, they have diverged from the truth. For, in consequence of not learning the mysteries of ecclesiastical knowledge, and not having capacity for the grandeur of the truth, too indolent to descend to the bottom of things, reading superficially, they have dismissed the Scriptures. Elated, then, by vain opinion, they are incessantly wrangling, and plainly care more to *seem* than to *be* philosophers. Not laying as foundations the necessary first principles of things; and influenced by human opinions, then making the end to suit them, by compulsion; on account of being confuted, they spar with those who are engaged in the prosecution of the true philosophy, and undergo everything, . . . even going the length of impiety, by disbelieving the Scriptures, rather than be removed from the honours of the heresy and the boasted first seat in their churches; on account of which also they eagerly embrace that convivial couch of honour in the Agape, falsely so called," *Stromata* 7.16.

27. A. Cleveland Coxe observes: "The early disappearance of the Christian *agapae* may probably be attributed to the terrible abuse of the word, here referred to, by the licentious Carpocratians," Coxe, ed., *Fathers of the Second Century*, 403.

28. It is also likely that the practice of greeting each other with holy kiss was being abused by the Carpocratians, since Clement also writes about the proper way for believers to kiss one another (see section C below).

munication. "And the care of discipline is love," as Wisdom says; "and love is the keeping of the law." . . . Love (*agape*), then, is not a supper. But let the entertainment depend on love.[29]

The Christian Love Feast is not chiefly a supper where human love is celebrated; instead, the Love Feast bears witness to the inbreaking Kingdom of God and is characterized by righteousness, peace, unity, and joy. Participants are to fix their attention on "the holy assembly of love, the heavenly Church." Clement also does not advocate the abolishment of the supper because it appears that the Alexandrian community was still celebrating the Eucharist in the evening with the Love Feast.[30] The celebration of the Eucharist in the evening, with the Love Feast, better fits Clement's restrictions on drinking wine than does a pre-dawn eucharistic celebration.[31] We may conclude that Clement attempts to redeem the Love Feast, rather than rejecting it, in order to preserve the understanding of God's pure love and the practice of celebrating the Eucharist within a broader *agape* meal.[32]

8. *The Witness of the* Apostolic Tradition[33]

Finally, the *Apostolic Tradition* contains several helpful details about the fellowship meal practices of churches in Rome in the third century.

---

29. Clement of Alexandria *Instructor* 2.1.

30. Unlike Tertullian, Clement makes no mention of the Eucharist occurring in the morning.

31. Clement writes: "I therefore admire those who have adopted an austere life, and who are fond of water, the medicine of temperance, and flee as far as possible from wine, shunning it as they would the danger of fire. . . . And, besides, it suits divine studies not to be heavy with wine. 'For unmixed wine is far from compelling a man to be wise, much less temperate,' according to the comic poet. But towards evening, about supper-time, wine may be used, when we are no longer engaged in more serious readings," Clement of Alexandria *Instructor* 2.2.

32. Clement is perhaps the earliest theologian who advocates a *via media* (middle way) approach, because he attempts to guide Christians in a path that avoids both the scandalous abuses of the Love Feast and the disgraceful rejection of the Lord's Supper. He writes: "Our mode of life is not to accustom us to voluptuousness and licentiousness, nor to the opposite extreme, but to the medium between these, that which is harmonious and temperate, and free of either evil, luxury and parsimony," ibid., 3.10.

33. Hippolytus (~170–235) was an important third-century bishop in Rome who is generally credited with authoring the *Apostolic Tradition*. Although originally written in Greek, only a few Greek fragments are extant, which means that modern editions of the text are based on extant translations in Latin, Coptic, Ethiopic, and Arabic.

Chapters 25–38 make it clear that Roman Christians were gathering in the evening to celebrate the Lord's Supper, which involved both the Eucharist and a full fellowship meal. The celebration begins with the lighting of a lamp and a prayer by the bishop which is strikingly similar in content to the *Phos hilaron*.[34] In the *Apostolic Tradition*, the Eucharist is shared at the beginning of the meal, before any other food is eaten. Alistair Stewart-Sykes summarizes as follows:

> At the beginning of the meal a light is kindled with accompany-ing prayer and the offering of a cup is made before the meal by the bishop. After the offering of this cup, bread is distributed by the bishop. After the sharing of bread, individual graces are said over individual cups of wine, which are then consumed.[35] All of this action may be understood as eucharistic action. When the eucharist is concluded the meal begins, as individuals consume their own bread.[36]

The fellowship meal was most likely what we have come to refer to as a potluck meal, a conclusion that is supported by various passages in the *Apostolic Tradition* that indicate that believers brought offerings of food to the fellowship meal.[37] Chapter 28 contains material instructing the participants on proper mealtime behavior, which is quite similar to Paul's instructions to the Corinthian church:

> When you eat and drink, do so with integrity and do not get drunk so that you become ridiculous and cause grief to the one who in-vites you through your unruliness, but rather let him give thanks that he is worthy that the saints should come to him. . . . [I]f a por-

---

34. The *Phos Hilaron* was an early Christian hymn, see n. 2 above. After the church gathers and a deacon brings in a lamp, the bishop's opening prayer makes it evident that the church is gathering in the dark of evening, not morning: "We give you thanks, O God, through your child Jesus Christ our Lord, through whom you have illuminated us, revealing to us the incorruptible light. Therefore we have completed the length of the day and we have arrived at the beginning of the night, being sated with the day's light which you created for our satisfaction. And now, having arrived at the light of evening through your grace, we give you praise and glorify you through your child Jesus Christ, our Lord" (*Apostolic Tradition* 25:7–9). All quotations from the *Apostolic Tradition* are from the 2001 St. Vladimir's Seminary Press edition, Stewart-Sykes, ed.

35. As in Judaism, there is no common cup.

36. Stewart-Sykes, "Commentary on the Apostolic Tradition," 140.

37. Chapters 5, 6, 20, and 32 indicate that participants brought oil, cheese, olives, milk, grapes, figs, pomegranates, pears, apples, mulberries, peaches, cherries, almonds, and plums as offerings to the fellowship meal.

tion is offered to all in common, take from it. And if you are invited to eat, eat so that you have had just enough, and so that there is food left over, so that the one who invited you might send it out to all who want it as left by the saints, and he may confidently rejoice. Let those who are invited to eat do so in silence, and not wrangle with words. But when the bishop has exhorted, then, if anyone asks anything, he should be answered. And when the bishop is speaking, listen in silence until he is asked again. (28:1–4)

Participants are instructed not to drink too much nor eat too much, in both cases so that the dinner host may not be disgraced. The meal is also eaten in silence, which is probably a restriction that emerged out of a need to maintain order, similar to the instructions concerning orderly worship mentioned in 1 Cor 14:27–35. This is also evident by the instruction that when the bishop is speaking, the members of the church are to listen in silence. In the *Apostolic Tradition*, then, is evidence that the Roman church in the third century continued to celebrate the Eucharist in the context of a fellowship meal.

9. Archaeological Evidence

A variety of pictorial representations, sarcophagi, and other inscriptions provide evidence that the fellowship meal was important in the life of the church prior to Constantine. The depictions and descriptions of meals include fish, bread, and wine. In fact, there is no early representation of the meal that does not contain fish.[38] Thus, these early depictions are not of the classic bread-and-cup Eucharist, but rather are more akin to the feeding of the five thousand and Jesus' post-resurrection meal with the disciples at Lake Tiberias. Graydon Snyder explains: "The art and symbols of third-century Christianity simply do not reflect the *anamnesis* eucharist. The art does portray a eucharist, but that consists of fish, loaves of bread, baskets of bread, and wine. In terms of biblical origins, the eucharist so pictured probably refers to the 'feeding of the five thousand.'"[39] In addition to Christian artwork showing fish at the meal, the Abercius inscription—which was carved into a stone stele prior to 216 CE and was discovered in the city of Hierapolis (in southwestern Turkey)—also indicates that fish was a part of the holy meal.[40] When bread is shown in

38. Snyder, *Ante Pacem*, 25.
39. Ibid., 16.
40. In this inscription, Abercius describes a journey to Rome in which "faith was

the meal, there are often five or seven loaves/baskets, which again point back to the feeding miracle. And as the quotation from Cole pointed out in the previous chapter, most meal depictions contain seven men, which can be taken as a reference to the meal at Lake Tiberias.

Early archaeological evidence also reveals that Christians shared meals in cemeteries and catacombs. Several of the Roman catacombs contain rooms (*cubicula*) which contain artwork depicting a fish and bread meal eaten by seven men. The remains of bones in these *cubicula* reveal that memorial meals were eaten there. In Salona (in modern-day Croatia), a triclinium was built in the catacombs so that the meal for the dead (*refrigerium*) could be celebrated. This meal was likely related to the *agape*. Some of the sarcophagi had flat lids that served as tables for the meal, and several of the lids also had depressions (*tessellae*) used for holding food and wine. A few of these *tesselae* had holes for food or wine to be dropped into the sarcophagus, allowing the departed one to "share" in the meal of his or her remembrance.[41] Thus, the earliest archaeological evidence helps us to understand that the fellowship meal was based on the feeding miracles of Jesus and was often celebrated in burial sites, which emphasized the belief that the living could continue to have *koinonia*/communion with those who had passed on before them. Our focus now shifts to the celebration of Communion in the early church.

B. *COMMUNION/EUCHARIST*

The liturgical celebration of the bread and cup began as a suppertime practice and gradually shifted into a morning-time practice separated from a meal. By the early second century the term Eucharist (thanksgiving) had emerged as a name for the celebration of the bread and the cup. In some sources, including the *Didache* and the *Apostolic Tradition*, the Eucharist is still described as a mealtime celebration. Other sources, such as Justin Martyr and Irenaeus, show that the Eucharist was becoming a celebration apart from a meal. Because of challenges posed by Gnosticism and Docetism—two philosophies that denied the incarnation of Christ and looked down on the physical nature—several church leaders in the

---

everywhere my guide and everywhere she laid before me food, the Fish from the Fountain, the very great, the pure, which a holy virgin seized, and she gave this to friends to eat forever, having a goodly wine, giving it mixed with water, with bread," ibid., 25, 139–40.

41. Ibid., 90–91.

second century stressed that the bread and cup were the actual body and blood of Jesus. This emphasis was also strongly connected to the doctrine of the physical resurrection of believers after death.

1. The Witness of the Didache Concerning the Eucharist

Beginning around the turn of the second century we see the emergence of the term "Eucharist" as a name for the celebration of the bread and cup. The earliest example is found in the *Didache*, written between 70 and 100 CE:

> Now about the Eucharist (*eucharistias*): This is how to give thanks (*eucharistesate*): First in connection with the cup: "We thank you, our Father, for the holy vine of David, your child, which you have revealed through Jesus, your child. To you be glory forever." Then in connection with the piece [broken off the loaf]: "We thank you, our Father, for the life and knowledge which you have revealed through Jesus, your child. To you be glory forever. As this piece [of bread] was scattered over the hills and then was brought together and made one, so let your Church be brought together from the ends of the earth into your Kingdom. For yours is the glory and the power through Jesus Christ forever." (*Didache* 9.1–4)

As noted above, although the Gospels address the bread before the cup (except Luke), this passage begins with the cup first, followed by the piece (of bread). Another interesting peculiarity of the *Didache* is that it does not use "blood" and "body" language concerning the cup and piece; language that is present in the Synoptics and 1 Corinthians. Instead, the cup and the piece are connected to: (1) the holy vine of David, (2) life, and (3) knowledge, all of which the Father has revealed through Jesus his child (9:2–3). Both the priority of the cup and the reference to the "holy vine of David" indicate that this early Eucharist was still closely associated with the mealtime practices of Judaism. Additionally, it is possible that the absence of "blood" and "body" language in the Didache is explained by Jewish restrictions on the drinking of (sacrificial) blood and an avoidance of cannibalistic themes. Whatever the reason, the author of the *Didache* wants to focus the participant's attention on the "big picture" of the Eucharist—the holy vine of David, life, and knowledge— and makes no attempt to connect the actual cup and bread with the spilt blood and broken body of Jesus Christ.

2. The Connection between the Eucharist and Physical Resurrection

When the early church fathers discussed the Eucharist as Christ's body and blood they were defending both the incarnational nature of Christ and the future resurrection of the flesh. The early church faced significant challenges from the Gnostics and Docetists—groups that denied the incarnation of Jesus and the physical resurrection of believers. For Ignatius and Irenaeus, understanding the bread and cup to be the body and blood of Jesus was a crucial part of their arguments against those who would deny the incarnation and resurrection of Christ. Early in the second century Ignatius of Antioch writes:

> [The Docetists] hold aloof from the Eucharist and from services of
> prayer, because they refuse to admit that the Eucharist is the flesh
> of our Savior Jesus Christ, which suffered for our sins and which,
> in his goodness, *the Father raised [from the dead]*. Consequently
> those who wrangle and dispute God's gift face death. They would
> have done better to love *and so share in the resurrection*.[42]

In another place Ignatius also refers to the Eucharist as "the medicine of immortality and the antidote which wards off death and yields continuous life in union with Jesus Christ."[43] For Ignatius it is clear that understanding the Eucharist as Christ's body is connected to the promise of the physical resurrection. When Christians partake of the flesh of Jesus they experience communion with Christ in such a way that even physical death cannot cause separation.[44]

Irenaeus of Lyon, writing around 180 CE, also makes a clear connection between the Eucharist as Christ's body and blood and the resurrection of Christians. He explains:

> How can [the Gnostics] say that the flesh which is nourished
> from the body of the Lord and from his flesh comes to corrup-
> tion and does not partake of life? Let them either change their
> views or avoid offering the bread and wine. But our view is in
> harmony with the eucharist, and the eucharist confirms our view.
> We offer to God his own things, proclaiming rightly the com-

42. *To the Smyrneans* 7.1 (emphasis added), cited from Richardson, *Early Christian Fathers*.

43. *To the Ephesians* 20, cited from Richardson, *Early Christian Fathers*.

44. We should also remember the discussion of the messianic banquet in chapter 2, which made the observation that numinous food and drink were connected to the eschatological banquet.

munion and unity of flesh and spirit. For as bread from the earth, when it receives the invocation, is no longer *common* bread but *the eucharist*, consisting of two things—*one earthly and one heavenly*—so also our bodies when they partake of the eucharist are *no longer corruptible but have the hope of the resurrection to eternity*. (*Against Heresies* 4.18.5, emphasis added)[45]

At this point what Irenaeus appears to describe is not the *conversion* of the bread when it is consecrated, but rather the *addition* of a spiritual reality to the common bread. Hence, when believers partake of the Eucharist, which is not just common bread, they are "no longer corruptible but have the hope of the resurrection to eternity." Both Irenaeus and Ignatius argue that the miracle of incarnation and resurrection of Jesus is mirrored in the celebration of the Eucharist. Christians can be assured of the resurrection because Jesus was raised in the flesh. In the eucharistic celebration, when the faithful consume the body and blood of Jesus, they are in essence receiving a heavenly down-payment which will be redeemed in the final resurrection. It is fair to conclude that in the second century the bread and cup, when consecrated, took on an additional spiritual reality as the body and blood of Christ, and that this incarnational understanding of the Eucharist primarily served to combat competing factions that challenged the physical nature of Christ and the resurrection of the flesh.[46]

3. The Witness of Tertullian Concerning the Eucharist

Although Justin Martyr implies that the Eucharist was celebrated in the morning, Tertullian is the first Christian author *explicitly* to state this.[47] In *De Corona* 3.3, he writes: "We take also, in congregations before daybreak, and from the hand of none but the presidents, the sacrament of the Eucharist, which the Lord both commanded to be eaten at mealtimes, and enjoined to be taken by all alike. . . . We feel pained should

45. Quoted in Ferguson, "The Lord's Supper in Church History," 25.

46. For a more thorough examination of these themes, including the views of Justin Martyr, Tertullian, and Clement of Alexandria, see ibid., 22–28.

47. Pliny's letter is the earliest pagan witness to the prayer service that occurred before daybreak, although he does not use the term Eucharist. While Justin Martyr does write that the Eucharist was celebrated on Sunday, he does not explicitly state that the Eucharistic celebration occurred in the *morning*, although this can be inferred from his discussion on the resurrection of Christ. Irenaeus makes no mention of time when he discusses the Eucharist.

any wine or bread, even though our own, be cast upon the ground."[48] It appears that Tertullian is referring to a combination of two separate practices: the Eucharist is to be celebrated *both* at the evening Love Feast *and* in the morning prayer service when all alike are able to participate (slaves, for instance, might have difficulties attending an evening meal). Andrew McGowan writes:

> Since the primary celebration of a sacral meal was the evening *agape*, the question may really be whether bread and wine were "eucharistized" at the morning events independently of the *agape*, rather than reserved from the banquet itself for later use. The answer is not clear. If, as seems to have been the case, bread alone was received and further reserved in the mornings, this may make it likely that the whole of the eucharistic actions (as later understood) were actually not performed, but that a distribution of the eucharistic bread held over from the *agape* was made in conjunction with the morning "sacrifices" (prayers) on stational days. If, on the other hand, there actually was a self-contained morning ritual over bread alone quite separate from the communal meal, then this would be the first instance recorded or alluded to of such a practice—but in any case it would certainly not make this event the main or only eucharistic celebration at Carthage. In either event, the morning assembly must be seen as a sort of subsidiary eucharistic ritual, rather than as a definitive separation of the eucharist from the communal meal, or a new primary liturgical focus.[49]

Observe also Tertullian's comment that Christians are "pained should any wine or bread, even though our own, be cast upon the ground." This is an early example of the veneration of the elements. It is significant, however, that Tertullian does not state that they are pained if the blood or body of Christ be cast upon the ground, but instead chooses to name the elements as wine and bread. This is consistent with his practice of describing the bread and wine as *figures* that represent the body and blood of Christ.[50] It is possible, then, that the clarification about the

48. Tertullian *De Corona* 3. It is generally assumed that Tertullian was the first theologian to translate the Greek word *mysterion* into the Latin word *sacramentum*.

49. McGowan, "Rethinking Agape and Eucharist," 171–72.

50. "[H]aving taken the bread and given it to His disciples, [Jesus] made it His own body, by saying, 'This is my body,' that is, *the figure of my body*. A figure, however, there could not have been, unless there were first a veritable body. An empty thing, or phantom, is incapable of a figure. . . . He likewise, when mentioning the cup and

wine and bread that are "our own" is Tertullian's way of indicating that the Eucharist is a figure of the blood and body of Christ, not the actual physical blood and body of Christ. If this is so, it is important to observe that even as figures, the wine and bread are treated as special.[51] It is also possible that the phrase "even though our own" refers to wine and bread that are eaten in the fellowship meal but are not the Eucharist proper. Understood this way, Tertullian is clarifying that they try to keep both the Eucharist and their own food and drink from falling to the floor. In either case, whether churches understood the Eucharist to be a figure of Christ's body and blood or his literal body and blood, by the third century we see various teachings emerge indicating the importance of keeping the eucharistic elements from falling to the ground.

4. The Witness of the Apostolic Tradition Concerning the Eucharist

The *Apostolic Tradition* indicates that, when celebrated concurrently, the Eucharist preceded the supper meal. There are two passages that point to this conclusion:

> [The faithful] shall take from the hand of the bishop a single frag-ment of bread, *before anyone breaks the bread which is in front of him.* For that [bread in front] is a blessing and not the eucharist, as is the body of the Lord. It is proper that all, before they drink, should take a cup and give thanks over it and in this manner to drink and to eat with purity. (26:2–3, emphasis added)

---

making the *new* testament to be sealed 'in His blood,' affirms the reality of His body. For no blood can belong to a body which is not *a body* of flesh. If any sort of body were presented to our view, which is not one of flesh, not being fleshly, it would not possess blood. Thus, from the evidence of the flesh, we get a proof of the body, and a proof of the flesh from the evidence of the blood. . . . Thus did [Jesus] now consecrate His blood in wine, who then . . . *used the figure of wine to describe His blood*," Tertullian *Anti-Marcion* 40 (emphasis added).

51. There are other sources, however, that indicate that the reason that the Eucharist is to be kept from falling to the ground is so that the body and blood of Christ are not despised. Chapters 37 and 38 of the *Apostolic Tradition* make such a connection to the body and blood of Christ: "Everybody should be concerned that one who is not of the faithful, nor a mouse nor any other animal, should eat of the eucharist, and that none of it should fall and be altogether lost. For it is the body of Christ to be eaten by the faithful, and not to be despised. For, blessing the cup in the name of God, you received, as it were, the antitype of the blood of Christ. For this reason, do not pour it out, that no alien spirit might lick it up because you despised it; you shall be guilty of the blood, like one who despises the price with which he has been bought" (*On the Apostolic Tradition* 37–38:2).

> Every faithful one should be concerned that, *before he [or she] consumes anything else*, [they] partake in the eucharist. For if [they partake] in faith, even if anything deadly is given [them, i.e., harmful food], after that it shall not overcome [them]. (36, emphasis added)

Taken together, these passages reveal that the celebration of the Eucharist came at the beginning of the meal. The first quotation is made clearer when it is understood that the non-eucharistic bread lies in front of the individual (to be eaten during supper), not the bread received from the bishop.[52] Unlike the *Didache, Apostolic Tradition* 26:2 treats the bread as "the body of the Lord," and in other places refers to the cup as "the likeness of the blood" (21:27) or "the antitype of the blood of Christ" (38:1). In ch. 36 we read the injunction that the Eucharist must be eaten first, and that doing so will protect the faithful from the deadly effects of eating unsafe food. In sum, the *Apostolic Tradition* instructs the church to begin their meals with the celebration of the Eucharist, which imparts to believers both spiritual and physical comfort, power and protection.

C. THE KISS OF PEACE

The holy kiss was a vital part of eucharistic worship in the second and third centuries. The early church fathers indicate that the holy kiss continued to serve as an important practice in eucharistic worship. In the previous chapter we saw that the New Testament references to the holy kiss are found at the end of several epistles, which seems to indicate that the kiss was shared in conjunction with the benedictions at the conclusion of worship services. Quite soon in the history of the church, however, the holy kiss became associated with the Eucharist. As a result, its location during the worship service moved forward in time to the celebration of Communion. This correspondence between the kiss and

---

52. In his commentary on this passage, Alistair Stewart-Sykes explains that it is best to understand 26:2b as "referring to the bread which is 'their own'; that is to say, their own meal is not the eucharist. This is blessed, we may assume, by virtue of the saying of grace, but since it is not the body of the Lord it is not to be eaten or broken until the eucharist has first been received. The implication is that the fragments received from the bishop's hand actually are the Body of the Lord," Stewart-Sykes, "Commentary on the Apostolic Tradition," 139. This interpretation clearly corresponds with the above quotation from Tertullian (*De Corona* 3), who states: "We feel pained should any wine or bread, even though our own, be cast upon the ground."

the Eucharist is understandable in that both were expressions of unity in the church. Stephen Benko writes:

> The Holy Spirit guaranteed that unity, for one Spirit baptized Christians into one body, "and all were made to drink of one Spirit" [1 Cor 12:13]. In the kiss, the Spirit was mingled, and the church became in a proleptic way a unity, the living body of Christ. This explains why the holy kiss occurred most frequently in the Eucharistic service. In the Eucharist the unity of the church was impressed on the senses of the believers as they drank from the same cup and ate of the same loaf of bread. The bread was a particularly important symbol because it represented "one body" that was consumed by all who thus became "one body" themselves. At the same time the Eucharist was a meal, and it reminded Christians of the time when the first believers ate together with Jesus after his Resurrection, which itself was a foretaste of the great messianic meal that believers will celebrate with Jesus in the kingdom of God.[53]

Let us examine several texts in the early church that inform our understanding of the holy kiss.

Writing in the mid-second century, Justin Martyr is the first author after the New Testament era to mention the holy kiss. In his *Apology*, Justin describes a worship service following baptism in which the kiss occurs in the middle of the worship service, after the prayers and before the Eucharist:

> [The worshipers] earnestly offer common prayers for themselves and the one who has been [baptized] and all others everywhere, that we may be made worthy, having learned the truth, to be found in deed good citizens and keepers of what is commanded, so that we may be saved with eternal salvation. On finishing the prayers we greet each other with a kiss. Then bread and a cup of water and mixed wine are brought to the president of the brethren and he, taking them, sends up praise and glory to the Father of the universe through the name of the Son and of the Holy Spirit, and offers thanksgiving at some length that we have been deemed worthy to receive these things from him. (*Apology* 65)

In addition to Justin, Tertullian also connected the holy kiss to prayer, calling it the "seal of prayer." Opposing those who would abstain from the holy kiss when they were fasting, he writes: "What prayer is complete if

53. Benko, "The Kiss," 86.

divorced from the 'holy kiss?' . . . What kind of sacrifice is that from which men depart without peace?" (*On Prayer* 18). Here Tertullian refers to the kiss as "peace," and it also is clear that the "sacrifice" of the people is their offering of prayer to God. Since Tertullian is clear here that prayers are sealed with the kiss, it seems likely that the prayers associated with the *agape* meal in *Apology* 39 would also conclude with the peace, although it is not mentioned in that specific text.[54]

Let us examine more closely this connection between the kiss and peace. In the previous chapter we saw that the command to greet one another with a "kiss of love" in 1 Pet 5:14 was immediately followed by "Peace to all of you who are in Christ." Above, Tertullian refers to the kiss as peace, and in another place in the treatise *On Prayer* he indicates that before leaving a house, Christian guests are to give the kiss and to say "peace to this house" (*On Prayer* 26). In the *Passion of Perpetua*, in a vision prior to her martyrdom, Perpetua receives a kiss from a heavenly being, accompanied with the words "peace be with you (*pax tecum*)" (*Martyrdom of Perpetua and Felicitas* 10.13). Edward Phillips comments: "Although these examples are few, they are extremely important, since the verbal exchange of 'peace' with a kiss appears to be a Christian innovation, there being no clear example in pre-Christian literature."[55]

Overall, in the first three centuries of the church the holy kiss was associated with the peace and unity given by the Holy Spirit to the congregation. Justin recounts the role of the kiss during the reception of newly baptized members into eucharistic fellowship; Tertullian speaks of the kiss as the "seal of prayer" and as the "peace"; and the *Apostolic Tradition* (ch. 4) tells us that the holy kiss was shared by the congregation upon the ordination of a bishop. Beginning in the third century, the kiss of peace began to be understood as a preparation to partake of the Eucharist. According to Kreider, "Peace, reconciliation, and unity were of the very essence of the church's life; without them communion would have been a sham. Bestowed by the Spirit and experienced in prayer, their liturgical expression—which pointed forward to the eucharist—was the holy kiss."[56]

54. Although his statement that Christian brothers and sisters acknowledge "God as their common Father, [and] have drunk in one spirit of holiness" in ch. 39 may be a reference to the holy kiss, which united members by forming new familial bonds.

55. Phillips, "The Kiss of Peace," 179.

56. Kreider, "Kiss of Peace," 34.

Several examples in the writings of the early fathers indicate that the church experienced some difficulties with the holy kiss. The Christian apologist Athenagoras wrote around 177 CE that

> On behalf of those, then, to whom we apply the names of broth-
> ers and sisters, and other designations of relationship, we exercise
> the greatest care that their bodies should remain undefiled and
> uncorrupted; for . . . "If anyone kiss a second time because it has
> given him pleasure, [he sins]. . . Therefore the kiss, or rather the
> salutation, should be given with the greatest care, since, if there
> be mixed with it the least defilement of thought, it excludes us
> from eternal life." (*A Plea for the Christians* 32)

Athenagoras implies that improper kissing between men and women could lead some members to lust. Clement of Alexandria also shares this conclusion. In *The Instructor*, he writes about the proper way to kiss, that is, with closed mouths.[57] We can infer that Christians in Alexandria are no longer meeting in homes for worship since Clement relates that some make the "churches" (i.e., buildings) resound with the sound of improper kissing. These loud kisses, these unchaste kisses, these kisses that inject the "poison of licentiousness," are leading to "foul suspicions and evil reports." We can reasonably guess that the so-called *agape* of the Carpocratians mentioned above, that feast of wickedness and not of godly love, also featured such unholy kissing.

Likely as a result of some these abuses, in the early- to mid-second century several limitations began to appear connected to the holy kiss. We see these limitations in the *Apostolic Tradition*. First, the kiss was clearly distinguished as a ritual for baptized believers; catechumens were not to participate. After catechumens received instruction from a

---

57. "[T]here are those that do nothing but make the churches resound with a kiss, not having love itself within. For this very thing, the shameless use of a kiss, which ought to be mystic, occasions foul suspicions and evil reports. The apostle calls the kiss holy. When the kingdom is worthily tested, *we dispense the affection of the soul by a chaste and closed mouth*, by which chiefly gentle manners are expressed. But there is another unholy kiss, full of poison, counterfeiting sanctity. Do you not know that spiders, merely by touching the mouth, afflict men with pain? And often *kisses inject the poison of licentiousness*. It is then very manifest to us, that a kiss is not love. For the love meant is the love of God. 'And this is the love of God,' says John, 'that we keep His commandments'; not that we stroke each other on the mouth. 'And His commandments are not grievous.' But salutations of beloved ones in the ways . . . of foolish boldness are characteristic of those who wish to be conspicuous to those [outside], and have not the least particle of grace," Clement of Alexandria *The Instructor* 3.11 (emphasis added).

church leader, they were to pray by themselves, separate from the faithful: "When they have prayed they shall not give the kiss of peace for their kiss is not yet holy" (18:3). Second, the holy kiss was limited to members of the same sex: "The faithful should greet one another, the men with each other and the women with each other. No man should greet a woman" (18:4). This is the earliest example of separating the sexes during the Christian greeting. Evidently this greeting—which was supposed to demonstrate outwardly that members from a variety of circumstances were now brothers and sisters in Christ and that they were reconciled one to another—was too difficult to maintain as the church grew in size. What once was an intimate gesture among a small group of Christians could too easily become a kissing catastrophe in a larger group setting, so some boundaries were set up to keep the kiss among men or among women. Even with these newer boundaries, the kiss was still shared physically between members, a kiss on the mouth that bore witness to the reconciliation of God in their midst as the congregation prepared to take Communion.

D. FEETWASHING

We have already seen that feetwashing was a common practice of hospitality in the ancient Near East and that it received special attention in the Gospel of John. Feetwashing customarily occurred at the door when guests entered a home, and guests either washed their own feet or had them washed by a servant. In an age when people wore sandals and walked on dirty streets, it would have been absurd for feetwashing not to have been practiced prior to the Love Feast; after all, when one reclines on couches to share a meal, diners want both their own feet and their neighbors' to be clean (smelling stinky feet does not make for a good mealtime experience!). Although it is mentioned relatively infrequently, the writings of Tertullian, Clement, and Cyprian reveal that feetwashing was practiced by Christians, and not just ordinary feetwashing but ritual feetwashing based on Jesus' actions at the Last Supper (John 13). Let us take a closer look in order better to understand feetwashing as a practice connected to the Love Feast.

1. The Witness of Tertullian Concerning Feetwashing

Of all the early fathers, Tertullian has the most to say regarding feet-washing. In a letter written around 207 CE, not only does Tertullian refer to the Lord's Supper as a "nocturnal convocation," but he also writes that one practice of Christian women is to "offer water for the saints' feet" (*To His Wife* 2.4).[58] Although this particular reference implies that feetwashing may have been a practice of women in the community (see 1 Tim 5:10), other examples in Tertullian's writings make no mention of gender in connection with feetwashing. In another work Tertullian counters the charge that feetwashing in Christian worship is simply a repackaged form of pagan worship. He writes:

> If at once, of every article of furniture and each household vessel, you name some god of the world as the originator, well, I must recognize Christ, both as He reclines on a couch, and when He presents a basin for the feet of His disciples, and when He pours water into it from a ewer, and when He is girt about with a linen towel—a garment specially sacred to Osiris. It is thus in general I reply upon the point, admitting indeed that we use these articles, along with others, but challenging that this be judged [as some-how participating in pagan worship]. (*De Corona* 8)

It seems somewhat ridiculous for Tertullian's opponents to imply that the simple use of towels during feetwashing connects Christians with the cult of Osiris. Nonetheless, Tertullian feels the need to defend the practice of feetwashing from being associated with this cult, and responds that Christians use towels in order to "supply what is simply useful and affords real assistance and honourable comfort, so that they may be well believed to have come from God's own inspiration" (*De Corona* 8).

Another allusion to feetwashing is found in the passage from *De Corona* 3, quoted above, where Tertullian describes the Eucharist taking

---

58. In this letter Tertullian describes the difficult circumstances that are present in the marriage of a pagan husband and a Christian wife. He writes, "For who would [allow] his wife, for the sake of visiting the brethren, to go round from street to street to other men's, and indeed to all the poorer, cottages? Who will willingly bear her being taken from his side by nocturnal convocations, if need so be? Who, finally, will without anxiety endure her absence all the night long at the paschal solemnities? Who, without some suspicion of his own, dismiss her to attend that Lord's Supper which they defame? Who will suffer her to creep into prison to kiss a martyr's bonds? nay, truly, to meet any one of the brethren to exchange the kiss? To offer water for the saints' feet? To snatch (somewhat for them) from her food, from her cup?," *To His Wife* 2.4.

place in a mealtime context. Immediately after discussing the celebration of the Eucharist he writes: "At every forward step and movement, at every going in and out, when we put on our clothes and shoes, when we bathe, when we sit at table, when we light the lamps, on couch, on seat, in all the ordinary actions of daily life, we trace upon the forehead the sign [of the cross]" (*De Corona* 3). For several reasons it is logical to conclude that this description, which on the surface applies to signing the cross, also indicates the practice of feetwashing in the community. First, the reference to going "in and out" must mean entering and exiting the house where worship was held, and we know that feetwashing commonly occurred when guests entered a home. Second, Tertullian writes that worshipers "put on our clothes and shoes," which implies that they had been removed for the mealtime worship.[59] When guests entered a house and removed their outer cloak and shoes, it was customary to have a basin of water available for feetwashing. Third, he indicates that believers make the sign "when they bathe." Certainly this does not mean a full bath, for this bathing takes place in a eucharistic context. Because the word "bathe" follows on the heels of the word "shoes," it seems logical that Tertullian is referring to washing feet. Finally, this feetwashing occurs in the context of the Christian meal, for Tertullian continues by stating, "when we sit at table." Hence, it should be clear that feetwashing was an important practice in Carthage during the time of Tertullian, as evidenced by the references to bathing in the context of the Eucharist, the offering of water for the saints' feet, and the admission that Christians use linen towels during their imitation of the feetwashing performed by Christ.

59. The putting on of clothes and shoes was done when guests left dinner. Margaret Visser, *The Rituals of Dinner*, 110–11, writes, "There are various ritual ways in which entry into a house is noted and 'managed.' In Japan or in the Middle East, one takes off one's shoes. Outside the house is dirt, and leaving shoes at the door not only respects cleanliness, but also ritually recognizes the sacrality of 'inside.' . . . The taking off of shoes is a very practical gesture, but it also means to a Middle Eastern guest that he is disarming himself, showing respect, and making himself similar to the host, who himself is shoeless." She writes later, "In many cultures there are clothes designed only for eating, just as we have special outfits to sleep in. . . . In ancient Rome, guests changed into a tunic and shawl for dinner. . . . Roman guests were given thin slippers to put on in their host's house, but these too were removed by slaves before the meal proper began. If a guest 'called for his slippers,' it was a sign that he wanted to leave the dining room, change into his street clothes, and then go home," pp. 114–15.

2. Clement of Alexandria: Feetwashing and Spiritual Cleansing

Even though Clement of Alexandria does not *explicitly* name feetwashing as a Christian practice,[60] in a sermon on the prodigal son he connects feetwashing with spiritual cleansing. When the wayward son repents and returns home, the father welcomes him by giving him gifts signifying his renewed status:

> Wherefore the Father bestows on him the glory and honour that was due, putting on him the best robe, the robe of immortality; and a ring, a royal signet and divine seal . . . and shoes, not those perishable ones . . . but such as wear not, and are suited for the journey to heaven, becoming and adorning the heavenly path, *such as unwashed feet never put on, but those which are washed by our Teacher and Lord.*[61]

The text in Luke 15 only mentions the father bidding for new sandals to be given to his son, yet Clement expounds on the parable by describing these non-perishable shoes that are only fit to be worn by those who have had their feet washed by Jesus, the Teacher and Lord. This inter-position of feetwashing into the narrative makes sense if we assume that feetwashing was a part of Christian practice in Alexandria. Moreover, it is clear that Clement understands feetwashing to relate to a change in behavior, not simply a physical cleansing. Relating the parable to his hearers, Clement preaches that after repentance and cleansing by Jesus, believers are to "wear the shoes," so to speak, of a heavenly, changed life.[62] Since Jesus did not physically wash the prodigal son's feet, nor the feet of the people listening to Clement, this sermon is a powerful ex-ample that Christians in the third century understood feetwashing to be connected to repentance and to involve spiritual cleansing by their Teacher and Lord.

---

60. Clement does, however, make several references to John 13 and to Jesus washing the disciples' feet.

61. Clement of Alexandria *Sermon on Luke* 15 (emphasis added).

62. "Now the shoes which the Father bids the servant give to the repentant son . . . do not impede or drag to the earth (for the earthly tabernacle weighs down the anxious mind); but they are buoyant, and ascending, and waft to heaven, and serve as such a ladder and chariot as he requires who has turned his mind towards the Father," ibid.

3. Cyprian: Feetwashing as Humble Service

Around 256 Cyprian, the bishop of Carthage and pupil of Tertullian, wrote a treatise (*On the Advantage of Patience*) in which he describes feetwashing as an act that Jesus performed to teach loving service to his disciples. He explains: "[Jesus] ruled over His disciples not as servants in the power of a master; but, kind and gentle, He loved them with a brotherly love. He deigned even to wash the apostles' feet, that since the Lord is such among His servants, He might teach, by His example, what a fellow-servant ought to be among his peers and equals."[63] Here we see a theological reflection on the act of feetwashing in Carthage, a generation after Tertullian. If Jesus, through feetwashing, taught his disciples what a fellow servant ought to do and be among his peers, then in order for the lesson to be learned, the act must be continually practiced. According to Cyprian, Jesus' feetwashing is not meant to teach the mind how to think, but rather to teach the hands how to act in service.

4. Feetwashing and Worship Setting

Feetwashing is an act that requires some degree of preparation; it cannot occur as spontaneously as prayer because a basin, water, and a towel are needed to perform the action. During the earliest centuries of the church most Christians worshiped in believers' homes, and every household would have had the proper materials needed for washing feet. In the mid-third century Christians in some locations began to build edifices especially designed for worship, and evidence exists demonstrating that some early church buildings contained a fountain for washing hands and feet. Philip Schaff notes:

> [T]he historian Eusebius, gives us the first account of a church edifice which Paulinus built in Tyre between a.d. 313 and 322. It included a large portico; a quadrangular atrium surrounded by ranges of columns; a fountain in the centre of the atrium for the customary washing of hands and feet before entering the church; interior porticoes; the nave or central space with galleries above the aisles, and covered by a roof of cedar of Lebanon; and the most holy altar.[64]

63. Cyprian *Treatise* 9.
64. Schaff, *Ante-Nicene Christianity*, 200–201.

While feetwashing is undeniably a domestic action, this account reveals that Christians continued to practice feetwashing even as they moved out of homes and into church buildings for worship. However, as the basilica became the primary model for worship buildings, feetwashing gradually declined as a worship practice.

5. Conclusions

Based on cultural norms, it is reasonable to conclude that when the Eucharist was a part of an evening meal, feetwashing would have been practiced at the beginning of the celebration. The writings of Tertullian, Clement, and Cyprian indicate that Christians had a unique understanding of the practice of feetwashing which was based on the actions of Jesus during the Last Supper. These authors understood feetwashing as a demonstration of humble, loving service. Also, although the evidence is weak, it does seem to be the case that some early church buildings contained fountains used for feetwashing. While these sources give us some clues that feetwashing was a Christian practice for the early church, there does not exist any clear source describing exactly how early Christians washed one another's feet. As the Eucharist shifted to a morning celebration, apart from a meal, feetwashing fades out of view. While washing feet before an evening meal made sense in the cultural surroundings, there was little need to wash one's feet in the morning before they became dirty from a day's work. Although feetwashing may not have been a universal practice for Christians before Constantine, it is nevertheless clear that in some communities it was an important practice serving to remind members of Christ's cleansing and to teach them how to be humble servants.

E. EUCHARISTIC PREPARATION/EXAMINATION

We now turn to examine the development of processes for preparing to celebrate the Eucharist. A significant development that occurred in the late first century was the requirement that only those who had been baptized could celebrate the Eucharist. The practice of confessing sins before celebrating the Eucharist had also emerged by the early second century. Similarly, Tertullian writes that those who had committed especially grave sins were subject to a period of *exomologesis* (public confession) during which they were excluded from Communion.

1. Limiting the Eucharist to the Baptized

Early in Christian history it became the norm to limit the celebration of the Eucharist to those who had been baptized. The *Didache* contains the earliest example of this restriction: "You must not let anyone eat or drink of your Eucharist except those baptized in the Lord's name. For in reference to this the Lord said, 'Do not give what is sacred to dogs' [Matt 7:6]" (9:5). Even though it appears that the author of the *Didache* has inappropriately applied Jesus' words to the Eucharist,[65] it is clear nonetheless that the celebration is understood to be holy, that is, set apart for those who are baptized. Several other examples, including Justin Martyr (*Apology* 66) and the *Apostolic Tradition* (37), indicate that this practice became widespread in the early church. This limitation had both theological and practical purposes. Theologically speaking, the belief was that the church could not truly gather as Christ's body on earth if pagans were included in the celebration of Communion. In a practical sense, remembering that the church experienced periodic persecution after Nero, it made sense to keep outsiders from participating in the Eucharist. When the Eucharist was celebrated in the morning, apart from a meal, the unbaptized and the catechumens were dismissed from the liturgy before the congregation shared the bread and the cup. However, in earlier times when the Eucharist was a part of an evening meal, it is possible that catechumens were allowed to observe the Eucharist without participating.

While it is clear that the early church prohibited the unbaptized from partaking in the Eucharist, it may be the case that some churches allowed catechumens to be present to observe the celebration without participating. This argument can be made from the *Apostolic Tradition*, which is somewhat perplexing because it both calls for the dismissal of the catechumens from gatherings after a time of instruction (18–19),[66] and yet also indicates that catechumens were present at the Lord's Supper:

> *Exorcized bread and a cup should be given to catechumens.* A catechumen shall not *sit* at the Lord's Supper. But throughout every meal the one who eats [i.e., the catechumen] should *be mindful*

---

65. The original context makes no reference to the bread and cup. Jesus' admonition most likely is a warning to avoid the careless exposition of Christian teaching to those who could not care less.

66. "Whenever the teacher ceases to give instruction the catechumens should pray by themselves, separated from the faithful . . . When the teacher lays his hand on the catechumens after their prayer he should pray and dismiss them," (18.1; 19.1).

of the one who invited him; for this reason he was asked to come
under the other's roof. (26:3–27:2, emphasis added).

While this passage reveals that catechumens are present at the meal,
it is made clear that only the faithful are to share the Eucharist. The bread
and cup that the catechumens consume are not the Eucharist, but rather
only "exorcized" bread and drink. Anglican scholar Alistair Stewart-
Sykes believes that catechumens were present during the Eucharist as
observers. He writes:

> We have already suggested that the eucharist precedes the meal,
> which makes [excluding catechumens] rather difficult if the
> catechumens are present for the meal. Rather than implying an
> exclusion from the premises, these words may be interpreted
> as suggesting that the catechumens should not sit at the same
> table as the faithful but that they remain present,[67] just as they
> pray separately from the faithful at 18:1. . . . In this respect the
> catechumens are in an analogous situation to that of freedmen at
> a meal given by their master who, whilst present, might receive
> inferior food and seating.[68]

This is a helpful explanation. I would like to add to this a conjecture
that retains part of the dismissal found in 19:1. Because most catechumens underwent instruction and examination for a period of three years
(17:1), perhaps the more novice catechumens who had yet to demonstrate a deep commitment to the Christian "Way" were dismissed after a
time of instruction, while those who were nearly ready for baptism were
allowed to remain to observe the celebration of the Eucharist and to
participate in the meal. In any case, the *Apostolic Tradition* indicates that
catechumens were present during the evening worship meal, although
they were not allowed to partake of the Eucharist.

2. Confession in the Didache

The *Didache* contains the first explicit connection of confession of sins
with the Eucharistic celebration. Chapter 14 reads:

> On every Lord's Day—his special day—come together and break
> bread and give thanks (*eucharistesate*), *first confessing your sins*

67. Another alternative is that the catechumens stood while the faithful sat to eat; cf.
Easton, *The Apostolic Tradition of Hippolytus*, 100.

68. Stewart-Sykes, "Commentary on the Apostolic Tradition," 143.

so that your sacrifice may be pure. *Anyone at variance with his neighbor must not join you, until they are reconciled*, lest your sacrifice be defiled. For it was of this sacrifice that the Lord said [Mal 1:11, 14], "Always and everywhere offer me a pure sacrifice; for I am a great King, says the Lord, and my name is marveled at by the nations." (14:1–3, emphasis added)

Here the author of the *Didache* expounds on Paul's earlier instruction to the Corinthians[69] by stating specifically that believers are to confess their sins before breaking bread and giving thanks. There are also connections to 1 Cor 5 where Paul writes that "our paschal lamb, Christ, has been sacrificed" (5:7) and instructs the church to avoid eating with Christians who are blatant sinners.[70] The *Didache* repeats this instruction, essentially stating that in order for members to be true companions, any and all disagreements must be resolved before the breaking of bread; participating otherwise made a mockery of the bread of communion ("As this piece [of bread] was scattered over the hills and then was brought together and made one, *so let your Church be brought together*" 9:4, emphasis added). The admonition to confess sins in order to offer a pure sacrifice (14:1) is mirrored by an earlier passage in which confession of sins precedes prayer time: "At the church meeting you must confess your sins, *and not approach prayer with a bad conscience*" (4:14). Stated differently, this internal evidence indicates that only in bad conscience would one approach prayer with unconfessed sin. Consequently, offering prayers to God without having confessed one's sins could be understood as offering to God an impure sacrifice. Although the church would later apply this sacrificial understanding to the bread and the cup, at this early stage the sacrifice offered to God is best understood to be prayer.

69. "Examine yourselves, and only then eat of the bread and drink of the cup" (1 Cor 11:28).

70. "Your boasting is not a good thing. Do you not know that a little yeast leavens the whole batch of dough? Clean out the old yeast so that you may be a new batch, as you really are unleavened. For our paschal lamb, Christ, has been sacrificed. Therefore, let us celebrate the festival, not with the old yeast, the yeast of malice and evil, but with the unleavened bread of sincerity and truth. . . . [Do not] associate with anyone who bears the name of brother or sister who is sexually immoral or greedy, or is an idolater, reviler, drunkard, or robber. Do not even eat with such a one. For what have I to do with judging those outside? Is it not those who are inside that you are to judge? God will judge those outside. Drive out the wicked person from among you" (1 Cor 5:6–8, 11–13).

3. Confession, Sacrifice, and Prayer

The early church had a broad understanding of the meaning of sacrifice, including the offering of food for the fellowship meal and the offering of one's entire life in service to God.[71] The sacrifice of the Eucharist primarily referred to the offering of prayers to God. Sacrifice was also linked with confession, a conjunction that had been made earlier in Hebrews: "Through him [Jesus], then, let us continually offer a sacrifice of praise to God, that is, the fruit of lips that confess his name" (Heb 13:15). In this passage sacrifice is understood as a vocal offering of praise, a confession of the name of Jesus.[72] In a similar fashion, the *Didache* links confession with offering a sacrifice of prayer to God, although there is now a shift from confessing praise to confessing sin. The *Didache* is not alone in addressing sacrifice and prayer as interchangeable; both Tertullian and Clement of Alexandria understood prayer to be a sacrifice unto God. Tertullian (*On Prayer* 28, ~192 CE) writes:

> We are the true adorers and the true priests, who, praying in spirit, sacrifice, in spirit, prayer,—a victim proper and acceptable to God, which assuredly He has required, which He has looked forward to for Himself! This victim, devoted from the whole heart, fed on faith, tended by truth, entire in innocence, pure in chastity, garlanded with *agape*,[73] we ought to escort with the

71. The *Apostolic Tradition* reveals that like the Israelites, who offered God their first-fruits (which fed the Levitical priests), so too the early Christians brought food as an offering to God. Food brought as an offering would have been consumed in the fellowship meal. Believers also understood sacrifice as offering their lives to God; Paul encourages believers in Rome to "present your bodies as a living sacrifice, holy and acceptable to God, which is your spiritual worship" (Rom 12:1). The author of Hebrews also writes, "Do not neglect to do good and to share what you have, for such sacrifices are pleasing to God" (Heb 13:16).

72. Hebrews is clear that the continual sacrifice of believers is distinct from Christ's own sacrifice, which occurred once for all, ending the repeated sacrifices of atonement in Judaism. "[Christ does not] offer himself again and again, as the high priest enters the Holy Place year after year with blood that is not his own; for then he would have had to suffer again and again since the foundation of the world. But as it is, he has appeared once for all at the end of the age to remove sin by the sacrifice of himself" (Heb 9:25–26).

73. It is quite likely that when Tertullian uses the word *agape*, he is referring to the Love Feast. After all, he uses *agape* in *Apology* 39 when his is describing the Love Feast. If Tertullian simply means "love," there would be no need to insert the Greek word *agape* into the Latin text.

pomp of good works, amid psalms and hymns, unto God's altar,
to obtain for us all things from God.

Clement of Alexandria also encourages Christians to offer sacrifices
of prayer to God and to approach prayer with souls that are "immaculate
and stainlessly pure."[74] In sum, during the first centuries of the church
the practice of confessing sins was intricately linked with the offering
of sacrificial prayer to God. When the church gathered to celebrate the
Eucharist/Love Feast, the confession of sins prior to corporate prayer
served as an act of ritual purification so that the prayers of the church
might be an acceptable sacrifice unto God. However, as time passed the
understanding of eucharistic sacrifice began to change, especially as the
identification of the elements with the body and blood of Christ became
more prominent.[75]

4. *Confession and Repentance:* Exomologesis

In his treatise *On Repentance*, Tertullian discusses the process of repentance in the life of Christians. Tertullian understood repentance to be a
plank of salvation which God offers to the Christian "shipwrecked" by
sin; those who cling to the plank of repentance will be born into "the
port of divine clemency" (*On Repentance* 4). The process of demonstrating repentance was quite difficult in Tertullian's day. He writes:

> [This act of repentance], which is more usually expressed and
> commonly spoken of under a Greek name, is *exomologesis* [lit-
> erally "confession"], whereby we confess our sins to the Lord,
> not indeed as if He were ignorant of them, but inasmuch as by
> confession satisfaction is settled, of confession repentance is
> born; by repentance God is appeased. And thus *exomologesis* is a
> discipline for man's [*sic*] prostration and humiliation, enjoining
> a demeanor calculated to move mercy. With regard also to the
> very dress and food, *it commands (the penitent) to lie in sackcloth
> and ashes, to cover his body in mourning, to lay his spirit low in
> sorrows,* to exchange for severe treatment the sins which he has

74. Clement of Alexandria *Stromata* 7.7.

75. Philip Schaff, *History of the Christian Church*, 3:354, writes, "The ante-Nicene
fathers uniformly conceived the Eucharist as a thank-offering of the church; the congregation offering the consecrated elements of bread and wine, and in them itself, to
God. This view is in itself perfectly innocent, but readily leads to the doctrine of the
sacrifice of the mass, as soon as the elements become identified with the body and
blood of Christ, and the presence of the body comes to be materialistically taken."

committed; moreover, *to know no food and drink but such as is plain,*—not for the stomach's sake, to wit, but the soul's; for the most part, however, to feed prayers on fastings, *to groan, to weep and make outcries unto the Lord your God; to bow before the feet of the presbyters, and kneel to God's dear ones; to enjoin on all the brethren to be ambassadors to bear his deprecatory supplication (before God).* All this *exomologesis* (does), that it may enhance repentance . . . Therefore, while it abases the man, it raises him; while it covers him with squalor, it renders him more clean; while it *accuses*, it *excuses*; while it condemns, it absolves.[76]

Tertullian acknowledges that many people shrink from this form of confession and repentance on account of its uncomfortableness; yet he pleads for them to reconsider in light of the even greater punishment that will befall them if they enter eternity with an unrepentant heart. In the early church, while all believers were to confess sins to God, *exomologesis* was understood as the path of reconciliation for those members who had committed especially grave sins. In addition to wearing sackcloth and ashes, fasting, and giving alms, the penitent was barred from sharing Communion with the church until their penance was deemed completed by the bishop (a process that could last for months or even years).[77] Only then was the penitent allowed back into the ranks of the faithful, once again able to participate in the Eucharist. With few exceptions, *exomologesis* was only offered once to a fallen member. Thus, in the third century *exomologesis* emerged as a tool of reconciliation through which those who had committed grave sins were restored to the communion of the church.

F. SUMMARY

Perhaps the best way to summarize the preceding material is to describe, in general, the overall order of a Love Feast in the first centuries, recognizing that some elements may not have been included in certain

76. *On Repentance*, 9 (emphasis added).

77. "After the sinner had asked the bishop for Penance, he was enrolled in the order of the penitents, excluded from Communion, and committed to a course of prayer, fasting, and almsgiving; after a period whose length was determined by the gravity of the sin, the sinner was reconciled and rejoined the congregation," Livingstone, *Concise Oxford Dictionary of the Church*, 438. The practice of separating penitents from the congregation has carried over into the modern criminal justice system, hence the name penitentiary.

places and times. The Love Feast was the name given by some churches to their evening worship meal. Whether believers gathered in homes or in rented spaces for this meal, social customs would have required the washing of feet before the meal. In the church, however, it appears that feetwashing was understood not only as an act of hospitality, but also as a distinct Christian discipline that emphasized both spiritual cleansing and humble service. The evening service likely began with several forms of confession. The confession *Kyrios Jesous* ("Lord Jesus") functioned as a greeting and welcome, acknowledging the Lord's presence in the gathering. Also, according to the *Didache*, before the meal began believers were to confess their sins so that their worship service would be a pure offering to God. After lamps were lit and an opening prayer was offered, the supper began. At some point during the meal, either at its opening or at its conclusion, the Eucharist was shared by all those who had been baptized. Prior to the celebration of the Eucharist, those present greeted one another with a holy kiss. The church understood the bread and the cup to be the body and blood of Christ, in particular, because this gave witness to the truth that just as Jesus' physical body was raised by God, so too their own bodies, having taken in the Eucharist, would be resurrected upon Christ's return. The fellowship meal that was shared consisted of food that was supplied by the various members of the church. Care was taken to ensure that participants did not eat or drink too much, and the leftovers from the meal were gathered to share with the poor and others unable to be present. After the meal the worship continued with the offering of prayers, the reading of letters and the Hebrew Scriptures, the singing of hymns, and instruction from the bishop or presbyter. The Love Feast concluded in a quiet and orderly fashion.

From the beginning, the celebration of the Love Feast presented challenges for the church. The Christian worship meal was radically inclusive of the more humble members of society—women, slaves, and the poor—and the mere gathering of these different groups to eat and worship together was socially awkward. Sustained by God's grace and power, the Love Feast was a provocative witness of God's upside-down Kingdom. Apart from God's active grace and power, such suppers became occasions where elitism, selfishness, and drunkenness prevailed. In addition to these internal difficulties, several external challenges also threatened the institution of the Love Feast. Roman restrictions on associations made it difficult for Christians in some cities to gather for evening meals. There were also sects, such as the Carpocratians, that celebrated a love feast in which licentiousness, and not the love of God, ruled the night. Both Tertullian and Clement defend the modesty and goodness of the Christian Love Feast against rumors of its extravagance and lewdness. Perhaps in response to such charges, beginning in the second century some churches began to celebrate the Eucharist in the morning, apart from an evening meal. Separated from the Eucharist, the focus of the evening Love Feast then became providing food for the poor (baptized and unbaptized), and remembering the martyrs and other Christian forebears. The practice of Christian feetwashing began to decline as the weekly remembrance of Jesus shifted from an evening supper in homes to a token meal celebrated in the early morning.

5

Over-Spiritualizing the Meal

The Decline of the Love Feast

B EGINNING IN THE FOURTH century, the Love Feast began to decline and the morningtime celebration of the Eucharist became solidified as the primary worship service of the church. I have chosen a provocative title for this chapter, not because I negate or neglect the spiritual value of the Eucharist, but rather because as the church left behind the actual meal, it left behind many of the practical aspects that provided balance to the spiritual realities also present in the celebration of Communion. Thus, the Roman Mass and/or the Liturgies of the Eastern church that emerged tended to overemphasize the spiritual dimension of the Eucharist and to undervalue the practical and economic dimensions that had been present in the earlier celebrations of the Love Feast. This chapter explores how the developments that occurred during and after the Constantinian shift contributed to the decline of the Love Feast. Hence the chapter begins by defining the Constantinian shift so that we may better understand how it impacts the celebration of the Love Feast. Following this is an examination of the developments in five main elements of the Love Feast: namely, the fellowship meal, Eucharist, holy kiss, feetwashing, and examination.

A. THE CONSTANTINIAN SHIFT

Understanding the Constantinian shift is crucial to our analysis of the decline of the Love Feast. Scholars and theologians, most notably John Howard Yoder and Stanley Hauerwas, have used the term "Constantinian shift" to describe changes in the church that occurred as Christianity developed from an illicit religion to the religion of the masses in the

Roman Empire. Because of his significant contributions, Constantine's name is attached to this transformation. The term "Constantinian shift" serves as an appropriate label for the transformation that began before 200 CE and lasted over 200 years.

1. The Life of Constantine

A brief look at several important events in the life of Constantine will aid our understanding of the Constantinian shift. In 312 CE, on the eve of the battle of the Milvian Bridge, Constantine reportedly had a vision in which Jesus told him to inscribe the first two letters of Christ (XP in Greek) on the shields of his troops. Following his victory in battle, Constantine became a supporter of the Christian faith, although he did not technically become a Christian until he was baptized on his deathbed in 337.[1] In 313 he issued the Edict of Milan which mandated tolerance of Christians throughout the Roman Empire. Constantine soon began to use his power to make decisions concerning the church: in 316 he intervened in the Donatist controversy and decided the legitimate bishop of Carthage; he declared Sunday to be a day of rest in 321; and in 325 he convened the first ecumenical council of Nicaea, which condemned the heresy of Arianism. Even though Constantine contributed significantly to the growth of the Christian church, as an unbaptized man he was never able to participate in the church's highest act of worship, namely, the celebration of the Eucharist. Under the favorable policies of Constantine, the church soon had thousands of catechumens and baptized Christians who celebrated the Eucharist on Sunday mornings. Yoder summarizes the changes effected by Constantine:

> Before [Constantine], Christians had been a minority—some scholars estimate no more than ten percent of the empire's population—and intermittent persecution worked against making anyone's adherence cheap. It took at least a degree of conviction to belong. After Constantine the church was everybody. Being counted as "Christian" was the rule, not an exception. Paganism

---

1. Justo Gonzalez writes of Constantine, "Even after the battle of the Milvian bridge, and throughout his entire life, he never placed himself under the direction of Christian teachers or bishops. . . . Constantine reserved the right to determine his own religious practices, and even to intervene in the life of the church, for he considered himself 'bishop of bishops.' Repeatedly, even after his conversion, he took part in pagan rites in which no Christian would participate, and the bishops raised no voice of condemnation," Gonzalez, *The Story of Christianity*, 1:121.

was soon declared illegal [by Theodosius I in 392], and [before long] the government was actively repressing heresies, i.e., ruling on what constitutes orthodox belief and punishing dissent. Henceforth, it would take exceptional conviction not to be counted as Christian.[2]

2. Constantinian Changes in the Church

The Constantinian shift affected the church in a variety of ways. First, the process for becoming a Christian was drastically changed. In the early church it was normal for an individual to undergo intense instruction and scrutiny, lasting from six months to three years, before being baptized. This process was condensed significantly in the fourth and fifth centuries, so that one could become a Christian in a matter of days or weeks.[3] Second, the expansion of the church impacted the ethical teaching of the church. In the earliest centuries of the church, Christians were strictly forbidden to kill another human. According to the *Apostolic Tradition*, a man who was a soldier prior to baptism could continue to stay in the army only as long as he refused to kill, and any individual who willfully joined the army after being baptized was put out of the church.[4] However, by 416 only Christians were allowed to

2. Yoder, "The Constantinian Sources of Western Social Ethics," 135–36. On the next page Yoder summarizes this shift by stating: "Before Constantine, one knew as a fact of everyday experience that there was a believing Christian community but one had to 'take it on faith' that God was governing history. After Constantine, one had to believe without seeing that there was a community of believers, within the larger nominally Christian mass, but one knew for a fact that God was in control of history," 137.

3. By 496 it was even possible to become a Christian simply because one's leader decided to convert. (When Clovis I of France decided to be baptized, 3,000 of his soldiers were baptized at the same time.) For an insightful look at the impact of the Constantinian shift on the process of conversion and the catechumenate, see Kreider, *The Change of Conversion*.

4. "A soldier in command must be told not to kill people; *if he is ordered so to do, he shall not carry it out*. Nor should he take the oath. If he will not agree, he should be rejected. Anyone who has the power of the sword, or is a civil magistrate wearing the purple, should desist, or he should be rejected. If a catechumens or a believer wishes to become a soldier they should be rejected, for they have despised God (16:8–10)," Hippolytus, *On the Apostolic Tradition*, 100 (emphasis added). The whole of v. 8 makes it clear that the instruction is for a soldier *under* command, even though the literal translation reads "in command"; see the note in Stewart-Sykes, "Commentary on the Apostolic Tradition," 101.

enlist in the Roman army.[5] These are but two examples of many that illustrate what Yoder considers to be the most significant result of the Constantinian shift, namely, that the categories of "church" and "world" are fused together.[6] Because of the Constantinian shift, he argues, "the meaning of the word 'Christian' has changed." Yoder continues:

> Its moral, emotional, and even intellectual meanings were changed by the reversal of the sociological and political pressures. This shift called forth a new doctrinal refinement, namely the doctrine of the invisibility of the true church. Whether defined from the godward side (the "elect") or the [hu]manward (those whose faith is sincere), the class of *true* Christians continues to be a minority. Though we are unable to determine just who they are, we can have some notion of the signs which suggest who are not of their number. The major architect of the concept of the *ecclesia invisiblis*, Augustine, thought that perhaps the true church would be five percent of the visible one.
>
> The definitions of the faith could thus no longer take the assembly of believers at its base. As a result, therefore, the eyes of those looking for the church had to turn to the clergy, especially to the episcopacy, and henceforth "the church" meant the hierarchy more than the people.[7]

This last sentence has particular relevance to our examination of the Love Feast during this time. As the hierarchy of bishops became increasingly understood as the true "church," and as Christian worship began to be influenced by imperial protocol, practices like the Love Feast that were associated with the "primitive" age of the church were gradually abolished.[8] Let us examine more closely the decline of the Love Feast.

5. *Theodosian Code* 16.10.21.

6. "The most pertinent fact about the new state of things after Constantine and Augustine is not that Christians were no longer persecuted and began to be privileged, nor that emperors built churches and presided over ecumenical deliberations about the Trinity; what matters is that the two visible realities, church and world, were fused. There is no longer anything to call "world"; state, economy, art, rhetoric, superstition, and war have all been baptized," Yoder, "The Otherness of the Church," 57.

7. Yoder, "The Constantinian Sources of Western Social Ethics," 136.

8. Justo Gonzalez writes, "After Constantine's conversion, Christian worship began to be influenced by imperial protocol. Incense, which was used as a sign of respect for the emperor, began appearing in Christian churches. Officiating ministers, who until then had worn everyday clothes, began dressing in more luxurious garments. Likewise, a number of gestures indicating respect, which were normally made before the emperor, now became part of Christian worship. The custom was also introduced of beginning

B. THE GRADUAL DECLINE OF THE FELLOWSHIP MEAL

The decline of the Love Feast was not immediate; in fact, during the fourth and early fifth centuries there were still examples of its practice in Christian communities.[9] We will look at a few of these examples of the continuation of the Love Feast before turning to examine how the Constantinian shift eventually shifted the location and meaning of worship in such a way that the Love Feast became viewed as primitive, obsolete, and unnecessary.

1. Church Councils Supporting the Agape

There is evidence in the canons of several early church councils that the *agape* was still considered an important practice of the church. Early references to the Love Feast in canon law appear to encourage its celebration in order to counter the emerging ascetic communities, which were rejecting feasting and eating meat. Canon 14 of the Council of Ancyra (314 CE) addresses a Love Feast problem, namely, some church leaders were refusing to eat meat at the feast, or even vegetables that had been cooked with meat.[10] The canon instructs church leaders to taste a sample of meat and not to refuse to eat vegetables cooked with meat, otherwise they are to be removed from their office. Hence, it was important for leaders not to disgrace the Love Feast by allowing dietary stipulations to restrict the fellowship meal. Similarly, canon 11 of the Council of Gangra (~325–381 CE) reads: "If anyone shall despise those who out of faith make love-feasts and invite the brethren in honour of the Lord, and is not willing to accept these invitations because he despises what is done, let him be anathema" (the Ancient Epitome reads, "Whoso spurns those who invite to the *agape*, and who when invited

---

services with a processional. Choirs were developed, partly in order to give body to that procession. Eventually, the congregation came to have a less active role in worship," Gonzalez, *The Story of Christianity*, 1:125.

9. It appears that in the Armenian Church the *agape* meal continued into the modern era. See Conybeare, "Survival of Animal Sacrifices."

10. "It is decreed that among the clergy, presbyters and deacons who abstain from flesh shall taste of it, and afterwards, if they shall so please, may abstain. But if they disdain it, and will not even eat herbs [vegetables] served with flesh, but disobey the canon, let them be removed from their order," Percival, ed. *Seven Ecumenical Councils*, 69. Johannes Zonaras, a twelfth-century Byzantine canonist and historian, observed that this canon chiefly applies to the Love Feast.

will not communicate with these, let him be anathema").[11] The canon primarily appears to condemn those who, out of false asceticism, spurn invitations to the love-feast, either to avoid eating meat, or (more likely) to avoid the social stigma of attending a feast held to honor the poor. The Ancient Epitome implies that Communion was celebrated at the Love Feast. Thus this canon anathematizes both the refusal of the rich to eat with the poor and the disgraceful refusal of some members to share the Eucharist with the poor.

2. Augustine and the Agape

Around the turn of the fifth century, Augustine still has a generally positive view of the Love Feast. Before moving to Milan, his mother had been accustomed to celebrating the memory of the saints with cakes, bread, and watered-down wine in North Africa (the *agape*).[12] Although Augustine recommends that feasting in cemeteries be discontinued because it has become scandalous,[13] he does not favor stopping the *agape* meal entirely. Writing from Hippo around 400, Augustine responds to the charges of Faustus the Manichean, who accuses Christians of turning pagan sacrifices into Love Feast celebrations:

> We do not turn the sacrifices of the Gentiles into love-feasts, as Faustus says we do. Our love-feasts are rather a substitute for the sacrifice spoken of by the Lord, in the words already quoted: "I will have mercy, and not sacrifice." At our love-feasts the poor obtain vegetable or animal food; and so the creature of God is used, as far as it is suitable, for the nourishment of man, who is also God's creature. You have been led by lying devils, not in self-denial, but in blasphemous error, "to abstain from meats which God hath created to be received with thanksgiving of them which believe and know the truth. For every creature of God is good, and nothing to be refused, if it be received with thanksgiving." In return for the bounties of the Creator, you ungratefully insult Him with your impiety; and because in our love-feasts flesh is

11. Ibid., 96.

12. However, when the family moved to Milan Augustine's mother was prohibited from continuing this practice by Bishop Ambrose (*Confessions* 6.2).

13. In a letter to Bishop Aurelius (~392) Augustine writes, "Since, however, these drunken revels and luxurious feasts in the cemeteries are wont to be regarded by the ignorant and carnal multitude as not only an honour to the martyrs, but also a solace to the dead, it appears to me that they might be more easily dissuaded from such scandalous and unworthy practices in these places," Augustine *Letters* 22, 240.

often given to the poor, you compare Christian charity to Pagan
sacrifices. (*Reply to Faustus the Manichaean* 20.20)

Augustine writes that the Love Feast was primarily an occasion for the
poor to receive food. The fact that meat was served was problematic for
the Manicheans, whose ascetic dietary laws prohibited eating meat. The
record shows that in Ancyra and Gangra (modern-day Turkey) and in
North Africa in the fourth and fifth centuries, the Love Feast was still
practiced among Christians, mainly as a charity meal for the poor.[14]

3. Socrates Scholasticus's Ecclesiastical History

In his *Ecclesiastical History*, written around 439 CE, Socrates Scholasticus
indicates that there were still Christians who were celebrating the
Eucharist on a Saturday evening in the context of a full meal. Writing
from Constantinople, his account of church history bears the influence
of the Eastern church. He reports:

> For although almost all churches throughout the world celebrate
> the sacred mysteries on the Sabbath of every week [Saturday], yet
> the Christians of Alexandria and at Rome, on account of some
> ancient tradition, have ceased to do this [and instead worship on
> Sunday]. The Egyptians in the neighborhood of Alexandria, and
> the inhabitants of Thebaïs [the region around Thebes], hold their
> religious assemblies on the Sabbath, but do not participate of the
> mysteries in the manner usual among Christians in general: for
> after having eaten and satisfied themselves with food of all kinds,
> in the evening making their offerings they partake of the myster-
> ies. (*Ecclesiastical History* 5.22)

14. Emperor Julian the Apostate (361–363 CE) understood that the Love Feast, as
a charity meal, was drawing people away from paganism. In 362 he wrote to the pagan
priests: "As a child might be lured by a cake from home, on board ship, and so sold
into slavery in some foreign port . . . In the same manner, beginning with their Agape,
as it is called among [Christians], and their entertainment and ministry of tables . . .
they have led the faithful into atheism," Cole, *Love-Feasts*, 121. In another place Julian
writes: "Why do we not observe that it is their benevolence to strangers, their care for
the graves of the dead, and the pretended holiness of their lives that have done most to
increase atheism [i.e., disbelief in pagan gods]? . . . For it is disgraceful that, when no
Jew ever has to beg, and the impious Galileans [Christians] support not only their own
poor but ours as well, all men see that our people lack aid from us. Teach those of the
Hellenic faith to contribute to public service of this sort," *The Works of Emperor Julian*,
LCL 3, 67–71, quoted in Witherington III, *Making a Meal of It* (2007), 89.

This account indicates that even into the fifth century the debate over whether to worship on Saturday or Sunday was still an active one in some places. More importantly, Socrates reports that some Christians in Egypt continue to worship on a Saturday evening. Their worship order consists of a meal followed by the sacramental bread and cup. It is striking to find this account so late in the record. It can be argued that as the eucharistic celebration developed into a Sunday morning celebration apart from a meal in the larger cities, Christians in more rural settings (like these described in Egypt) resisted such changes and kept the primitive practice of celebrating on Saturday evening with a meal followed by the Eucharist.

4. Changes in Worship Setting and the Decline of the Love Feast

One of the most significant developments in Christian worship resulting from the Constantinian shift was the change from worshiping in homes to worshiping in basilicas. The changes that Constantine made to imperial policy resulted in multitudes of people joining the church. The growing number of worshipers made it impractical—and all but impossible—to continue worshiping in homes; consequently Constantine and the church leaders chose the basilica as the style of building in which to house Christian worship.[15] The basilica was a large rectangular building which, prior to its Christian use, functioned as a courtroom or a community forum. The far end of the basilica had seats for officials and a raised platform with an altar, where sacrifices were made to the Emperor. With a few changes, the basilica became a house of Christian worship; the seats were now used by the bishop, presbyters, and deacons, and the altar was used for the eucharistic celebration.[16] Meeting in the

15. Constantine's involvement stems from his decision in 326 to expand vastly the city of Byzantium in order to make it his new capital city. He decided that the basilica would be the model for Christian churches built in the new city, which became the capital in 330 and was later called Constantinople.

16. Leland Roth writes, "Christians required not only buildings that would accommodate large numbers of converts but also enclosed spaces that would facilitate hearing the spoken word and chanted psalms. Clearly, the ancient Roman temple form could not be used, for it was doubly unsuitable: First, it did not have broad internal spaces suitable for housing scores or hundreds of people, and second, it so thoroughly symbolized pagan gods and Roman emperor worship. Constantine and church officials looked to secular public buildings, and the type they selected was the basilica. . . . The basilica had originally been devised for public gatherings, and its symbolic connotation, having to do with the equitable administration of earthly justice, was positive. It

basilica was beneficial for accommodating the increasing membership of the church, but the shift also changed the meaning and experience of worship.

When the basilica, and not the home, became the chief setting for Christian worship, the Eucharist became further separated from its original mealtime context. Basilicas did not have kitchens or tables, and this, combined with the large number of worshipers, presented significant logistical difficulties for worshiping at table. Moreover, Christian basilicas began to be understood as especially sacred places, so much so that eating in the basilica soon became viewed as sacrilegious. Worship in the basilica was much more institutional and structured than the early Love Feast, and the roles of bishops, presbyters, and deacons grew in importance. The eucharistic celebration, which was originally a joyous and spontaneous occasion, became much more formal and austere, and the role of the bishop began to be likened to that of a ship captain who manages his mariners.[17] The Love Feast proved difficult to manage effectively, and consequently church leaders began to limit its practice.[18]

---

was a simple matter to replace the small altar devoted to the emperor with one at which the Eucharist, or ritual communal meal, could be celebrated," Roth, *Understanding Architecture*, 279–80.

17. The *Apostolic Constitutions*, a bishop's handbook originating in Syria around 385 CE, reads: "When you [the bishop] call an assembly of the church, as one that is the commander of a great ship, charge the deacons as mariners to prepare place for the people as passengers. Let the building be long, with its head to the east, with its vestries on both sides at the east end, and so it will be like a ship. In the middle let the bishop's throne be placed, and on each side of him let the presbytery sit down; and let the deacons stand near at hand, in close and small-girt garments, for they are like the mariners and the managers of the ship. Let the laity sit on the other side [of the fence] with all quietness and good order. And let the women sit by themselves, they also keeping silence. If anyone be found sitting out of place, let him be rebuked by the deacon, as a manager of the ship, and be removed into the place proper for him. For the church is not only like a ship, but also like a sheepfold. For as the shepherds place all the brute creatures distinctly, I mean goats and sheep, according to their kind and age, so it is to be in the church. Let the deacon oversee the people, that nobody may whisper, slumber, laugh or nod. All ought to stand wisely and soberly and attentively. . . . After the prayer is over, let some of [the deacons] attend upon [the altar], and let others of them watch the multitude, and keep them silent," *Apostolic Constitutions* 2.7, quoted in Kreider, *Communion Shapes Character*, 53.

18. Ben Witherington III writes, "The more ascetical the church became, the more concern there was about the potential bad witness of the agape, and this in fact was to lead to the separation of the agape from the celebration of the Lord's Supper altogether as it became a 'church ceremony' rather than a part of a Christian family meal," Witherington III, *Making a Meal of It* (2007), 106.

5. Agape Restrictions in Canon Law

In the mid-fourth century, prohibitions concerning the Love Feast began to appear in the canons of church councils, and by the late-fifth century the Love Feast was virtually abolished as an official function of the church.[19] Canon 28 of the Synod of Laodicea (~363) is the first to forbid the celebration of the Love Feast in church buildings: "It is not permitted to hold love feasts, as they are called, in the Lord's Houses [*kyriaka*], or Churches, nor to eat and to spread couches in the house of God."[20] This canon does not forbid the Love Feast outright, just the celebration of the feast in the *kyriaka*, the Lord's House (from which the English word "church" is derived). The Love Feast was not entirely banned, however, because the previous canon (27) states: "A clergyman invited to a love feast shall carry nothing away with him; for this would bring his order into shame."[21] Since worship in homes was declining, it is logical to assume that the practical impact of canon 28 was the cessation of the *agape* for many Christians around Laodicea. Lastly, the fiftieth canon of Laodicea prohibits feasting on Maundy Thursday.[22] Apparently some Christians were holding a feast on Maundy Thursday to commemorate the Last Supper; a feast that included meat and the celebration of the Eucharist. Although later councils would mandate that the Eucharist be taken fasting, the Synod of Laodicea prohibits the Maundy Thursday feast on the grounds that it breaks the Lenten fast.

The Council of Carthage (419) contains several canons that relate to the Love Feast. Canon 42 states: "No bishops or clerics are to hold feasts in churches, unless perchance they are forced thereto by the necessity of hospitality as they pass by. The people, too, as far as possible, are to be prohibited from attending such feasts."[23] While the first part

---

19. It is noteworthy that none of the seven ecumenical councils contains a prohibition concerning the Love Feast.

20. Percival, ed. *Seven Ecumenical Councils*, 148. Also compare to canon 41 of the Council of Carthage (419 CE) and canon 74 of the Council of Trullo (692 CE).

21. Ibid. For a clergyman to take food home with him would both exhibit covetousness and would diminish the food that would have been distributed to the poor and others who were not present (see Justin, *Apology* 1:67).

22. "The fast must not be broken on the fifth day of the last week in Lent [i.e., on Maundy Thursday], and the whole of Lent be dishonoured; but it is necessary to fast during all the Lenten season by eating only dry meats," Percival, ed. 155.

23. Ibid., Canon 42. The Donatists seem to have taken communion with the *agape*, because Carthage canon 47 emphasizes that former Donatists who rejoined the Catholic

of the canon forbidding feasts in the church building is essentially the same as Laodicea (with the exception of the necessity of hospitality), the canon also encourages clerics to discourage the laity from attending such feasts. This additional prohibition indicates that the bishops gathered in Carthage were concerned to stop feasting in churches, homes, or cemeteries. In addition, canon 41 instructs that the Eucharist should be taken fasting, i.e., separate from the *agape* meal: "The Sacraments of the Altar are not to be celebrated except by those who are fasting, except on the one anniversary of the celebration of the Lord's Supper; for if the commemoration of some of the dead, whether bishops or others, is to be made in the afternoon, let it be only with prayers, if those who officiate have already breakfasted."[24] In a similar vein, canon 47 reads: "True it is that sacrifices are to be forbidden after breakfast, so that they may be offered as is right by those who are fasting, and this has been confirmed then and now."[25] Taken together, these canons instruct bishops to celebrate the Eucharist in the morning, before breakfast, so that any afternoon or evening worship services consisted only of prayers. Contrary to the Synod of Laodicea, the council of Carthage allows the Eucharist to be celebrated on Maundy Thursday evening.

Lastly, it is important to consider several canons from the Council of Trullo, held in the domed room (*trullus*) of the imperial palace at Constantinople in 692 CE.[26] Echoing the Synod of Laodicea, canon 74 states: "It is not permitted to hold what are called Agapae, that is love-feasts, in the Lord's houses or churches, nor to eat within the house, nor to spread couches. If any dare to do so let him cease therefrom or be cut off."[27] Canons 28, 57, and 99 clarify that the celebration of the Eucharist should not be accompanied by any other foods or drinks (i.e., grapes, milk, honey, or meat). Thus, the Council of Trullo reemphasizes the

Church must take communion fasting.

24. Ibid., 461. This is canon 28 of the Synod of Hippo (393 CE). Although the Synod of Laodicea ruled against celebrating the *agape* on Maundy Thursday, the bishops gathered in Carthage allowed Maundy Thursday to be an exception to the rule prohibiting eating before celebrating the sacraments of the altar.

25. Ibid., 462.

26. The council of Trullo established the basic code for the Eastern churches that is still normative for the Orthodox today. It is not recognized as authoritative by the Roman church. Trullo gave formal approval to several previous canons concerning the Love Feast.

27. Percival, ed. *Seven Ecumenical Councils*, 398.

canons of previous centuries by prohibiting the celebration of a fellowship meal with the Eucharist.[28] Eleanor Kreider comments, "As the *agape* meal faded away, the churches suffered irretrievable losses both in the intimacy of fellowship and in the free, informal worship characteristic of the love feasts."[29]

C. THE DEVELOPMENT OF THE EUCHARIST

Although the morning celebration of the Eucharist had been celebrated since the second century, it was only in the fourth century that the practice became the norm in Christian worship. As the Eucharist moved from a home celebration to a large-group liturgical celebration, and as restrictions were placed on the Love Feast, the theological understanding of the Eucharist began to change. Rather than providing a detailed examination of the development in the Eucharist, this section only examines two interrelated developments.[30] These two changes are the emergence of calling the Eucharist the "unbloody sacrifice" of Jesus Christ and the emphasis on the bread and cup *transforming into* the body and blood of Christ *when* the prayer of consecration is offered.

28. Interestingly, the practices of the *antidoron* in the Eastern church and the *pain benit* in French and Canadian churches appear to be echoes of the early *agape* tradition. In these churches, the bread which is later consecrated for the Eucharist is cut out of a larger loaf, and at the end of the liturgy the remaining bread is distributed to everyone present, including those who did not partake of the Eucharist. See Coxe, ed. *Fathers of the Second Century*, 403.

29. Kreider, *Communion Shapes Character*, 42–43. It should be noted that at the same time that the agape meal was fading away, other expressions of Christian hospitality were emerging, such as hospitals, hospices, and hostels. Christine Pohl observes that Christians established many hospitals in the fourth century to care for strangers and the poor. Chrysostom writes that the church at Antioch, though not wealthy, took care of three thousand widows and virgins daily, as well as those who were in prison, sick, or disabled. From 400 to 403 Chrysostom ordered the construction of a number of hospitals in Constantinople so that strangers and orphans, the sick, the poor and the invalid could receive care. There was a downside to this development, however, because Chrysostom's parishioners seem to have excused themselves from the demands of hospitality by noting that the church had the ability to provide hospitality to those in need. Although he insisted that hospitality remained a personal responsibility, it appears that many Christians found it easier to have the church-at-large take care of the poor and the stranger. See the discussion in Pohl, *Making Room*, 44–47.

30. For a more thorough examination of the Eucharist, see Macy, *The Banquet's Wisdom*.

1. The Development of the Eucharist as Sacrifice

In the fourth century the understanding of the Eucharist as sacrifice began to change. As worship gradually moved from homes into basilicas, many aspects of worship became more refined: presbyters were now referred to as priests; the liturgy began to include a processional and recessional when priests and attendants entered and exited; ornate vestments were worn by priests, and ornate artwork began to adorn the basilica. In many ways these developments made the structure and worship of the church more like that of the Israelites in the Old Testament, as is evident in this passage from the *Apostolic Constitutions*, written in the late fourth century:

> You, therefore, O bishops, are to your people *priests and Levites*, ministering to the holy tabernacle, the holy Catholic Church; who stand at the altar of the Lord your God, and offer to Him reasonable and *unbloody sacrifices* through Jesus the great High Priest. You are to the laity prophets, rulers, governors, and kings; the mediators between God and His faithful people . . . *Those which were then the sacrifices now are prayers, and intercessions, and thanksgivings.* Those which were then first-fruits, and tithes, and offerings, and gifts, now are oblations, which are presented by holy bishops to the Lord God, through Jesus Christ, who has died for them. *For these [bishops] are your high priests, as the presbyters are your priests, and your present deacons instead of your Levites*; as are also your readers, your singers, your porters, your deaconesses, your widows, your virgins, and your orphans: but He who is above all these is the High Priest. (*Apostolic Constitutions* 2.4.2, emphasis added)

Not only does this quotation give witness to the rise of the priesthood in Christianity, it also reveals that the concept of sacrifice is developing. No longer are prayers, intercessions, and thanksgivings understood to be sacrifices, as they had been in the past. The sacrifice of the church now is understood to be the "unbloody" sacrifice of the Eucharist:

> Instead of a bloody sacrifice, He [Christ] has appointed that reasonable and unbloody mystical one of His body and blood, which is performed to represent the death of the Lord by symbols. Instead of the divine service confined to one place, He has commanded and appointed that He should be glorified from sunrise to sunset in every place of His dominion. (*Apostolic Constitutions* 6.4.23)[31]

---

31. Philip Schaff summarizes this development as follows: "According to this doctrine [of the sacrifice of the mass], the Eucharist is an unbloody repetition of the aton-

It is not coincidental that the practice of referring to the Eucharist as the unbloody sacrifice occurred at the same time that some pagan temples were being converted into Christian houses of worship and that pagan villagers were converting en masse to the Christian faith. This is not to say that the church simply baptized Jewish or pagan practices and called them "Christian." However, it is a recognition that in a context of great social and religious change, when people who had been accustomed to offering pagan sacrifices now were gathering to worship in Christian buildings, the sacrifice of the Eucharist was reinterpreted in such a way that the primary task of Christian priests became the repeated offering of the unbloody sacrifice of the eucharistic bread and cup. A central aspect of this theological development became the transformation of the substance of the elements into the body and blood of Christ.

2. The Transformation of the Eucharistic Elements

While the New Testament scriptures and the writings of the earliest Christians mysteriously connect or equate the bread and cup with the body and blood of Christ,[32] beginning in the fourth century theologians began to positively emphasize the *transformation* of the substance of the Eucharist during the prayer of consecration. When Irenaeus described the eucharistic prayer of consecration, he used language conveying that a spiritual reality is *added* to the bread and the cup, rather than their being transformed in nature. Remember too that when the bread and cup were described as Christ's body, this was often in defense of the incarna-

---

ing sacrifice of Christ by the priesthood for the salvation of the living and the dead; so that the body of Christ is truly and literally offered every day and every hour, and upon innumerable altars at the same time. The term *mass*, which properly denoted the *dismissal* of the congregation (*missio, dismissio*) at the close of the general public worship, became, after the end of the fourth century, the name for the worship of the faithful, which consisted in the celebration of the eucharistic sacrifice and the communion," Schaff, *History of the Christian Church*, 3:352–53.

32. Most Protestants tend to emphasize how the breaking of bread and the sharing of the cup are connected with Jesus' broken body and spilt blood, while Catholic and Orthodox Christians equate the bread with the body of Christ and the contents of the cup with the blood of Christ. We should observe, however, that some early church fathers do not connect the body and blood of Christ with the Eucharistic elements; Origen understands eating and drinking Christ's body and blood to be receiving the teaching and words of Christ, which nourish the soul (*Hom. on Matt.* 85), and Eusebius writes in the fourth century that the flesh and blood of Christ refers to the words and sermons of Jesus (*Eccles. Theo.* 3.12).

tion of Christ and the physical resurrection of his followers. By the 300s, however, these emphases had changed. Ben Witherington describes these developments:

> [I]t was precisely in the fourth century, and not accidentally or incidentally after Constantine became emperor and Christianity came out of the catacombs and into increasing public prominence, that we have Cyril of Jerusalem in the East, in about A.D. 346, and Ambrose of Milan in the West, in about A.D. 374, both saying that the prayer of consecration turns the ordinary elements into something they were not before. Cyril, speaking to his catechumens, says that they must be completely convinced and persuaded that "what seems bread is not bread, though bread by taste, but rather the body of Christ; and that what seems wine is not wine, though the taste will have it so, but rather the blood of Christ." He then goes on to explain how this change is wrought: "We call upon the merciful God to send forth his Holy Spirit upon the gifts lying before him, that he may make the bread the body of Christ, and the wine the blood of Christ. For whatsoever the Holy Spirit has touched is sanctified and changed" (*Mystagogical Catecheses* 4.1–9; 5:7). . . . Similarly, in seeking to answer the objection . . . "[How] is it that you assert that I receive the body of Christ?" Ambrose [writes]: "This is not what nature made, but what the blessing consecrated, and the power of blessing is greater than that of nature, because by blessing nature itself is changed" (*On the Mysteries* 8.48–49). Even more clearly in his *On the Christian Faith* (4.10.125) he says, "by the mysterious efficacy of holy prayer [the elements] are transformed into the flesh and the blood." . . . Of course, the whole problem with this is that the words Jesus spoke at his modified Passover meal did not in any way suggest a transformation—he simply said "this bread (is) my body" and similarly with the blood.[33]

From the fourth century onward, the prayer of consecration became a high point in the celebration of the Eucharist; the point where the substance of the bread and wine is changed into the body and blood of Christ, according to Roman Catholic belief.[34] Gone was the mealtime Eucharist that revealed communion with God through fellowship with

---

33. Witherington III, *Making a Meal of It* (2007), 115–16. In the original, the last sentence appears in the middle of the quotation.

34. The English phrase "hocus pocus" emerged as a barbarization of Jesus' words "This is my body" ("*hoc est corpus meum*"), which are spoken by the priest during the consecratory prayer of the Latin Mass.

the body of Christ, the church. In its place was the sacrifice of the Mass, which emphasized the conversion of the elements into the body and blood of Christ, and the power of these transformed emblems to secure eternal communion with God for the communicant.

D. THE DEVELOPMENT OF THE KISS OF PEACE

By the fourth century, the Christian salutation was almost universally practiced during the eucharistic liturgy and was frequently called the "kiss of peace", or simply the "peace" (*pax*). Alan Kreider has shown that the Syrian church orders of the third and fourth centuries—the *Didascalia Apostolorum* and the *Apostolic Constitutions*—both indicate that peace and reconciliation were central themes in the worship of Syrian church-es.[35] He argues that the kiss of peace was a vital liturgical practice that helped these congregations to live out the call to be peacemakers. That the kiss was associated with peacemaking is also clearly seen in the writing of Cyril of Jerusalem, who wrote in the mid-fourth century:

> You must not suppose that this kiss is the kiss customarily ex-changed in the street by ordinary friends. This kiss is different, effecting as it does a conmingling of souls and mutually pledged unreserved forgiveness. The kiss, then, is a sign of a true union of hearts, banishing every grudge. It was this that Christ had in mind when he said, "If, when bringing your gift to the altar. . . ." The kiss, then, is a reconciliation, and therefore holy.[36]

The greeting of peace exchanged before the celebration of the Eucharist functioned as an outward expression of the unity of the congregation as they prepared to partake of the holy mysteries.

It appears that there was variation in congregations as to whether the kiss of peace occurred before or after the anaphora (the prayer of consecration during which the priest offers up the eucharistic elements). In the East, John Chrysostom named six places where the *pax* greeting was given during the liturgy, including during the kiss of peace before the anaphora:

> When the president of the assembly enters, right away he says, "Peace to all"; when he preaches, "Peace to all"; when he blesses,

35. Kreider, "Peacemaking in Worship," 177–90.

36. *Lectures on the Christian Sacraments*, 72Q, quoted in Kreider, "Kiss of Peace," 34.

"Peace to all"; when he gives the command to exchange the kiss of peace, "Peace to all"; when the sacrifice [anaphora] is completed, "Peace to all"; and in between [the services of the word and table] again, "Grace to you and peace.[37]

In the West, on the other hand, Augustine describes the kiss of peace as following the anaphora:

Then, after the consecration of the Holy Sacrifice of God . . . we say the Lord's Prayer which you have received and recited. After this, the 'Peace be with you' is said, and the Christians embrace one another with the holy kiss. This is a sign of peace; as the lips indicate, let peace be made in your conscience, that is, when your lips draw near to those of your brother, do not let your heart withdraw from his.[38]

In either location, it is clear that the kiss was a demonstration of the peace that was to characterize relationships within the congregation.[39] Augustine put it beautifully when he said "do not let your heart withdraw" from that of another brother or sister when your lips approach theirs for the kiss of peace. This kiss was to express both outward and inward unity.

Because the kiss served as a powerful expression of Christian unity, its sharing also became a marker for who was and was not a member of the Christian community. In the previous chapter we saw that the *Apostolic Tradition* began to limit the kiss to the faithful, that is, those who were baptized and not the catechumens. However, as theological controversies began to appear in the church, questions also began to arise about whether Christians from one group should share the kiss of peace with Christians from another group. Michael Penn writes, "The ritual kiss emphasized that one was a member of the community. To be kissed by another Christian was not merely an action between two individuals; it also reaffirmed membership in a larger social body. In the often ambiguous world of fourth- and fifth-century theological controversies, the ritual kiss became an explicit expression of whether an individual was considered orthodox or heretical."[40] Penn goes on to

37. *In Col. Hom.* 3.4, as quoted in Phillips, "The Kiss of Peace," 178.

38. Augustine *Sermon* 227.

39. For a helpful analysis of the differences in practice between East and West, see Woolfenden, "The Sign of Peace," 242–46.

40. Penn, "Ritual Kissing," 627–28.

explore in further detail how the writings of Jerome, Rufinus, Augustine, and Paulinus of Nola indicate that the holy kiss had become intimately connected with controversies over orthodox belief.[41] Additionally, the kiss was withheld from those members of the church that were restricted from taking communion during their time of penance. Hence, because the kiss was such a powerful expression of peace and unity, important messages were communicated by whom one did or did not kiss.

Modifications to the practice of the holy kiss continued in the fourth century and beyond. The earlier practice of sharing the greeting between sexes was gradually replaced by the practice of men greeting men and women greeting women. Moreover, it became increasingly common for only clergy to exchange the kiss, with the laity merely observing the kiss.[42] Another development emerged in thirteenth-century England; the *pax* board. The *pax* board was a wooden tablet or metal plate with a representation of the crucifix upon it, which was kissed by the bishop or priest and then passed among communicants, where it was pressed to their lips.[43] This practice, which prevented improper kissing between members, allowed the holy kiss to focus on an object, and not a person, and thus was a far cry from the original practice that demonstrated unity and reconciliation between people. Many, if not all, Eastern Orthodox churches continue to celebrate the kiss of peace among the entire congregation at the end of the Easter Matins.[44] Most churches in the West do not practice the holy kiss anymore. In recent years, handshaking has become a common way to "pass the peace" in Western churches.

E. THE DECLINE OF CHRISTIAN FEETWASHING

Broadly speaking, as the Constantinian shift occurred, and worship moved out of houses and into basilicas, the practice of feetwashing fell out of practice in the church. This process took some time, however, because the writings of Ambrose, Augustine, and other fourth-century witnesses all indicate that feetwashing was still being observed. After the fifth century feetwashing seems to have continued mainly in monastic communities. In the Middle Ages there also emerged a feetwashing

41. Ibid., 628–40.

42. *Apostolic Constitutions* 8.11.9. See Ibid., 627.

43. Kreider, "Kiss of Peace," 44.

44. Ibid., 325.

practice performed by the bishop on Maundy Thursday. Let us examine more closely these developments in the practice of feetwashing.

1. The Witness of Ambrose

In the late 300s, Ambrose of Milan was a strong proponent of feetwashing. In his treatise *On the Holy Spirit* (c. 381), he explains beautifully their practice:

> Let us come to the Gospel of God. I find the Lord divesting Himself of His garments, and girding Himself with a towel, pouring water into a basin, washing the feet of his disciples. . . . And now let the feet of our souls be extended. *The Lord Jesus wishes to wash our feet also*, for not to Peter alone but to each one of the faithful does he say: "If I wash not thy feet, thou shalt have no part with me."
>
> Come, therefore, O Lord Jesus, divest Yourself of Your garments . . . [B]e You naked, that You may clothe us with Your mercy. Gird Yourself with a towel for our sakes, that You may gird us with Your gift of immortality. Pour water into the basin; wash not only our feet but also the head, and not only of the footprints of the body, but also of the mind. . . .
>
> How great is that majesty! As a servant, You wash the feet of Your disciples; as God, You pour dew from heaven. Not only do You wash the feet, but You also invite us to recline with You, and You exhort us by the example of Your graciousness saying: "You call Me Master, and Lord, and you say well, for so I am. If I then, being Lord and Master, have washed your feet, you also ought to wash one another's feet."
>
> *I also, then, wish to wash the feet of my brethren*; I wish to fulfill the mandate of the Lord; I do not wish to be ashamed of myself, nor to disdain what He Himself did first. Good is the mystery of humility, because, *while I wash the filth of others, I wash away my own*. . . . [Lord,] Wash the steps of my mind, that I may not sin again. Wash off the heel of my spirit, that I may be able to abolish the curse, that I may not feel the bite of the serpent on my inner foot, but, as You Yourself have ordered your followers that I may have the power with uninjured foot to tread upon the serpents and scorpions. You have redeemed the world; redeem the soul of one sinner. (*On the Holy Spirit* 1.12–16, emphasis added)

Just as the Lord washed the feet of Peter, Ambrose believes that Jesus also desires to wash the feet of fourth-century Christians (as they enter the baptismal waters), in order that they might have a part with him.

Feetwashing is not just an ethical example of humility, but rather a command of the Lord to be obeyed, regardless of the shame. This feetwashing is *physical* and *spiritual*; physical in that it is literally performed in and by the church, and spiritual in the way in which Christ mysteriously participates and cleanses the soul from sin. For Ambrose, feetwashing cleanses "the heel of [the] spirit" in order to erase the hereditary curse of original sin, which he traces back to the serpent striking the heel of Eve's offspring (Gen 3:15).

It appears that in Ambrose's context feetwashing was practiced immediately after baptism.[45] Baptism was understood to wash the neophyte of their personal sin, after which feetwashing was performed to cleanse the individual of original sin inherited from Adam:

> Peter was clean, but he must wash his feet, for he had sin by succession from the first man, when the serpent overthrew him and persuaded him to sin. His feet were therefore washed, that hereditary sins might be done away, for our own sins are remitted through baptism. Observe at the same time that the mystery consists in the very office of humility, for Christ says: "If I, your Lord and Master, have washed your feet; how much more ought you to wash one another's feet." For, since the Author of Salvation Himself redeemed us through His obedience, how much more ought we His servants to offer the service of our humility and obedience. (*On the Mysteries* 6.32–33)

Observe that Ambrose commends feetwashing as a practice of cleansing *and* as a practice of humility and obedience. He is aware that the Roman Church does not have the custom of washing feet, yet he attributes this decline to the fact that people were uncomfortable with the humble act of feetwashing.[46] Ambrose, however, commends feetwashing as both an act

---

45. *The Sacraments* 3.4. See also the discussion in Thomas, *Footwashing in John 13*, 162–63.

46. "We are not unaware of the fact that the Roman Church (whose character and form we follow in all things) does not have the custom of washing the feet. So note: perhaps on account of the multitude this practice declined. Yet there are some who say and try to allege in excuse that this is not to be done [as a sacrament], nor in baptism, nor in regeneration, but the feet are to be washed as for a guest. But one belongs to humility, the other to sanctification: 'If I wash not thy feet, thou shalt have no part with me' [John 13:8]. So I say this, not that I may rebuke [the Roman Church], but that I may commend my own ceremonies. In all things I desire to follow the Church in Rome, yet we, too, [are not without discernment]; what is preserved more rightly elsewhere, we too preserve," Ambrose *The Sacraments* 3.5. The first sentence is slightly adapted for

of sanctification and humility which should be practiced by those who desire to follow obediently the example and the command of Christ.

2. The Witness of Augustine

Saint Augustine, who was baptized by Ambrose in Milan before moving to North Africa, also understood feetwashing to be an important practice. In a letter written around 400 to Januarius of Benevento, Augustine gives the following instruction:

> As to the feetwashing . . . the question has arisen at what time it is best, *by literal performance of this work*, to give public instruction in the important duty which it illustrates, and this time [of Lent] was suggested in order that the lesson taught by it might make a deeper and more serious impression. Many, however, have not accepted this as a custom, lest it should be thought to belong to the ordinance of baptism; and some have not hesitated to deny it any place among our ceremonies. Some, however, in order to connect its observance with the more sacred association of this solemn season, and at the same time to prevent its being confounded with baptism in any way, have selected for this ceremony either the eighth day itself, or that on which the third eighth day occurs, because of the great significance of the number three in many holy mysteries. (*Letters* 55.33, emphasis added)

Whereas Ambrose performed feetwashing immediately after baptism (which was performed on the Sabbath, the seventh day), Augustine argues that feetwashing should be a separate practice carried out on either the Sunday after baptism (the eighth day) or the third Sunday after baptism. Accordingly, the cleansing dimension of feetwashing is not highlighted by Augustine, but rather its demonstration of humble service. While he acknowledges that some Christians do not practice feetwashing, in a sermon on John 13 (*John: Tractate* 58.4), he strongly praises those who do wash feet in obedience to Christ, noting the way in which it awakens and strengthens humility:

> And wherever [feetwashing] is not the practice among the saints, what they do not with the hand they do in heart, if they are of the number of those who are addressed in the hymn of the three blessed men, "O ye holy and humble of heart, bless ye the Lord."

---

greater clarity. The first and last bracketed insertions come from the 1919 translation (*On the Mysteries*) by T. Thompson, 98–99.

> But it is far better, and beyond all dispute more accordant with
> the truth, that it should also be done with the hands; nor should
> the Christian think it beneath him to do what was done by Christ.
> For when the body is bent at a brother's feet, the feeling of such
> humility is either awakened in the heart itself, or is strengthened
> if already present.

Augustine can be identified as a defender of feetwashing as a Christian
practice, performed both to obey the command of Christ and to engen-
der humility among those who offer the service.

3. Other Fourth-Century Examples of Feetwashing

In addition to Ambrose and Augustine, there are several other fourth-
century examples indicating that feetwashing was a valuable practice
in certain locations. In Constantinople, John Chrysostom urged his
listeners to wash one another's feet, even if it meant washing the feet
of slaves (*Homilies on John* 71 [c. 391]).[47] In the *Apostolic Constitutions*
(3.19), written in Syria in the last half of the fourth century, feetwashing
is described as a task that the deacons are to perform for the church, particularly for those who are "weak and infirm."[48] According to the *Canons*

---

47. "'Let us wash one another's feet,' [Jesus] said. 'Those of slaves, too?' And what
great thing it is, even if we do wash the feet of slaves? For He Himself was Lord by nature, while we were slaves, yet He did not beg off from doing even this . . . Yet what shall
we then say, we who have received the example of such great forbearance, but do not
imitate it even slightly, and who, on the contrary, adopt the opposite attitude: both mag-
nifying ourselves unduly and not rendering to others what we ought? For God made
us debtors to one another—after He Himself had begun this process—and debtors in
regard to a smaller amount. He Himself, to be sure, was Lord, whereas if we perform
an act of humility we do it to our fellow slaves. Accordingly, He made an indirect reference to this very thing, also, by saying: 'If therefore, I the Lord and Master,' and again:
'So you also.' Indeed, it would have followed logically for us to say: 'How much rather
we slaves,' and He left this conclusion to the consciences of His hearers," Chrysostom,
Commentary on St. John, 261, quoted in Thomas, *Footwashing in John 13*, 130–31.

48. "Let the deacons be in all things unspotted . . . that they may minister to the
infirm as workmen that are not ashamed. . . . [Deacons] ought therefore also to serve
the brethren, in imitation of Christ. For says He: 'He that will be great among you, let
him be your minister; and he that will be first among you, let him be your servant.' For
so did He really, and not in word only, fulfill the prediction of, 'serving many faithfully.'
For, 'when He had taken a towel, He girded Himself. Afterward He puts water into a
basin; and as we were sitting at meat, He came and washed the feet of us all, and wiped
them with the towel.' By doing this He demonstrated to us His kindness and brotherly
affection, that so we also might do the same to one another. If, therefore, our Lord and
Master so humbled Himself, how can you, the laborers of the truth, and administrators

of Athanasius, written c. 366–373 in Alexandria, the bishop is to demonstrate his service to priests under his authority by, among other things,
washing their feet several times a year.[49] These last two examples indicate
that as time passed, feetwashing was increasingly being performed by
persons in ecclesial authority upon those who were under their authority. These examples preserve the scandal of Jesus, the Teacher, stooping
to wash the feet of his disciples. And there is the archaeological evidence
of smaller pools located next to baptismal fonts in Northern Italy, North
Africa, and Switzerland, which were likely used for feetwashing in connection with baptism.[50] By the sixth century the practice of feetwashing
appears no longer to be a regular practice for most Christians, except
perhaps by some bishops and monks.

4. Feetwashing in the Monastic Tradition

Even as feetwashing fell out of practice for the majority of Christians, it was
being continued as an important practice in some monastic communities.
In Egypt in the mid-fourth century, Pachomius, the father of coenobitic
monasticism (that is, communal monasticism), indicates that the feet of
visiting clerics or monks were washed "according to the Gospel precept."[51]

---

of piety, be ashamed to do the same to such of the brethren as are weak and infirm?,"
Apostolic Constitutions 19.

49. "This bishop shall eat often with the priests in the Church, that he may see their
behavior, whether they do eat in quiet and in the fear of God. And he shall stand there
and serve them; and if they be weak (if he can), he shall wash their feet with his own
hands. And if he is not able to do this, he shall cause the archpriest or him that is
after him to wash their feet. Suffer not the commandment of the Savior to depart from
you, for all this shall ye be answerable, that they likewise may see the lowliness of the
Savior in you," *The Canons of Athanasius of Alexandria*, 43, 131, quoted in Thomas,
Footwashing in John 13, 130.

50. Ferguson, *Baptism in the Early Church*, 785, 837, 846.

51. "When people come to the door of the monastery, they are to be received with
greater honor if they are clerics or monks. Their feet shall be washed, according to
the Gospel precept, and they shall be brought to the guest house and offered everything suitable to monks," Pachomias, *Pachomian Koinonia*, 153, quoted in Thomas,
Footwashing in John 13, 132. Pachomius, who was born in a pagan family, first inter-
acted with Christians as an imprisoned military conscript in Thebes around 312 CE. He
was impressed by the kindness of strangers who came to the prison to encourage the
conscripts and give them food (an *agape!*), and made a vow to serve God and humanity
if God would free him from prison. He was released the following year, and he soon
became a catechumen and was later baptized (*The Boharic Life* 7–8). See Goehring,
"Withdrawing from the Desert," 271–72.

The French coenobitic monk John Cassian (360–433) also established feetwashing as a weekly practice within the monastic community:

> But each one who undertakes these weeks is on duty and has to serve until supper on Sunday, and when this is done, his duty for the whole week is finished, so that, when all the brethren come together to chant the Psalms (which according to custom they sing before going to bed) those whose turn is over wash the feet of all in turn, seeking faithfully from them the reward of this blessing for their work during the whole week, that *the prayers offered up by all the brethren together may accompany them as they fulfill the command of Christ [to wash feet], the prayer that intercedes for their ignorances and for their sins committed through human frailty*, and may commend to God the complete service of their devotion like some rich offering.[52]

In this passage, the monk whose turn it was to serve the community (in the kitchen) also had the job of washing all the monks' feet on Sunday evening. One significant aspect of this feetwashing is the offering of prayers made by the community, interceding for the sins of human weakness that the washer has committed "through human frailty." Thus, like Ambrose, feetwashing in this context is connected with the forgiveness of sins. One final example of feetwashing in monastic communities is found in the *Rule of St. Benedict* (c. 540), which became the standard for Western monasticism. In its list of communal rules are two of particular import:

> 35. Of the Weekly Servers in the Kitchen: Let the brethren so serve each other in turn that no one be excused from the work of the kitchen unless on the score of health . . . Let him who is ending his week's service clean up everything on Saturday. He must wash the towels with which the brethren wipe their hands and feet: and both he who is finishing his service, and he who is entering on it, are to wash the feet of all. . . .
> 53. Of the Reception of Guests: Let all guests that come be received like Christ Himself . . . Let the Abbot pour water on the hands of the guests; let both the Abbot and the whole community wash the feet of all guests.[53]

52. John Cassian, "Institute of the Coenobia," quoted in Thomas, *Footwashing in John 13*, 160-61 (emphasis added).

53. Benedict of Nursia, *The Rule of Saint Benedict*, 254–57, 330, quoted in ibid., 145–46. Perhaps this is the origin of the "double mode" of feetwashing that was prevalent in the nineteenth-century Brethren Love Feast, see chapter 6 below.

Overall it is clear that feetwashing continued to be a practice of humility and hospitality in monastic communities, even as the practice declined in the mainstream church.

5. Liturgical Feetwashing.

Sometime around the seventh century feetwashing emerged as a regular practice performed by bishops on Maundy Thursday. The *Catholic Encyclopedia* reads:

> The liturgical washing of feet . . . seems only to have established itself in the East and West at a comparatively late date. In 694 the Seventeenth Synod of Toledo [Spain] commanded all bishops and priests in a position of superiority, under pain of excommunication, to wash the feet of those subject to them. . . . In the latter half of the twelfth century the pope washed the feet of twelve sub-deacons after his Mass and of thirteen poor men after his dinner [on Maundy Thursday]. The "Caeremoniale episcoporum" directs that the bishop is to wash the feet either of thirteen poor men or of thirteen of his canons.[54]

By the late Middle Ages many European monarchs also performed the Royal Maundy (washing feet and distributing alms; derived from the Latin *mandatum novum*, "new command," John 13:34) on Maundy Thursday, and the practice continued into the twentieth century in Austria and Spain. From 1570 to 1955 the Roman Missal printed a rite of washing feet following the text of the Holy Thursday Mass. In 1955 Pope Pius XII revised the Missal to include the feetwashing rite in the Mass itself, after a homily on John 13. Christian groups that practice feetwashing include: Anglicans, Brethren, Church of God (Cleveland, Tennessee), Church of God in Christ, Lutherans, Mennonites, Methodists, Presbyterians, Primitive Baptists, Seventh-Day Adventists, the True Jesus Church, and others.

F. THE DEVELOPMENT OF CONFESSION AND PENANCE

The understanding of confession and eucharistic preparation also experienced changes during the Constantinian shift. With the Roman government helping to promote Christianity, individual confession of faith

---

54. Thurston, "Washing of Feet and Hands."

became less important, and confession became increasingly tied to the sacrament of Penance. The previous chapter revealed that in the early church, confession (*exomologesis*) and penance involved fairly severe actions, including fasting, wearing sackcloth and ashes, giving alms to the poor, and restriction from Communion. These practices were strict in order to maintain the purity of the church and to help the sinner to grow through their acts of penance. The practice of confessing sins prior to celebrating the Eucharist, and of restricting penitents from partaking of Communion, continued during the Constantinian shift and afterward. The current analysis of confession will focus on two key developments: (1) the shift to understanding confession primarily as confessing sin, and (2) the shift to introspective confession.

1. Confession Reduced to Confessing Sin

After the Constantinian shift, the broad concept of confession became understood primarily as confessing sin. After Christianity became legal, confessing faith in Jesus no longer entailed the danger of earlier times. In those times the church greatly esteemed confessors—that is, those who had confessed the faith and had suffered for their confession. After Constantine, when the state became actively involved in promoting Christian doctrine and practice, it became less important for individual Christians to confess their faith publicly. The sacrament of Penance grew in importance during this period, placing a greater emphasis on confessing sin. While the New Testament and the early church generally understood confession to entail publicly confessing Jesus as Lord, beginning in the fourth century the general connotation of confession shifted to the act of confessing personal sins.

2. Introspective Confession

It is only after the Constantinian era that we begin to see a noticeable shift toward focusing on the inward dimensions of confession.[55] Around

---

55. Yoder comments on the shift toward inwardness, writing: "After Constantine, one had to believe without seeing that there was a community of believers, within the larger nominally Christian mass, but one knew for a fact that God was in control of history. Ethics had to change because one must aim one's behavior at strengthening the regime, and because the ruler himself must have very soon some approbation and perhaps some guidance as he does things the earlier church would have disapproved of. *The conception of a distinctive lifestyle befitting Christian confession had to be sweepingly*

400 Augustine published his *Confessions*, which Krister Stendahl calls "the first great document in the history of the introspective conscience."[56] From this point forward confession gradually moved away from the public witness of faith to the practice of internal examination and the confession of sins to a priest. In the Western church this confession remained somewhat public until the seventh century, when Irish missionaries introduced to continental Europe the practice of private penance between the confessor and the priest. This practice, inspired by the Eastern monastic tradition, did not require the public and prolonged completion of penitential works before reconciliation with the church.[57] From that time onward, the sacrament of Penance and Reconciliation in the Roman Catholic Church has been performed in secret between penitent and priest. Moreover, because of the requirement that confession and penance precede the Eucharist, examination, which had once been a practice of the worshiping community, was now chiefly an individual, introspective act.

G. SUMMARY

Many of the changes that occurred in the church as a result of the Constantinian shift proved detrimental to the celebration of the Love Feast. The fellowship meal gradually died away as the church placed restrictions against holding Love Feasts in the Lord's House. The role of the clergy also became much more important after the fourth century, especially as they played a central role in offering the prayer of consecration, which was understood to transform the elements of bread and wine into the true body and blood of Christ. The kiss of peace was gradually limited to members of the same sex, then only passed between the clergy, and later became expressed by kissing the *pax* board. These developments added symbolic layers on top of the earlier practice, which was a physical demonstration of reconciliation between members and a witness to the spiritual unity of the church. Along with the decline in

---

redefined. It could no longer be identified with baptism and church membership, since many who are 'Christian' in that sense have not themselves chosen to follow Christ. Its definition will tend to be *transmuted in the definition of inwardness.* Its outward expression will tend to be assigned to a minority of special "religious" people [i.e., the clergy]," Yoder, "The Constantinian Sources of Western Social Ethics," 137 (emphasis added).

56. Stendahl, "Paul and the Introspective Conscience."

57. Ratzinger, ed. *Catechism of the Catholic Church,* 363.

the *agape* meal, feetwashing too became less important as a Christian practice, although it did continue to be practiced among some monastic communities. After the Constantinian shift, confession became increasingly focused on the confession of sin, which was an important prerequisite to an individual partaking of communion. Confession also became much more introspective in the manner in which it was practiced. All of these developments contributed to an over-spiritualization of the Christian meal. With the decline of the Love Feast and its related practices, many of the physical and practical aspects of the early church meal were left behind. The liturgical practices that remained tended to overemphasize the spiritual nature of the Eucharist and to overlook the importance of fellowship between members of the church.

6

Reclaiming the Feast

Historical Recoveries of the Love Feast

DURING THE REFORMATION, WHEN scholars throughout Europe were debating Christian theology and practice, some Christians started to rediscover practices of the early church, like the Love Feast, that had been neglected over time. Groups like the Anabaptists, Pietists, Brethren, Moravian Brethren, and Methodists began to reclaim aspects of the Love Feast in their worship services. In the early 1520s the Anabaptists began to reemphasize the importance of unity and holiness in the faith community. With their emphasis on following the scriptures, they began to reclaim earlier practices, including the fellowship meal, feetwashing, and the holy kiss in connection with the Lord's Supper. Building on the practices of the Anabaptists and the Pietists, in the early 1700s the Schwarzenau Brethren began celebrating a Love Feast consisting of feetwashing, a simple supper, the holy kiss, and Communion. A few years later, the Moravian Brethren and the Methodists also started celebrating Love Feasts. In this chapter we will look back over several centuries to see the efforts made by several Christian groups to recover the Love Feast. But before this, we will briefly look at the celebration of the Mass in the Western church.

A. THE MASS IN THE SIXTEENTH-CENTURY

By the early 1500s the celebration of the Mass had developed into something quite different from the simple celebration of the Lord's Supper in the early church. The Fourth Lateran Council (1215) significantly shaped the celebration of the Mass in two ways. First, this council formally introduced the language of "transubstantiation" to express the real presence of Christ in the Eucharist that had been understood for centuries.[1] Thus, from this point on the Roman church's official position was that when a properly ordained priest spoke the prayer of consecration, the substance of the bread and wine were converted into the true body and blood of Jesus, while the outward appearance of the elements remained unchanged. Second, the council *required* all members of the church to make confession before a priest *and* to partake of communion at least once a year. Because people had been avoiding taking communion for a variety of reasons,[2] the church found it necessary to require, at minimum, an annual participation in confession and the Mass.

The liturgy of the Mass was also fairly difficult for the common people to understand. The congregation primarily observed the worship service, and did not participate. The most sacred part of the service, the prayer of consecration, was not visible to the laity because the priest had his back to the congregation, facing the altar. They often could not understand the words spoken in Latin because they were fluent in other languages. One notorious example of this language barrier is the English phrase "hocus pocus," which came about as a parody of the words spoken by the priest (*hoc est corpus meum*, "This is my body") during the prayer of consecration.[3] On most occasions, communicants only received the communion bread, while the wine was reserved for the clergy (this was done to avoid people spilling the blood of Christ on the floor). The bread was placed in communicants mouths by the priest as an additional measure of protection to keep it from falling on the floor. Many of these aspects of the Mass made it fearsome or awkward. Almost all evidence of the original fellowship meal was gone, and what remained was a formal worship service that had diminished lay involvement. With this in mind,

---

1. "In [the universal church] Jesus himself is both priest and sacrifice, whose body and blood are truly contained in the sacrament of the altar under the species of bread and wine by the transubstantiation of bread into body and wine into blood through divine power: that through the perfecting of the mystery of unity we receive of him from himself, that which he received from us. And certainly no one is able to accomplish this sacrament, except a priest, who has been properly ordained, according to the keys of the Church, which Jesus Christ gave to the Apostles and their successors," quoted in White, *Documents of Christian Worship*, 194–95.

2. For example, fear of taking communion unworthily, fear of confessing sins and doing the required penance, and/or delaying confession and communion until just prior to death to maximize the salvific benefit.

3. Witherington III, *Making a Meal of It* (2007), xi.

let us look at the ways in which the Anabaptists and Pietists worked to recover the Lord's Supper practices of the early church.

B. EARLY RECOVERIES OF THE LOVE FEAST

1. *The Anabaptist Movement*

The early Anabaptists contributed much to the recovery of the Love Feast. In the early 1520s, during the period when Luther and Zwingli were challenging Catholic worship practices, several other religious leaders (i.e., Conrad Grebel, Hans Denck, and Balthasar Hubmaier) began to preach against church practices in Switzerland, Germany, and Austria. Originally known as the Brethren or the Swiss Brethren, they did not believe that the Bible supported the practice of infant baptism and the celebration of the Mass. They were later called Anabaptists (re-baptizers) because they insisted on adult believer's baptism, even for those who had previously been baptized as infants. Because they refused to accept the hierarchy of the church and the authority of civil bodies in religious matters, they were accused of sedition and heresy, and were persecuted and even executed. For our purposes, we will look at the ways in which the Anabaptist Lord's Supper reemphasized the importance of the eucharistic community, the ban, the holy kiss, and feetwashing.

A. THE EMPHASIS ON THE EUCHARISTIC COMMUNITY.

The Swiss Anabaptists, like Zwingli, understood the Lord's Supper to be a memorial supper. Unlike Zwingli, however, they more strongly emphasized the presence of Christ in the community of believers gathered to celebrate the Lord's Supper.[4] Arnold Snyder summarizes the Lord's Supper in the Anabaptist tradition:

> The Anabaptists refused to honour the elements and the ceremony as such, convinced as they were that too much power had been given to lifeless elements and clerics in the preceding tradition. But on the other hand, they valued the visible ceremony enough that they carefully examined all participants and excluded from participation all those who gave evidence that they were not in

---

4. For a helpful examination of the Anabaptist Lord's Supper, including the practices of the ban and feetwashing, see the chapter "The Body of Christ" in Snyder, *Following in the Footsteps of Christ*, 85–110.

spiritual communion. The Anabaptist Lord's Supper was thus a celebration of remembrance and communion in which the elements of inner renewal, eating and drinking of the bread and wine, were simultaneously conjoined among those who honestly witnessed to a new life with a good conscience. . . .

There was no presence of Christ *in the elements* of the Anabaptist Lord's Supper. The bread and the wine were not seen as instruments to *convey* grace. This does not mean, however, that the Anabaptists denied the living presence of Christ in and with their celebration of the Supper, only that observers were looking for the presence of Christ in places where the Anabaptists did not expect to find that presence.[5]

Like their Reformed neighbors, who celebrated the Lord's Supper quarterly, the Anabaptists also rejected a weekly Eucharistic celebration.[6] While some Anabaptists preferred an evening celebration of the Lord's Supper, which was closer to the Scriptural practice, there was flexibility concerning the time of the actual celebration.[7] When the Lord's Supper was celebrated in the evening, however, the participants did not share a full meal together but still continued the tradition of sharing only bread and wine. Although the Anabaptists did not celebrate Communion as a part of a fellowship meal, nor use the terms *agape* or Love Feast (*Liebesmahl*) to name their eucharistic worship, their renewed focus on the church as the body of Christ helped to reclaim a significant aspect of the Love Feast tradition that had been largely neglected.

B. The Ban and the Community.

Along with placing a renewed focus on the body of Christ present in the gathered community, the Anabaptists reclaimed "the ban" as an aspect of Christian discipleship. Anabaptists understood the ban as a process instituted by Christ for the preservation and growth of the church's integrity and witness. They were dissatisfied with the ability of the penitential system of the Catholic Church to help believers struggling with sin to correct their errors. To them, it was all too evident that many so-called Christians in the local community were making little effort to live ac-

---

5. Ibid., 102–3 (emphasis in original).

6. George, *Theology of the Reformers*, 319.

7. Conrad Grebel writes to Müntzer in 1524, "As for the time, we know that Christ gave it to the apostles at supper and that the Corinthians had the same usage. We fix no definite time with us," Williams and Mergal, eds., *Spiritual and Anabaptist Writers*, 77.

cording to the teachings of Jesus. Accordingly, the Anabaptists insisted that the "rule of Christ," described in Matt 18:15–18, should always accompany the church's celebration of the Lord's Supper. Snyder explains:

> The Anabaptist ban took the place of the earlier sacrament of penance. It was by means of fraternal admonition and public repentance that the process of confession, absolution and the forgiveness of sins was carried out in the baptizing communities. Those who had been 'inadvertently overtaken' by sin needed to demonstrate contrition and repentance, in a humble spirit, before the brothers and sisters. They could then be readmitted by the wider community into full fellowship in the Body of Christ. This practice found its scriptural warrant in Matt 18:18: whatever you bind on earth will be bound in heaven. The penitential 'binding and loosing' function regarding sins and their forgiveness thus fell to the church community as a whole—it was not a clerical function or a privilege. The congregation of baptized, committed believers was also the forgiving, reconciling and absolving community, with the power to 'bind and loose'. . . . The process was fraught with danger, and did lead to schism and division. Nevertheless, the positive side of the story must also be told: the Anabaptists and their descendents came to be known for their piety, sobriety, modesty and honesty, living in communities where fraternal admonition and discipline were the norm. Admonition and loving discipline were instruments, when they functioned as intended, that served to maintain the integrity between the Spirit of Christ, born within, and the life of Christ that was to be lived in the world.[8]

In the same way that Penance preceded the celebration of the Mass in Catholic practice, *The Schleitheim Confession* (1527) reveals that the early Swiss Anabaptists also understood the ban to be closely related to the Lord's Supper: "But this [the practice of the ban] shall be done according

---

8. Snyder, *Following in the Footsteps of Christ*, 87–90. The importance of the ban for early Swiss Anabaptists is evident in *The Schleitheim Confession*, where it is addressed in Article 2: "We have been united as follows concerning the ban. The ban shall be employed with all those who have given themselves over to the Lord, to walk after (him) in his commandments, those who have been baptized into the one body of Christ, and let themselves be called brothers or sisters, and still somehow slip and fall into error and sin, being inadvertently overtaken. The same (shall) be warned twice privately and the third time be publicly admonished before the entire congregation according to the command of Christ (Matt 18). But this shall be done according to the ordering of the Spirit of God before the breaking of bread, so that we may all in one spirit and in one love break and eat from one bread and drink from one cup," Klaassen, *Anabaptism in Outline*, 215.

to the ordering of the Spirit of God before the breaking of bread, so that we may all in one spirit and in one love break and eat from one bread and drink from one cup."[9] Although it was not universal among Anabaptists, many groups strongly emphasized the importance of confession and fraternal admonition in their celebration of the Lord's Supper.

c. The Holy Kiss.

Although the early Anabaptists do not give us any extended discussion of the holy kiss, there are several sources that indicate that they practiced the kiss of peace in their communities. Article 11 of the Strasbourg Discipline of 1568 reads: "The brethren and sisters, each to each, shall greet each other with a holy kiss; those who have not been received into fellowship shall not be greeted with a kiss, but with the words, 'The Lord help you.'"[10] The *Martyrs Mirror* contains a "Confession of Faith According to the Holy Word of God" which was apparently written around 1600. Article 23 of this confession describes the holy kiss as a welcome to believers entering a home and connects the greeting to feetwashing. Article 29 of the confession also mentions that the holy kiss is to be withheld from those who are under the ban of the church, until they are readmitted into the communion of the church. Menno Simons also mentions the holy kiss twice in his writings; both times it is listed as a greeting to be withheld from a disfellowshipped member.[11] From these few sources we see that the holy kiss was recovered as a greeting in some Anabaptist circles and that it symbolized communion for them.

d. Recovering Feetwashing.[12]

Beginning in the sixteenth century, some Anabaptists began to reclaim the practice of feetwashing as a Christian discipline, although this was not practiced universally.[13] The earliest record of feetwashing performed

9. Klaassen, *Anabaptism in Outline*, 215.

10. Bender, "The Strasbourg Discipline," 65.

11. Wenger, ed. *The Complete Writings of Menno Simons*, 480, 971.

12. Two pre-Reformation sects in France practiced feetwashing—the Albigenses and Waldenses. The Albigenses washed feet following the Lord's Supper in obedience to Jesus' example. The Waldenses washed the feet of itinerant ministers when they arrived at congregations, similar to the practice of monastic groups at the time. For a more thorough account of the Waldenses, see Durnbaugh, *The Believers' Church*, 41–50.

13. Arnold Snyder observes, "Although the practice of footwashing was not widely practiced as a church ordinance by Anabaptists until later in the sixteenth century, in

by an Anabaptist dates to April 1525 in Waldshut, Germany, when Balthasar Hubmaier washed the feet of newly (re)baptized believers and gave them communion.[14] Apparently the practice of feetwashing continued, for a 1531 treatise written against the Anabaptists claimed that they washed feet according to the letter of the Scriptures.[15] From 1531 to 1547 Anabaptist leader Pilgram Marpeck wrote various tracts and letters in which he refers to feetwashing at least seven times, considering the practice to be an ordinance instituted by Christ.[16] In his 1560 treatise "The Church of God," Anabaptist leader Dietrich Philips names feetwashing as an ordinance that emphasizes the need for Christians both to be cleansed continually by Jesus and humbly to serve one another.[17] Anabaptist feetwashing was most often connected to the Lord's Supper (usually occurring afterward), although Menno Simons does mention feetwashing as a practice of hospitality.[18] By 1632 the *Dordrecht Confession*, which was

retrospect the broad acceptance of the rite of washing one another's feet seems a natural development, given the biblical bases of spiritual practice the Anabaptists sought to institute," Snyder, *Following in the Footsteps of Christ*, 104.

14. "From this and like references to contemporary chronicles it should seem that the practice of feetwashing in connection with the Supper had been previously introduced at Waldshut, and was still retained," Vedder, *Balthasar Hubmaier*, 112. In later years, however, it does not appear that Hubmaier continued to practice feetwashing with the Supper.

15. Snyder notes, "In his *Chronicle* of 1531, published in Strasbourg, Sebastian Franck notes that some Anabaptists 'claim the apostolic life' and 'go by the letter of Scripture, washing each other's feet', lending first-hand testimony to the occasional practice at that time," Snyder, *Following in the Footsteps of Christ*, 204 n. 48. For Franck's *Chronicle*, see Snyder, ed., *Sources of South German/Austrian Anabaptism*, 235.

16. Marpeck, *The Writings of Pilgram Marpeck*, 51, 79, 98, 264–65, 340, 453–54. See the discussion of Marpeck in Graber-Miller, "Mennonite Footwashing," 152–53.

17. For Philips, feetwashing is the third of seven Christian ordinances. He writes, "The *third ordinance* is the foot washing of the saints, which Jesus Christ commanded his disciples to observe, and this for two reasons. First, he would have us know that he himself must cleanse us after the inner man, and that we must allow him to wash away the sins which beset us (Heb 12:1) and all filthiness of the flesh and the spirit, that we may become purer from day to day . . . The second reason why Jesus instituted foot washing is that we should humble ourselves toward one another (Rom 12:10; Phil 2:3; 1 Pet 5:5; Jas 4:10–11), and that we should hold our fellow believers in the highest respect, for the reason that they are the saints of God and members of the body of Jesus Christ," Williams and Mergal, eds., *Spiritual and Anabaptist Writers*, 245 (emphasis in original).

18. Wenger, ed. *The Complete Writings of Menno Simons*, 417. Keith Graber-Miller writes that in current practice, Mennonite footwashing usually occurs after the twice-yearly communion service. Generally men and women only wash the feet of same-sex members. It is common for pairs to approach the basin and towel, for one member

widely accepted among Dutch Anabaptists, included a separate article naming feetwashing as an Anabaptist ordinance.[19]

2. The County Feasts in England

Although the county feasts that flourished in England from the mid-1650s to the early 1700s are not as significant as the other examples of the recovery of the Love Feast mentioned in this chapter, we should still briefly discuss them. The county feasts occurred in cities (mostly in London) and were annual occasions in which natives of a particular county (i.e., Oxford, Warwick, Wiltshire, etc.) gathered for a sermon, dinner, and to raise money for a local charity.[20] These feasts were like a "homecoming" ceremony, allowing people to catch up with others who hailed from their home county. Newton Key has documented 193 such feasts that occurred between 1654 and 1714.[21] The feasts would be advertised in various London newspapers, and tickets for the dinner were available for purchase at coffeehouses and taverns. The county feast began in a London church with a sermon by a noteworthy preacher, often from the same county as those who were feasting. Concerning the feast sermons, Key writes:

> Feast sermons often praised the contemporary virtues of the na-
> tives' county, as well as its past glories. . . . But the center of each
> feast sermon, of course, was an explication of a biblical text. Three
> subjects were most discussed in these sermons: unity, charity, and
> feasting. The sermons often used the Greek word *agape*, meaning
> "brotherhood," "charity," and, as one preacher noted, "in the plural
> signifieth Feasts." . . . The text most applicable to the feasts' chari-
> table purpose was the ambivalent section of Jude 12 ("These are
> spots in your feasts of charity"); and perhaps a majority of all ser-
> mons at least referred to Jude 12. The sermons compared county
> feasts to "Christian Love-feasts" of "Primitive times."[22]

to wash and dry the other's feet, and then for the service to be reciprocated. After the washing, they stand and embrace, exchanging a handshake or the holy kiss. In general, Mennonite footwashing is only practiced by baptized members of the church. See Graber-Miller, "Mennonite Footwashing," 160–61.

19. Article 11 of the *Dordrecht Confession* reads: "We also confess a washing of the feet of the saints . . . as a sign of true humiliation; but yet more particularly as a sign to remind us of the true washing—the washing and purification of the soul in the blood of Christ," quoted in Snyder, *From Anabaptist Seed*, 34.

20. Key, "County Feasts and Feast Sermons," 224.

21. Ibid., 226–27, 35.

22. Ibid., 241–42.

After listening to the sermon in a London church, those present would march to the nearby dining hall of a livery company (merchant guild), where the feast was eaten. A charity subscription was one of the final events of the county feast.

Because so many of the county feast sermons referenced Jude 12 and the Love Feast, we should not overlook these events in our discussion of recovering the Love Feast. However, the main thrust of Newton Key's research shows that these county feasts often were more political than they were religious. They became occasions for county natives to gather and talk politics, and the choice of which livery company hall to dine in often had political overtones (the Merchant-Tailors' Hall, which held the majority of the London feasts, was strongly associated with the Tory party).[23] Nevertheless, it is helpful to know that such county feasts, with their sermons on Jude 12 and the early church Love Feast, were celebrated in London decades before John Wesley started his Methodist love-feasts (see section D below).

3. The Pietist Movement

Some in the German Pietist movement of the late 1600s and early 1700s also were interested in reclaiming the Love Feast. Marcus Meier, a Lutheran scholar who has done tremendous scholarship in the fields of Radical Pietism and Brethren history, notes, "As early as 1670, after the celebration of a love feast in the circle of supporters gathered around Jean de Labadie in Herford, there occurred 'Christian jubilation, jumping, dancing, and kisses.'"[24] The English Philadelphian Society, founded in 1694 and led by Jane Leade, also "practiced the holy kiss on the model of the original apostolic congregation."[25] In 1705 in Calw, Germany, a small group of around twenty people began to celebrate a simple fellowship meal, although they were clear to distinguish it as a "love feast" and not as the Eucharist.[26] The writings of Radical Pietist and historian Gottfried Arnold (1666–1714) also were influential upon those who were interested in recovering the form and practice of the apostolic church.[27] In his

---

23. Ibid., 232.

24. Meier, *Origin of the Schwarzenau Brethren*, 112.

25. Ibid.

26. Ibid., 114.

27. For more on Arnold, see Bach, "Agape in the Brethren Tradition," 162–63; Erb, "Arnold, Gottfried," 57.

1696 book *Die Erste Liebe* (*The First Love*), Arnold discussed the worship of the early church and the writings of Tertullian and Hippolytus, noting that in the early church the holy kiss was practiced by communicants before and after the Eucharist, that the *agape* or Love Feast (*Liebesmahl*) was the setting for early Christian worship, and that feetwashing was also practiced in the early church.[28] He concluded that the first Christians had celebrated the Eucharist in the context of a communal meal. Within several decades, two "Brethren" groups in Germany who were influenced by Arnold's writings (the Schwarzenau and Moravian Brethren) had initiated their own Love Feast celebrations.

C. THE LOVE FEAST IN THE BRETHREN TRADITION

The Schwarzenau Brethren recovered the celebration of the Love Feast in 1708, and those who trace their church history to these original eight members can claim the longest continued practice of the Love Feast in the modern era.[29] What distinguished the early Brethren Love Feast from other expressions of the Lord's Supper was the way in which it combined feetwashing, a fellowship meal, the holy kiss, and Communion. This Love Feast was shared in a community of believers who understood the church to be the household of God, a household that could only function when obligatory rules and ordinances existed for its members. The Brethren enforced these rules with congregational discipline, that is, the ban. Our examination of the Brethren Love Feast begins by looking at earliest accounts of the practice. Focus then turns to the process of the deacon's visit, which developed in the late eighteenth-century and was connected to the Love Feast. After this we examine the general structure of the Love Feast in the nineteenth century. The section concludes by looking at several twentieth-century developments to the Brethren Love Feast.

1. Love Feast and the Formation of the Brethren

The Love Feast was of central importance to the original eight women and men who started the Brethren movement in the village of Schwarzenau

28. Meier, *Origin of the Schwarzenau Brethren*, 112–15.

29. For a general look at the history of the Brethren see Durnbaugh, *Fruit of the Vine*; Brumbaugh, *A History of the German Baptist Brethren*; Durnbaugh, *European Origins of the Brethren*; Durnbaugh, *The Brethren in Colonial America*; Sappington, *The Brethren in Industrial America*.

in 1708. Even before their first baptism, the proto-Brethren were wrestling with how to celebrate the Love Feast (*Liebesmahl*). Hochmann von Hochenau, the spiritual advisor of the early Brethren leaders George Grebe and Alexander Mack, wrote the following to them in a letter dated July 24, 1708 (a few weeks before the first Brethren baptisms in August):

> One must . . . first carefully count the cost, if one will follow after the Lord Jesus in all the trials which will certainly follow from [baptism]. Without this true following of Jesus Christ, the water baptism will help little or not at all, even if it were to be performed on adults after the example of the first Christians. *God does not look on the outward but rather on the inward—the change of heart, and the sincerity of the heart.*
>
> I have the same opinion concerning the Lord's love feast—the foundation must be based on the love of Jesus and the appropriate community of members. I will not oppose it, if they want to hold the outward love feast in the memory of the Lord Jesus, as it corresponds with the Scriptures in every respect. Where the love of Christ unites the hearts inwardly and they are impelled by the laws of Christ—when they are willing thereby to sacrifice their lives for Christ and His church, and desire to proclaim the death of Christ with heart, mouth, and deed—in sum, where they pledge and bind their properties and lives to Jesus and His church, I shall not be against it. *When, however, only an outward, legalistic work is made of it without the spirit of Christ and love prevailing and ruling in the hearts, then I can in truth not think much of it.*[30]

Here von Hochenau emphasizes that the inward change of heart, resulting from the presence of the Spirit of Christ, must be the foundation for the Lord's Love Feast. From this counsel it can be presumed that the first Brethren were careful to avoid making the Love Feast "an outward, legalistic work." Instead, following von Hochenau's advice, the Brethren Love Feast flowed from *sincere* hearts and showed their willingness to sacrifice their lives for Christ and the church.

The exact date of the first Brethren Love Feast is not known. The writings of Brethren opponents indicate that it happened in the autumn of 1708, within months of the first baptism in August. In April 1709, rival separatist John George Gichtel wrote a letter to his followers, which concluded: "I have received a detailed report about the new Anabaptists in the Schwarzenau area. They also observe feet-washing

---

30. Durnbaugh, *European Origins of the Brethren*, 113 (emphasis added).

and communion, but refuse to let anyone participate who has not been baptized by them with water."[31] In 1710 Charles Louis, Count of Sayn-Wittgenstein, also decried the Brethren as religious fanatics who had rejected the communion practices of the established churches in favor of their own *agape* celebration.[32] By 1719, religious persecution had forced twenty Brethren families to migrate to America, and on Christmas Day, 1723, in Germantown, Pennsylvania, the Brethren gathered to celebrate their first baptism and Love Feast in America.[33] Marcus Meier explains that for the early Brethren:

> Jesus' word was an irrefutable command, just as his example [in John 13] was a binding law. After the Love Feast meal, they washed one another's feet and then greeted each other with the kiss of peace. Then followed the distribution of the bread and wine. Love Feast and feetwashing, as well as the kiss of peace, harmonized with each other, had a relation to each other, and symbolized the all-encompassing community of love represented by the group.[34]

After emigrating to the United States, it appears that Brethren Love Feasts were held fairly often in the eighteenth century, but by the nineteenth century the pattern was for each congregation to celebrate the Love Feast once or twice a year, although members would go to great effort to travel to other congregations to participate in their services.[35] Also, by the mid-1700s the practice had emerged of holding an annual meeting around Pentecost for all Brethren to gather for worship and

31. Ibid., 129. Gichtel was a lawyer in Amsterdam who left the Lutheran church to follow the teachings of Jacob Böhme. He founded a rival separatist group called the "Angel Brethren" (*Engelbrüder*).

32. "[The Brethren] not only abstain from the most holy communion of our Lord and Savior Jesus Christ, but also revile it most blasphemously as a swine's feast or cold broth, which one makes of the bread and wine in one's mouth. Some of them maintain that this sacrament can bring no salvation, but is rather a symbol of Christian brotherhood. Therefore they prefer to receive the *agape*, as they call it, in their secret meetings. . . . [T]hey commit nothing but scandalous acts in those meetings and the redeeming ordinance of the Savior and the benefit of this most holy sacrament are soiled by their blasphemous conduct," ibid., 142.

33. Brumbaugh, *A History of the German Baptist Brethren*, 155–56. Brumbaugh writes, "Doubly memorable Christmas Day, 1723! Christ's anniversary and the . . . birth of His church in America!" (p. 155).

34. Meier, *Origin of the Schwarzenau Brethren*, 116.

35. Durnbaugh, *Fruit of the Vine*, 104.

discussion of church polity. A prominent feature of these annual meetings was the celebration of the Love Feast, which occurred on Saturday evening before Pentecost. In sum, it is clear that the Love Feast was a central practice for the earliest Brethren in Europe, and continued to be important as they migrated to America.

2. The Emergence of the Deacon's Visit Preceding Love Feast

By the nineteenth century it was common for the deacon's visit (or annual visit) to occur before the Brethren Love Feast. The deacon's visit helped to preserve the peace and unity of the church and of the Love Feast. The Brethren believed strongly that unrepentant sinners and those who had unresolved conflict with members of the church should not participate in the Lord's Supper.[36] Prior to celebrating the Love Feast, deacons went in pairs to visit all the members of the congregation to inquire as to each member's spiritual health. Henry Brumbaugh wrote in 1887:

> The end desired [of the deacon's visit] is that all the members may be in unity and peace, so that they may participate in the Communion services in a worthy manner (1 Cor 11:27). . . . The importance of this visit cannot be overestimated, and therefore it should be made with great care, taking time enough at each house, when practicable, to have a season of worship with the family. As a guide to the character of the visit the following form of questions has been submitted:
>
> 1. Are you still in the faith of the Gospel, as you declared when you were baptized?
> 2. Are you, as far as you know, in peace and union with the Church?
> 3. Will you still labor with the Brethren for an increase of holiness, both in yourself and others?
> 4. Liberty should be given to members to bring anything they may desire to, and they may think the good of the Church requires, before the visiting brethren.[37]

---

36. In his longest work, *Rights and Ordinances*, written in 1715, Alexander Mack states: "Obvious sinners cannot be permitted at the Lord's Supper, even if but one work of the flesh is evident in them (about which Paul writes in Galatians 5), if repentance or improvement does not take place after admonishment," 63.

37. Brumbaugh, *The Brethren's Church Manual*, 17–19, quoted in Ramirez, *The Love Feast*, 22–23.

Although the wording of these three questions was not standardized until 1887, records indicate that this practice had already been observed for quite some time.[38] After all the members had been visited, the deacons reported back to a congregational council meeting concerning the spiritual condition of the membership. If during the visitation some personal transgression or interpersonal conflict arose, the council would consider each case. Those who were brought before the council would either be admonished, given a course of discipline and invited to participate in the Love Feast, or they would be ordered to "sit back from the table" until they had demonstrated repentance.[39] In rare circumstances the Love Feast was postponed until the conflict had been appropriately resolved. Carl Bowman summarizes well:

> [T]he intangible theme of perfect union was tied to a quality-control apparatus, the deacon's visit, that helped to make unity a reality. Being a member wasn't enough—one had to be "still in the faith" professed at baptism and in harmony with one's Brethren. Annual Meeting's ruling that "no member should be permitted to remain at the communion table, when he is known to . . . have been guilty of a violation of the order of the house of God" was taken seriously.[40]

3. The Typical Nineteenth-Century Brethren Love Feast

It will help to provide a brief overview of the typical nineteenth-century Brethren Love Feast. While the Brethren had no official liturgical calendar, the Love Feast was clearly a liturgical high point in their lives. By the nineteenth century most congregations held one Love Feast a year, although it was common for Brethren to attend several more during a year

38. Ramirez, *The Love Feast*, 22.

39. Clarence Kulp describes the typical Brethren practice up until the twentieth century: "One thing that would happen years ago sometimes is that people would be turned away from the table. In the time I was growing up, there was still church discipline, and so there were reasons that you were not permitted to take communion. . . . The Brethren had two orders of excommunication. One was full excommunication for a major transgression, when a person was stubborn and would not repent (as they say, 'make his things right') and you were totally cut off from the fellowship. That was full excommunication or, in German, *absonderung*. The lesser excommunication was called literally 'to be set back from the table' or *zurichstellt vom disch*. Until you confessed and were absolved, you would not be permitted to take communion, and you were also not to be given the holy kiss during that period." quoted in ibid., 31.

40. Bowman, *Brethren Society*, 62.

because congregations were mindful to stagger the dates of observance so that members from neighboring congregations could participate. Hence, the Love Feast served to strengthen the bonds of community, both within the congregation and across a network of sister congregations. Though the earliest Brethren met in homes and barns to celebrate the Love Feast, it became necessary to build meetinghouses (sometimes called "Love Feast houses") as congregations grew larger. Frank Ramirez writes, "It is possible that the church kitchen, now a fixture in churches of all denominations, had its origins in the Brethren love feast. . . . The first meetinghouses resembled houses and, like houses, included kitchens so that members could prepare the most important meal of the year, the Lord's Supper." Perhaps the oldest church kitchen in America is the one at the Pricetown (PA) Church of the Brethren, which was built in 1777.[41]

There is hardly a more thorough, yet concise, description of a mid-nineteenth century Love Feast than in Carl Bowman's *Brethren Society*. He describes:

> [T]he Dunker love feast was a celebration of the purity, unity, and continuing regeneration of the saints. It was without a doubt the sacred climax of Brethren worship and devotion. Always consisting of three parts (feetwashing, the Lord's Supper, and communion), the love feast simultaneously expressed the love the Brethren felt for their Maker and for each other. It was both a ritual of spiritual cleansing and a celebration of unity with Christ and the faith community. All members who were "in love and peace" with their Brethren and constant in the "faith once delivered to the Saints" were not only invited but expected to participate.
>
> The love feast consisted of a series of services, beginning on Saturday morning and ending the following day. Saturday began with a preaching service, followed by dinner, which was prepared in a small kitchen attached to the meetinghouse. The dinner, typically consisting of beef, bread, butter, apple butter, pies, and coffee, would last for a couple of hours, the Brethren being in no hurry to end their time of visiting with Brethren from their own and neighboring congregations. Eventually, they would move into an "examination" service during the late afternoon, during which they would prepare their hearts for the sacred services to follow. A short break followed, until a hymn signaled the Brethren that it was time to take their seats at the communion tables, the

41. Ramirez, *The Love Feast*, 98, 117.

brothers at their tables and the sisters at theirs. Solemn, serene, and expectant, the Brethren waited.

Following a hymn, the first thirty verses of John 13 were read, suitable admonitions were given, and the feetwashing service began. Washing occurred in the "double mode," with two Brethren leading off, one washing and one drying. They would wash the feet of from six to ten persons, after which they were relieved by another two, and so forth until all the saints' feet were washed. After a brother's or sister's feet had been washed, he or she greeted the washer with a holy kiss.[42]

When the feetwashing service was completed, the Lord's Supper, consisting of bread, beef (or mutton), and sop (broth) was eaten.[43] Compared with the fellowship dinner that had occurred earlier in the day, this was a solemn, spiritual time of reflection and meditation. More hymns were sung while the tables were cleared to make room for the communion bread and wine. After these were in place, more Scripture was read and exhortations heard, this time focusing on Christ's sufferings on the cross. When all was ready, the elder greeted the brother next to him with a holy kiss; the brother did the same to the one next to him; and likewise, forming a chain of unity and brotherly love that was passed all the way around the table and back to the elder that

42. The best evidence, however, indicates that the Brethren originally washed feet according to the "single mode," where each individual brother or sister washes *and* dries their neighbor's feet, who in turn does the same to their neighbor, until all have received *and* given the service. In the mid 1800s there was considerable debate among Brethren as to whether the feetwashing should be performed following the single mode or the double mode. In the early 1800s the Annual Meeting had prescribed the double mode, but after evidence emerged that the mother church in Germantown had originally washed feet following the single mode, most Brethren shifted to this method. All Brethren today, except for the Old German Baptist Brethren, wash feet in the single mode. See Allison, "Feetwashing," 481.

43. Alexander Mack, Jr. reports that feetwashing was initially practiced after the *agape* meal and the Eucharist, although it eventually came to be observed before these elements of the Love Feast. In an 1860 English translation of an open letter published in the 1774 German edition of his father's *Rights and Ordinances*, he writes: "I am able to write this in truth out of experience, namely, when we were in the beginning of our baptism, we washed one another's feet in blessing and in the awakening of love *after the meal and after the breaking of bread* [similar to Mennonite practice]. Later we saw more clearly and, with blessing, washed one another's feet after the meal and *before the breaking of bread*. Later, after Reitz had published his New Testament translation, and a brother joined us who knew Greek and properly explained to us that Jesus washed the feet before supper, then we were humble and did it always *before the meal*. Now no brother will think ill of us if we do not wish to begin all over again," Durnbaugh, *The Brethren in Colonial America*, 467 (emphasis added).

began it. The same action, sometimes called "passing the peace," was repeated among the sisters. When the unity and harmony of the Brethren had thus been sealed, communion could begin.

Appropriate remarks were made by the presiding elder. Then the bread was passed among the brothers and sisters. More remarks were heard, and then the Brethren drank of the symbolic wine. For this part of the service only two cups were used, one for the brothers and one for the sisters, and they were passed all the way around until all present had partaken of the ordinance. Spontaneous singing of hymns occurred throughout, until the elder eventually signaled the service's closing with the scriptural quote, "And they sang a hymn and went out." A final prayer was heard, a final hymn sung, and then the Brethren considered themselves dismissed. Visiting Brethren retired to the homes of hosts from the local congregation or stayed in the meetinghouse . . .

The following morning . . . the Brethren turned out for a great preaching service. Typically this was the biggest service of the year with Brethren standing in the doorway and peering through the windows. Much fine preaching was heard. Joyous voices were raised in song. Eventually the service would wind to a close, signaling the end of another sacred love feast.[44]

Thus, the celebration of the Love Feast was a liturgical highlight for the Brethren, similar in character in many ways to the yearly revival meetings of other Protestant churches in America. Of course, the Brethren Love Feast was unique in combining feetwashing and a fellowship meal with the practice of Communion.[45]

4. Twentieth-Century Developments in the Brethren Love Feast

In the last century the Love Feast in the Church of the Brethren has experienced some significant changes. The earlier two-day celebration involving Brethren from around the region gradually gave way to a single evening celebration involving primarily (often exclusively) members from a single congregation. It has become common for many Church of the Brethren congregations to hold the Love Feast twice a year: during Holy Week and during the weekend of World Communion Sunday (the

44. Bowman, *Brethren Society*, 58–60. Bowman's description is a paraphrase of the account by Holsinger, *History of the Tunkers*, 249–55.

45. This summary names the key aspects of the Brethren Love Feast, although there were minor variations in practice between congregations. For a closer look at some of these variations, see Ramirez, *The Love Feast*.

first Sunday in October). During the 1900s the practice of the annual visit gradually declined. It was removed from the list of official deacon responsibilities in 1947, and the preparation element of Love Feast shifted to a time of self-examination and confession at the beginning of the service.

A number of modifications have been made to the elements of feet-washing, the fellowship meal, the holy kiss, and communion. Regarding feetwashing, a handful of churches do not continue the practice, mainly because members find it culturally irrelevant. Some congregations have experimented with handwashing as an alternative for those who have physical difficulties or personal uneasiness washing feet. In a few cases, there are churches that allow men and women to wash each other's feet. Although most congregations continue to separate men and women for the practice of feetwashing, a larger number of congregations now allow men and women to sit together during the fellowship meal. Many churches are broadening the Love Feast menu to include other foods besides beef (or lamb), bread, and broth. While the early Brethren ate the Lord's Supper in reverent silence, today it is more common for hearty conversation to be a part of the supper meal. Some congregations have chosen to have one "contemporary" Love Feast and another "traditional" Love Feast. In many Brethren churches, the holy kiss is no longer shared in connection to the bread and cup Communion, but there are still occasions when members will greet one another with the holy kiss following feetwashing.[46]

Regarding the celebration of the bread and cup, in 1951, Annual Conference formally discarded the requirement of "close communion," allowing Brethren to share communion with Christians from other denominational backgrounds. Another significant development occurred in 1958, when Annual Conference decided that congregations could introduce a Sunday morning bread-and-cup Communion service (prior to 1958 the Brethren had only celebrated Communion within the context of the Love Feast). And in some congregations the previous requirement that Communion be shared only by the baptized has fallen by the wayside. In other words, some congregations continue to instruct participants that the bread and the cup are only to be taken by baptized Christians, while other churches provide no such instruction, and thus open the "meal" to anyone who wishes to eat it.

46. See Kettering, "Greet One Another with a Holy Kiss," 208.

So far we have focused in large part on the Brethren Love Feast, which is the longest continuing example of a recovered Love Feast in modern times. Before we finish the chapter, however, there are several other examples of recovering the Love Feast that we should examine.

D. THE LOVE FEAST IN OTHER TRADITIONS

1. The Community of True Inspiration

In 1714 a group of Pietists known as the Community of True Inspiration (later known as the Amana Society) formed in Germany. The group was founded by two key men, Eberhard Ludwig Gruber and Johann Friedrich Rock.[47] A year before founding the Community of True Inspiration, Gruber had written a pamphlet titled "Basic Questions" in which he sought to clarify the different perspectives on baptism held by the Brethren and another separatist living in Schwarzenau at the time, Christoph Seebach.[48] Thus, with one of their founders having knowledge of the beliefs and practices of the Schwarzenau Brethren, it is no surprise that the love feast of the Community of True Inspiration also bears similarities to the Brethren Love Feast. Marcus Meier reports that between 1714 and 1716 the members of the Community of True Inspiration held five love feasts, including two in the town of Schwarzenau.[49] Their early love feasts included feetwashing, but in 1716 they gave up the practice of washing feet.[50] In 1842 the Community of True Inspiration began moving to Buffalo, New York, and in 1854 the group moved to Iowa, where

---

47. Perkins and Wick, *History of the Amana Society*, 10.

48. See Meier, "Eberhard Ludwig Gruber's *Basic Questions*: Report of a Discovery," 64–67; Schneider, "Basic Questions," 31–63.

49. Meier, *Origin of the Schwarzenau Brethren*, 195 n. 81.

50. "In October 1715 the third love feast was held. These feasts were held, not at any stated time or place, but when it was thought desirable for the strengthening of the members, or when new converts were made, and when their ministers were released from prison. There was generally a week's preparation, when the members were tested by the elders to see if they were prepared. If the members were not in a spiritual mood, they could not take part. After this examination, a day was spend in prayer, when they had feet-washing, and finally the love feast," Perkins and Wick, *History of the Amana Society*, 13. For the cessation of feetwashing, see Meier, *Origin of the Schwarzenau Brethren*, 116.

they founded the town of Amana.[51] Members of the Amana Society continue to celebrate the Love Feast today.

2. The Moravian Lovefeast

Another group of Christians that continues to celebrate the Love Feast today is the Moravian Church. The Moravian Church webpage explains that "the lovefeast of Apostolic times was resuscitated in its original simplicity by the Moravian Church in 1727."[52] After celebrating Holy Communion on the morning of August 13, 1727, several of the participants continued to talk about the great spiritual blessing that they had experienced, and were therefore reluctant to return home to eat lunch. Count Zinzendorf, the leader of the Moravians, sent them food from his manor house and they partook together, continuing to share in prayers, the singing of hymns, and religious testimony. The incident reminded Zinzendorf of the early church *agape*, and henceforth celebrating the lovefeast has been a vital practice of the Moravian Church. The early Moravians also included the kiss of love with their celebration of the Eucharist,[53] and they practiced feetwashing before celebrating Communion until 1818, when it was discontinued by the Moravian synod.[54]

The Moravian lovefeast, as celebrated today, is primarily a service of song. The lovefeast opens with prayer, and the hymns in the service provide the subject matter for devotional thoughts. There is rarely a sermon in the lovefeast, although a minister sometimes gives an address on lovefeasts held on special occasions (such as the anniversary of the founding of the Moravian Church or other anniversary days). During the lovefeast participants partake of sweetened buns and coffee, although other forms of bread and drinks may also be served. It is common for men to handle the trays of mugs, and women the baskets of buns. Usually a choir sings an anthem as the congregation partakes of the bun and coffee. The food and drink served are not consecrated, as in

51. Perkins and Wick, *History of the Amana Society*, 45–57.

52. From www.moravian.org/faq/lovefeast.phtml. The Moravians prefer to spell lovefeast as a single word.

53. Meier, *Origin of the Schwarzenau Brethren*, 113.

54. Cole, *Love-Feasts*, 275. We should also recall that the group from which the Moravians emerged, the *Unitas Fratum* (the League of Brethren) practiced feetwashing as part of the Eucharist; see ibid., 271.

Communion. The Moravians allow children and members of any other Christian denomination to participate in the lovefeast.

3. THE GLASITES

Another group that recovered the Love Feast in their worship practice was the Glasites. The Glasites were followers of John Glas, a Scottish clergyman who broke away from the Church of Scotland in 1725. In 1730 he set up a church in Dundee, and their worship practices included feetwashing, the love-feast, and the holy kiss. In fact, because their love-feast often featured a broth made from the vegetable kale, their church became known as the "Kail Kirk" (the "kale church")![55] Some of the bread from the meal was reserved for the celebration of Communion, which occurred after the meal.[56] Glas's son-in-law Robert Sandeman also became a prominent leader in the church, and together they founded congregations in Edinburgh, London, and several other cities.[57] Although the movement largely dissipated in the late-nineteenth-century, several small churches continued on into the twentieth century. The Glasite congregation in Edinburgh continued until the late 1980s.[58]

4. THE METHODIST LOVE-FEAST

Beginning in 1738, the Methodists, under the leadership of John Wesley, held their first love-feast, and it continued to be a significant practice until the end of the nineteenth century. On August 8, 1737, while in Savannah, Georgia, on a missionary journey, Wesley was invited to join a group of German Moravians in their lovefeast celebration.[59] Wesley was impressed by the Moravian lovefeast, and he began experimenting

55. Cole, *Love-Feasts*, 281–82.

56. McMillon, "Discovery of the Earliest Extant Scottish Restoration Congregation," 47–48.

57. The Glasites later became known as the Sandemanians, and decades later Michael Faraday, the famous scientist, was a member and elder of the Sandemanian church in London.

58. See McMillon, "Discovery of the Earliest Extant Scottish Restoration Congregation," 51–52.

59. In his journal Wesley wrote, " . . . we joined with the Germans in one of their love-feasts. It was begun and ended with thanksgiving and prayer, and celebrated in so decent and solemn a manner as a Christian of the apostolic age would have allowed to be worthy of Christ," Wesley, *The Journal of the Rev. John Wesley*, 1:377, quoted in Parkes, "Watchnight, Covenant Service, and Love-Feast," 38.

with the practice upon returning to London later in the year.[60] In the Methodist love-feast, participants ate cake or bread and drank water or tea (in order to avoid confusion with the Eucharist, cake was preferred and wine was never used). Methodist love-feasts were held quarterly and became best known as testimony services. They were also characterized by open praise, singing, prayer, preaching and calls for discipleship. In order to help prevent intruders from listening in on the testimony of the faithful, some Methodists required individuals to have a ticket or a written note by an itinerant preacher in order to gain admittance to the love-feast.[61] By the late 1800s the Methodist love-feast gave way to straight prayer meetings and "tea gatherings," and very few Methodist churches continue the tradition today.[62]

E. SUMMARY

Beginning in the early 1500s and lasting for over two centuries, groups of Christian reformers made efforts to recover practices of the apostolic church that had been neglected in later years. In 1708 the Brethren Love Feast emerged as a combination of several of these reforms. The Brethren incorporated several aspects of Anabaptist worship in their Love Feast: their practice of the deacon's visit was rooted in the concept of the ban, they included feetwashing as a part of their service, they greeted one another with the holy kiss, and during Communion they emphasized the presence of Christ in the body of believers gathered to worship. The

60. On January 1, 1738, Wesley wrote in his diary: "Mr. Hall, Kinchin, Ingham, Whitefield, Hutchins, and my brother Charles were present at our love-feast at Fetter Lane, with about sixty of our brethren. About three in the morning, as we were continuing instant in prayer, the power of God came mightily upon us, inasmuch that many cried out for exceeding joy, and many fell to the ground. As soon as we were recovered a little from that awe and amazement at the presence of His majesty we broke out with one voice: "We praise Thee, O God; we acknowledge Thee to be the Lord," *The Works of John Wesley*, 1:93, quoted in Parkes, "Watchnight, Covenant Service, and Love-Feast," 39.

61. Lester Ruth explains that in addition to encouraging the unfettered testimony of believers, the love-feast restrictions were in place to guard the purity of the gathering: "Simply put, early Methodists considered that God was uniquely present in their midst when they gathered as God's distinct people. Mixture with unawakened outsiders voided the condition by which God was present and revealed. Methodists restricted admission to their [love-feasts] because there they experienced the glorious presence of God," Ruth, "A Little Heaven Below," 63–64.

62. The African Methodist Episcopal Church (AME) continues to practice a Wesley-style love-feast. For more on the Methodist love-feast, see the articles by Parkes and Ruth quoted above, as well as Baker, *Methodism and the Love-Feast*.

early Brethren also were influenced by Pietist author Gottfried Arnold, whose writings gave detail to the practice of the *agape* in the early church. The Brethren celebrated the first Love Feast in America in 1723. When they began to outgrow their homes, they became the first Christians in America to build meetinghouses with attached kitchens. By the 1800s, most Brethren congregations were celebrating the Love Feast once or twice a year, with the practice having developed into a Saturday–Sunday event attracting Brethren from the surrounding congregations. After sharing a lunch meal on Saturday, the Brethren would hold a several-hour examination service before moving into the feetwashing, fellowship meal (Lord's Supper) and Communion of the Love Feast proper. The service would conclude with the singing of a hymn, and the following morning there would be a large worship service, usually led by special guest preachers.

PART II

Celebrating the Love Feast Today

Formed to Embody Submission, Love, Confession, Reconciliation, and Thanksgiving

O UR LOVE FEAST JOURNEY continues as we "use the past to help us see what has been lost, in the hope that our imaginations will be renewed and begin to see what we must now do."[1] Thus, the focus of Part II will be how the church might celebrate the Love Feast today—hopefully with renewed imaginations that are open to new understandings of eucharistic worship. It is one thing to have a great deal of knowledge about the Love Feast, and another thing to have the wisdom that comes through experiencing the Love Feast. Anyone can research "Love Feast" on the Internet and learn about its history, but this information, divorced from actual experience, has little value. What the church should offer the world is the wisdom and character gained through experiences of celebrating the Love Feast.

Recovering the Love Feast is important because it has great potential to shape the habits and character of the church. The Love Feast can be a truly powerful practice that forms our worldview, both as individuals and as communities. Brethren author Ken Morse tells of one particularly prominent example of the formative witness of the Love Feast:

> Andrew W. Cordier, who helped draft the charter of the United Nations and who for seventeen years served as one of its top officials, once told an interviewer that he received his first world view at the Brethren love feast. . . . [In 1960 Cordier said] "utter

---

1. Hauerwas and Wells, "How the Church Managed before there Was Ethics," 49.

sincerity, utter fairness, and utter integrity are basic to commu-
nication, and I first learned them as prior conditions to coming
to the love feast tables. At these tables, after applying the rules of
Matthew 18, the Brethren dramatize the idea of brotherhood under God. I saw these concepts acted out before my eyes, by people
I loved and trusted, from the time I could remember. The ideas
stayed with me. . . . Such concepts of brotherhood at the conference table of the United Nations give peace a fighting chance."[2]

This is but one example, albeit a notable one, of the formative power
of the Love Feast. While most people will never be involved in shaping
global policy, they still have a variety of opportunities to witness lo-
cally for Christ. And this local Love Feast can be the *Feast of the World's
Redemption* (John Koenig).

Although we do not have a clear scriptural example of what the
Love Feast included, there are two passages in particular that give us
clues as to the central themes of early eucharistic worship. They are from
Philippians 2 and Colossians 3:

If then there is any encouragement in Christ, any *consolation
from love*, any *sharing* (*koinonia*) in the Spirit, any compassion
and sympathy, make my joy complete: be of the same mind, *having the same love* (*agapen*), *being in full accord* and of *one mind*.
Do nothing from selfish ambition or conceit, but *in humility
regard others as better than yourselves*. Let each of you look not
to your own interests, but to the interests of others. Let the same
mind be in you that was in Christ Jesus,
who, though he was in the form of God,
did not regard equality with God
as something to be exploited,
but emptied himself,
taking the form of a slave, being born in human likeness.
And being found in human form,
he humbled himself
and became obedient to the point of death—
even death on a cross.
Therefore God also highly exalted him
and gave him the name
that is above every name,
so that at the name of Jesus
every knee should bend,
in heaven and on earth and under the earth,

2. Morse, "Lessons Learned at the Love Feast," 765.

and every tongue should confess
that Jesus Christ is Lord,
to the glory of God the Father.

Therefore, my beloved, just as you have always obeyed me, not only in my presence, but much more now in my absence, work out your own salvation with fear and trembling; for it is God who is at work in you, enabling you both to will and to work for his good pleasure. *Do all things without murmuring and arguing*, so that you may be blameless and innocent, children of God *without blemish* in the midst of a crooked and perverse generation, in which you shine like stars in the world.... But even if I am being poured out as a libation over the sacrifice and the offering of your faith, I am glad and rejoice with all of you—and in the same way *you also must be glad (chairo) and rejoice with me.* (Phil 2:1–15, 17–18, emphasis added)

As God's chosen ones, holy and beloved, clothe yourselves with compassion, kindness, *humility*, meekness, and patience. *Bear with one another* and, if anyone has a complaint against another, *forgive each other; just as the Lord has forgiven you, so you also must forgive.* Above all, clothe yourselves with *love (agapen)*, which binds everything together in perfect harmony. And let the *peace of Christ* rule in your hearts, to which indeed you were called in the one body. And be *thankful (eucharistoi)*. Let the word of Christ dwell in you richly; teach and admonish one another in all wisdom; and with gratitude in your hearts sing psalms, hymns, and spiritual songs to God. And whatever you do, *in word* or deed, do everything in the name of the Lord Jesus, *giving thanks (eucharistountes)* to God the Father through him." (Col 3:12–17, emphasis added)

This is not the place for an extended exegesis of these passages. It must suffice to say that there is strong evidence pointing toward a mealtime setting for these passages.[3] When taken together, these passages give us a broad picture of the themes and connected practices of mealtime worship in the early church. From this broad range of themes, I would like to focus on five: submission, love, confession, reconciliation,

---

3. The reference to hymn-singing in both passages is a major clue pointing to a mealtime celebration. See especially the section "Cosmic hymnic imaginations of early Christianity at the Hellenistic meal," in Taussig, *In the Beginning was the Meal*, 104–12. Ralph Martin argues that the panoramic language about salvation used in the Phil 2 hymn indicates its connection to eucharistic worship; see Martin, *A Hymn of Christ*, 269. See the discussion in Koenig, *Feast of the World's Redemption*, 138–40.

and thanksgiving. Three of these (love, confession, and thanksgiving) are mentioned explicitly in the texts. Although submission and reconciliation do not explicitly appear, many phrases are found to support their inclusion as central themes.[4] Thus, from these texts one can make a strong argument that submission, love, confession, reconciliation, and thanksgiving were central themes in early Christian mealtime worship.

I will argue in Part II that these five themes can be linked with five practices of the early church: submission/feetwashing; love/fellowship meal; confession/eucharistic preparation; reconciliation/holy kiss; and thanksgiving/Eucharist. In the same way that early church worship emphasized these themes and practices, I believe that the contemporary celebration of the Love Feast should help the church to embody the disciplines of submission, love, confession, reconciliation, and thanksgiving. Of course, God is ultimately the one who forms us individually and communally in these aspects of Christian discipleship. At the same time, there is also personal and communal initiative and involvement in this process, for as Christians we are called to "work out [our] own salvation with fear and trembling" (Phil 2:12).

Celebrating the Love Feast today should not just be the peculiar emphasis of the Brethren and a few others; the Love Feast is a practice for *all Christians*, and one that can broaden our celebration of the Eucharist. Because of this, in the next several chapters I will not attempt to provide a detailed description of how the Love Feast should be practiced in churches today. Rather, in the next five chapters we look at the broader themes at the heart of the Love Feast while leaving room for differences in practice. Catholics may not be quite ready to meld the Mass to the meal, but that does not mean that local parishes cannot experiment with ways of celebrating fellowship meals that demonstrate Christian love and thanksgiving to the wider community. Some Presbyterians might not be ready to practice feetwashing just yet, but they might be open to celebrating a Love Feast that emphasizes submission in some other form. This is not to say that it does not matter how Christian worship embodies these disciplines; some practices are more valuable and meaningful than others. However, churches should not be discouraged from reclaiming the Love Feast simply because they are currently not ready to practice feetwashing or to celebrate Communion with a full meal.

4. For example, "taking the form of a slave", "humility", "being in full accord and of one mind," and "bear with one another and . . . forgive one another."

Before moving on, let me address two potential concerns relating to worship and formation. First, because I emphasize the formative nature of the Love Feast, it may seem that the Love Feast is something that the church does primarily for her own benefit, rather than an expression of worship for the glory of God. At the heart of this concern is whether the aim of worship is to glorify God or to sanctify our lives, to magnify the Creator or to form the worshiping community into a holy people. This is a false choice. Throughout history the church has understood worship to involve *both* of these dimensions. Luther referred to worship as revelation and response, both of which are empowered by the Holy Spirit.[5] Sixteenth-century Anglican Archbishop Thomas Cranmer explained that the goal of worship is the "setting forth of God's honor or glory, and the reducing of the people to a most perfect and godly living."[6] Pope Pius X wrote in 1903 that worship is for "the glory of God and the sanctification and edification of the faithful."[7] In sum, "Nothing glorifies God more than a human being made holy; nothing is more likely to make a person holy than the desire to glorify God. Both the glorification of God and the sanctification of humans characterize Christian worship. Apparent tensions between them are superficial."[8] This understanding of worship must guide our discussion of the contemporary celebration of the Love Feast.

Second, I will argue that the habit/practice of celebrating the Love Feast helps to form us more fully to embody the disciplines of submission, confession, love, reconciliation, and thanksgiving. It is important to mention, however, that there is not a *quid pro quo* relationship between our celebration and our formation. The Love Feast is not like a spiritual vending machine; we cannot expect that our mere celebration of it will bring about our formation in these five disciplines (like putting money into a vending machine to get a candy bar). Nor does the frequency of our celebration necessarily relate to our overall growth in practicing

5. He writes of Christian worship "that nothing else be done in it than that our dear Lord Himself talk to us through His holy word and that we, in turn talk to him in prayer and song of praise," WA 49, 588, 15–18, quoted in White, *Introduction to Christian Worship*, 22.

6. Cranmer, "Of Ceremonies," 326, quoted in White, *Introduction to Christian Worship*, 23.

7. Pope Pius X, "*Tra le sollecitudini*," 4, quoted in White, *Introduction to Christian Worship*, 24.

8. White, *Introduction to Christian Worship*, 24.

these disciplines. And, of course, the celebration of the Love Feast is not the only practice which forms us to submit, confess, love, reconcile, or give thanks. Nonetheless, the appropriate recovery of the Love Feast today has tremendous potential to form and reform congregations and individuals in the practical expressions of Christian discipleship. Having addressed these two potential concerns, let us begin the second half of our journey—the exploration of the ways we might recover the Love Feast in the twenty-first century.

7

Formed to Submit

The Relationship between Feetwashing and Submission

Submit yourselves therefore to God.

—JAMES 4:7A

Submit to one another out of reverence for Christ.

—EPH 5:21 NIV

[In 1834 Brethren pastor] Peter Nead wrote, "Feetwashing represents that state of purification through which the believer must pass, so as to be received at the coming of Christ." It was also a symbol of the Christian's willingness to go and help cleanse a brother or sister of trespasses by humble admonishment, a task sometimes as difficult and unpleasant as washing dirty feet. Feet washing meant both *cleansing from sin* and *service*.

—JAMES LEHMAN[1]

When Jesus immortalized the principle of the cross-life by washing the disciples' feet, he added, "I have given you an example, that you also should do as I have done to you" (John 13:15). The cross-life is the life of voluntary submission.

—RICHARD FOSTER[2]

1. Lehman, *The Old Brethren*, 82 (emphasis added), quoted from Nead, *Primitive Christianity*, 118.
2. Foster, *Celebration of Discipline*, 116.

Submission is a crucial and challenging discipline in the church—crucial because God cannot accomplish much of anything in our lives unless we submit to him, and challenging because we have a sordid history of botching submission. It is not easy to emphasize submission as a virtue in the church, particularly in the contemporary American context where individualism is such a strong force. When Christians in America do not like what their pastor or church teaches, rather than submit, they simply leave and find another church. When a politician's pastor or religious advisor says provocative things that challenge the views of potential voters, the politician simply resigns from his or her church or disavows their controversial endorser. Of course, submission is not a virtue in all circumstances; there are many examples in church and world history where authorities have abused their power. Richard Foster elaborates:

> Of all the spiritual disciplines, none has been more abused than the discipline of submission. Somehow the human species has an extraordinary knack for taking the best teaching and turning it to the worst ends. Nothing can put people into bondage like religion, and nothing in religion has done more to manipulate and destroy people than a deficient teaching on submission. Therefore, we must work our way through this discipline with great care and discernment in order to ensure that we are the ministers of life, not death.[3]

Foster goes on to provide a broad examination of the discipline of submission in chapter 8 of *Celebration of Discipline*. We will not attempt here to rehash Foster's argument. Instead, we will focus on one particular practice that helps to form submission in the character of the members of the church, namely, feetwashing.

The practice of feetwashing forms Christians to submit, both to Christ and to one another. This twofold submission begins with the believer's submission to God in Christ, who desires to wash away our sins. In the same way that Peter's feet had to be washed in order for him to have a share with Christ, so disciples today must also submit to the cleansing of Christ. This submission is poignantly demonstrated in the washing of feet. Submission to Christ can also be demonstrated in the believer's obedience to Jesus' command to wash one another's feet. Secondly, when Christians today wash one another's feet they are following the instruction to "Submit to one another out of reverence for

3. Ibid., 110.

Christ" (Eph 5:21 NIV). This practice forms church members to serve one another in love. It also shapes them to be people who are able to receive acts of service without necessarily having to reciprocate. Thus, when feetwashing is practiced during the celebration of the Love Feast, Christians rehearse their submission to Christ and to one another.

A. CHALLENGES CONCERNING AUTHORITY AND SUBMISSION

1. The Deconstruction of Authority

Before examining Christian submission, we must address our current context in which most claims of authority and obedience are challenged or rejected. In his chapter "Listening: Authority and Obedience" in the *Blackwell Companion to Christian Ethics*, Scott Bader-Saye describes the development of forces confronting authority in the modern and postmodern eras.[4] At the beginning of the modern era, the growth of Renaissance humanism and Enlightenment rationalism began to challenge traditional structures of authority (especially the authority of the church). René Descartes is "a particularly vivid illustration of the modern turn to the self, the ascendance of the individual as arbiter of truth and the decline of traditional authorities as trusted sources of knowledge and guidance."[5] It was Descartes, of course, who began his search for truth by first doubting everything that could possibly be doubted, and then famously concluding "I think, therefore I am" (or more accurately, "I doubt, therefore I am"). Immanuel Kant continued this process of rejecting authority, writing in 1784:

> Enlightenment is man's release from his self-incurred tutelage. Tutelage is man's inability to make use of his understanding without direction from another. Self-incurred is this tutelage when its cause lies not in lack of reason but in lack of resolution and courage to use it without direction from another. *Sapere aude!* "Have courage to use your own reason!" – that is the motto of enlightenment.[6]

4. Bader-Saye, "Listening: Authority and Obedience."

5. Ibid., 157.

6. Kant, "What is Enlightenment?," 85, quoted in ibid., 157.

Hence, Kant proclaimed that those who are "enlightened" have cast off the burden of having to submit to direction from outside or above. The call is essentially "Stand on your own two feet" (intellectually speaking)!

"Where modernism prepared the way for the suspicion of authority, a 'legitimation crisis,' in Jürgen Habermas's terms, postmodernism furnishes the coup de grâce," writes Kenneth Gergen.[7] The primary thinkers of postmodern thought (Jacques Derrida, Michel Foucault, and Jean-François Lyotard) set about to deconstruct sources of authority in society, that is, the authority of a text to say something specific, or the authority of an individual to command allegiance, or the authority of a grand narrative to give meaning to life. The deconstruction of authority is evident not only in the philosophical realm, but also in popular culture, where TV shows like *Seinfeld* and *Friends* normalize a world in which individuals are guided by no authority beyond their personal fulfillment.[8] "In a culture infatuated with autonomy," explains Bader-Saye, "personal experience and individual preference become the arbiter of what is true and right. In such a context all outside voices are treated with suspicion."[9] Thus, in both the philosophical and the cultural realms a strong skepticism toward authority exists, and therefore toward submission as a virtue.

2. Reclaiming Appropriate Authority

Even as our postmodern culture continues to undermine most forms of authority, we must recognize that the Christian church, like any community, requires structures of authority to function properly. Without any rules or guidelines, groups of self-interested individuals can hardly avoid becoming splintered by competition and conflict, as is evident in the *Lord of the Flies* or an episode of *Survivor*.[10] Richard Foster writes:

7. Gergen, *The Saturated Self*, 124.

8. "Indeed, part of the humor in these shows comes from the levity with which the characters treat such serious matters as sex and death: think of the death of George's fiancé in *Seinfeld* or Joey's inability to remember the names of women he sleeps with in *Friends*," Bader-Saye, "Listening: Authority and Obedience," 158.

9. Ibid.

10. John Howard Yoder, *The Politics of Jesus*, 174 n. 25, comments: "What if, e.g., the sweeping doctrinaire egalitarianism of our culture, which makes the concept of [place and role] seem either laughable or boorish, and makes that of 'subordination' seem insulting, should turn out really (in "the intent of God," or in long-run social experience) to be demonic, uncharitable, destructive of personality, disrespectful of creation,

The point is not that we are to do away with all sense of leadership or authority. Any sociologist would quickly demonstrate the impossibility of such a task. Even among Jesus and the disciples, leadership and authority are seen easily. *The point is that Jesus completely redefined leadership and rearranged the lines of authority.*

Jesus never taught that everyone had equal authority. In fact, he had a great deal to say about genuine spiritual authority and taught that many did not possess it. But the authority of which Jesus spoke is not the authority of a pecking order. We must clearly understand the radical nature of Jesus' teaching on this matter. He was not just reversing the "pecking order" as many suppose. He was abolishing it. The authority of which he spoke was not an authority to manipulate and control. It was an authority of function, not of status.[11]

Jesus explains this new understanding of authority during the Last Supper. In Luke, the disciples get into an argument about their respective positions of authority, and Jesus responds: "The kings of the Gentiles lord it over them; and those in authority over them are called benefactors. But not so with you; rather *the greatest among you must become like the youngest, and the leader like one who serves.* For who is greater, the one who is at the table or the one who serves? Is it not the one at the table? But I am among you as one who serves" (Luke 22:25–27, emphasis added). In the Gospel of John, Jesus demonstrates this servanthood authority by removing his outer clothes, tying a towel around his waist, and washing the feet of his disciples (13:1–20). This act of washing feet can still be a powerful reminder of the redefined spiritual authority in the Kingdom of God. As the church continues the practice of feetwashing, its members are formed to submit to Christ and to one another.

3. Revolutionary Submission or Revolutionary Subordination?

Although I have chosen to name submission as the discipline at the heart of feetwashing, subordination is an equally adequate term to name this discipline. In his chapter "Revolutionary Subordination" in *The Politics*

---

or unworkable? Must we still assume that in order properly to 'play twentieth-century occidentals' we must let this modern myth keep us from hearing what the apostle says about the christological basis of mutual subordination?"

11. Foster, *Celebration of Discipline*, 127 (emphasis added).

of Jesus, John Howard Yoder notes the following concerning the House-Table (*Haustafeln*)[12] moral instruction passages in the New Testament:

> In the *Haustafeln* . . . the center of the imperative is a call to willing subordination to one's partner [husband/wife, master/slave, etc.]. The term *hypotassesthai* is not best rendered by *subjection* [NRSV, NASB], which carries a connotation of being thrown down and run over, nor by *submission* [NIV, NKJV, ISV, NLT], with its connotation of passivity. Subordination means the acceptance of an *order*, as it exists, but with the new meaning given to it by the fact that one's acceptance of it is willing and meaningfully motivated.[13]

Yoder is correct in that the word *hypotassesthai* is a compound word in the Greek, consisting of *hypo* ("under, beneath") and *tasso* ("to place in order"). Thus, in the strictest sense, subordination is the best way to translate the term. Yoder goes on to explain how the New Testament addresses the subordinate person as a free moral agent, something that was revolutionary for the time.[14]

The term *submission*, however, seems preferable because of the fact that its imperative form (*Submit!*) is simpler and easier to understand than the correlative (*Subordinate!*). Submit to God! Submit to one another! To me these commands carry more meaning than: Subordinate to God! Be subordinate to one another! Perhaps this is why no major English translations of the Bible use "subordination" in the *Haustafeln*, choosing instead to use "subjection" or "submission." And although Richard Foster engages the work of Yoder in the *Celebration of Discipline*,

---

12. *Haustafeln* is a German word, coined by Martin Luther, meaning literally 'house-table," hence a table of rules for the Christian household. The term *Haustafeln* designates passages in the New Testament that include such moral instruction. See Eph 5:21–6:9; Col 3:18–4:1; Titus 2:4–10, and 1 Pet 2:18–3:7. Yoder refers to Eph 5:21.

13. Yoder, *The Politics of Jesus*, 172 (emphasis in original).

14. "The admonition of the *Haustafeln* is addressed *first to the subject*: to the slave before the master, to the children before the parents, to the wives before the husbands. Here begins the revolutionary innovation in the early Christian style of ethical thinking for which there is no explanation in borrowing from other contemporary cultural sources. The *subordinate* person in the social order is *addressed as a moral agent*. She is called upon to take responsibility for the acceptance of her position in society as meaningful before God. It is not assumed, as it was in both Jewish and Hellenistic thought, that the wife will have the faith of her husband, or that the slave will be part of the religious unity of the master's household. Here we have a faith that assigns *personal moral responsibility to those who had no legal or moral status* in their culture, and makes of them decision makers," ibid., 171–72 (emphasis in original).

in the end he chooses to call the discipline *submission*, not subordination. Thus, while recognizing the value of the term "revolutionary subordination," "submission" seems better for the sake of clarity.[15]

B. SUBMITTING TO CHRIST

1. Allowing Christ to Cleanse Us

When Jesus washed his disciples' feet, John reports that he was not simply sanitizing their feet, but also cleansing them spiritually. This is made evident when Peter refuses to allow Jesus to wash his feet. Paul Duke comments: "No wonder Peter resists. He has signed up to follow Jesus, not to have the unpleasantness down at the foot of his life exposed and handled for him. He prefers the dignity of self-reliance, the fantasy of being heroic."[16] But this is not just about Peter in the first century; it is also about each of us in the twenty-first century. For we too are faced with the scandal of Christ reaching out to touch us, to cleanse us, to perform a task that we would rather not allow someone of kingly status to perform. And while the physical Christ may not be kneeling in front of us, reaching for our feet, when Christians continue the practice of feetwashing, it is indeed Christ in our brother or sister who kneels before us; and we, like Peter, are faced with the challenge of submission.

Peter's first response is "No! You will never wash my feet!" We are also prone to refusing to submit to the cleansing that Christ offers. We

15. Indeed, if I have not adequately described submission in this chapter, please refer to Yoder to clarify any misconceptions, for his description of revolutionary subordination is exactly what I am describing as submission. He explains, "[Jesus'] motto of revolutionary subordination, of willing servanthood in the place of domination, enables the person in a subordinate position in society to accept and live within that status without resentment, at the same time that it calls upon the person in the superordinate position to forsake or renounce all domineering use of that status. This call is then precisely not a simple ratification of the stratified society into which the gospel has come. The subordinate person becomes a free ethical agent in the act of voluntarily acceding to subordination in the power of Christ instead of bowing to it either fatalistically or resentfully. The claim is not that there is immediately a new world regime which violently replaces the old; rather, the old and the new order exist concurrently on different levels. It is because she knows that in Christ there is no male or female that the Christian wife can freely accept that subordination to her unbelieving husband which is her present lot. It is because Christ has freed us all, and slave and free are equal before God, that their relationship may continue as a humane and honest one within the framework of the present economy, the structure of which is passing away (1 Cor. 7:31)," ibid., 186.

16. Duke, "John 13:1–17, 31b–35," 399–400.

would rather tell our dark secrets to a psychologist who will help us come up with a program to accept ourselves. As adults, we refuse to be wiped and cleansed like a baby. And we have been inculcated by a culture that loudly trumpets the freedom of the individual and the rejection of religious superstition, to such a degree that it is culturally backward to hold on to ideas of submission to God.[17] After all, who really wants to be humbled, to be stripped of power? Who wants to reveal their most intimate struggles? The path to atonement is treacherous.

But Jesus responds to Peter: "Unless I wash you, you have no share with me" (John 13:8). Paul Duke comments:

> Forget being a disciple, forget being a minister, forget the very name of Christ unless you will be touched where you loathe to be touched. We go down with Christ to our most painful secrets, to our ugliest drives, dreams, terrors, and sins, to be known there and embraced, to be probed, dealt with and died for, or we are excluded. As someone has said, either we come to terms with an atonement, or we spend the rest of our lives re-enacting it. We face our need, or die of it.[18]

Jesus tells Peter that the feetwashing is more than physical cleansing; it also cleanses the disciples spiritually and unites them with Christ (although Judas rejects this cleansing and leaves the meal after the feet-washing to betray Jesus). Like Peter, we face the challenge of submission to Christ. Will Jesus truly be the Lord of our lives, or will he simply be a religious consultant? In the Love Feast, our brother or sister comes as Christ, offering to cleanse us from sin, but this spiritual cleansing only occurs when we submit and allow Christ to wash our souls.

Over the last two years I have had the blessing of staying at home to raise our young daughter. One day when I was changing her diaper, I had an epiphany that helped me to understand further the connection of feetwashing and spiritual cleansing. We all know that babies soil their diapers and cannot clean themselves; they need a caretaker to clean them and get them dressed and going again. As children grow up they may no longer need an adult to change their diapers, but they still get dirty on occasion (or get into "dirty" situations) and need to be "cleaned up" again. As adults, however, we are fairly capable of cleaning and dressing ourselves, and only in extreme circumstances will we allow another

---

17. For a critique of this concept of freedom, see Hauerwas, *After Christendom?*
18. Duke, "John 13:1–17, 31b–35," 400.

person to wipe us like a baby. Yet I suppose that from God's perspective, there are many of us who are still immature in aspects of our spiritual life. Our own sin creates a spiritual mess in our lives, like a dirty diaper, which we are powerless to clean up. Thank God that Christ comes to us to cleanse us! When we submit ourselves to Christ, he washes our soles and our souls and makes us clean once again!

2. Washing Sins Away: Baptism, Feetwashing and Penance

Some might argue that feetwashing is not necessary for Christians because Christ has washed away all our sins at baptism. But what about the sins we commit after baptism? How do Christians in the Protestant tradition experience forgiveness and reconciliation for post-baptismal sin, especially since most of these groups have rejected the sacrament of Penance? While God graciously forgives the sin of the individual who confesses and repents, does not the church have a role in this process of reconciliation?

In his book *Promise and Presence: An Exploration of Sacramental Theology*, Baptist theologian John Colwell suggests that feetwashing should be understood as an element of the sacrament of cleansing (more commonly known as penance).[19] Because post-baptismal sin is inherently a sacramental problem (because it denies the sacramental/mysterious identity received by the Christian at baptism), it is appropriate for the church to identify a sacramental resolution, namely, the sacrament of cleansing/feetwashing. Colwell comments on feetwashing:

> Our identity as already "clean" [through baptism] does not negate the need to have our feet washed, it rather identifies that need: if we were wholly unclean our dirty feet would be a matter of consistency rather than of inconsistency; it is our essential and underlying identity as "clean" that itself identifies the need and necessity of having our feet washed by Christ. And only by Christ: he calls us to wash one another's feet but unless he himself, as our Lord and Teacher, washes our feet, we have no part with him. . . . Only Christ has the authority to forgive sin, only Christ has the authority to wash our dirty feet and to pronounce us clean— but Christ mediates this authority, by his Spirit, through those

---

19. Feetwashing was understood as a sacramental practice in the Milanese church (Ambrose), in North African churches (Tertullian) and in the Gallican church; see Schaff, *History of the Christian Church*, 3:334. In the twelfth century Bernard of Clairvaux believed, counter to Catholic theology, that feetwashing was a sacrament; see Schaff, *The Middle Ages: Part I (1049–1294)*, 355.

he has so called. In Christ's name and in the power of the Spirit the Christian . . . has the authority (and the responsibility) to . . . pronounce forgiveness, to enact restoration.[20]

When understood as an element of the sacrament of cleansing, feet-washing then becomes more firmly linked to the confession of sin. Feetwashing is thus understood to be a ritual act of absolution, cleansing the repentant Christian from their sin. Further research would be help-ful to understand better the sacramental character of feetwashing.

3. Christ's Cleansing and the Mode of Feetwashing

Forms of feetwashing that are not mutual, but rather involve one person washing the feet of many, place a greater emphasis on the cleansing of sin. In the Brethren tradition, feetwashing done in the double mode meant that two individuals would perform the act; one washing feet and the other drying them. These two members, often deacons, would wash and dry about ten pairs of feet, after which another two persons would con-tinue the practice. Performed this way, the majority of the congregation experienced feetwashing only as recipients of the action, not as washers themselves.[21] Accordingly, in the nineteenth century, when the double mode was predominant in Brethren practice, feetwashing was primarily understood to represent cleansing from sin. Although I believe mutual feetwashing is preferable in general, especially in the celebration of the Love Feast, on occasion there may be value in trying out different forms of feetwashing (like the double mode) that emphasize the cleansing di-mension of the practice.

4. Submitting to Christ by Obeying His Command to Wash Feet

Lastly, we must recognize that Christ *commands* his followers to wash feet. This command is repeated three times in John 13:

20. Colwell, *Promise and Presence*, 180, 187. I have adapted the last sentence to be more egalitarian. Colwell's original sentence reads, "In Christ's name and in the power of the Spirit the Christian minister has the authority (and the responsibility) to say "I absolve you' (*ego te absolvo*), to pronounce forgiveness, to enact restoration.

21. Although the Catholic, Orthodox and Anglican traditions all celebrate feet-washing on Maundy Thursday, in which bishops and priests wash the feet of (usually 12) laypeople or subordinates, the action is primarily a demonstration of the *humility* of church leaders, rather than an act of cleansing from sin. For that, these traditions all practice the sacrament of penance.

After he had washed their feet, had put on his robe, and had returned to the table, he said to them, "Do you know what I have done to you? You call me Teacher and Lord—and you are right, for that is what I am. So if I, your Lord and Teacher, have washed your feet, *you also ought to wash one another's feet.* For I have set you an example, that *you also should do as I have done to you.* Very truly, I tell you, servants are not greater than their master, nor are messengers greater than the one who sent them. If you know these things, *you are blessed if you do them.* (John 13:12–17)

In chapter 3 we saw that attempts to separate these commands from the act of feetwashing are inappropriate. The plain sense of the text is the best reading. Also, it is significant to observe that John 13 is the only occasion in the New Testament where Jesus says, "I have set you an example (*hypodeigma*)" to follow. He does not refer to any other action as an example to follow. As believers obey Christ's command to wash one another's feet, they are also formed to submit to one another.

C. SUBMITTING TO ONE ANOTHER

1. Feetwashing as Humble Service.

When Christians wash one another's feet, they are shaped to submit to one another. Most Christian communities that practice feetwashing today (e.g., Brethren, Church of God, Mennonites, Primitive Baptists, some Anglicans/Episcopalians) do so mutually, that is, members both wash feet and have their feet washed. When Christians stoop to wash the feet of a brother or sister, they voluntarily take a position of submission. They perform the task out of obedience to Christ and his command to wash feet. One should recall the hymn that Paul quotes in Philippians in which Christians are to have the same mind as Christ, who "emptied himself, taking the form of a slave" (2:7). Ephesians contains instructions for church members to: "Submit to one another *out of reverence for Christ*" (Eph 5:21 NIV, emphasis added). Thus mutual submission is based on the example of Christ, who humbled himself when he washed the disciples' feet and allowed himself to be crucified, demonstrating his deep love for humanity.

The call to revolutionary submission (or revolutionary subordination) is based on the person and work of Jesus Christ. "The Discipline of submission has been terribly misconstrued and abused from failure to see this wider context," writes Richard Foster.

Submission is an ethical theme that runs the gamut of the New Testament. It is a posture obligatory upon *all* Christians: *men* as well as women, *fathers* as well as children, *masters* as well as slaves. *We are commanded to live a life of submission because Jesus lived a life of submission*, not because we are in a particular place or station in life. Self-denial is a posture fitting for all those who follow the crucified Lord.[22]

This radical submission is to be evident in every aspect of the lives of Christians, but perhaps most vividly in their communal worship. When Christians break bread and drink the cup they are remembering the revolutionary submission of Christ on the cross.

2. Feetwashing as Sacrifice

When our understanding of eucharistic worship is broadened to include the practice of feetwashing, we are more able to see feetwashing as a sacrificial act. When Christians wash one another's feet, they are offering a sacrifice of their own pride and dignity to God. In the early church, Christians offered their prayers and their very lives as sacrifices unto God.[23] Paul told the Roman believers: "[P]resent your bodies as a living sacrifice, holy and acceptable to God, which is your spiritual worship" (Rom 12:1b). Submitting to one another in feetwashing is a powerful example of Christians offering their bodies as living sacrifices. Vernard Eller explains:

[I]n every way the feetwashing is a more graphic [i.e., visibly powerful] statement than is the breaking of bread. Consider how in the course of time the significance of the *breaking* of bread was lost even to the Lord's Supper; yet any reader of John 13 can immediately tell you what the feetwashing signifies. The action itself is very appropriate: in order to wash another's feet one must kneel, and to kneel is to break one's upright posture, one's posture of self-containment, of being for oneself. One must now break at the knee, break at the waist, break at the neck, break at the elbow. In as clear a way as could be devised, feetwashing says, "My body broken for you."[24]

Eller reminds us of the way that washing feet strengthens the practice of breaking the bread of thanksgiving. Christians most fully remember

22. Foster, *Celebration of Discipline*, 117 (the first emphasis is original).
23. See chapters 3 and 4 above.
24. Eller, *In Place of Sacraments*, 111.

the sacrificial death of Christ on the cross through the sharing of the bread and the cup, the body and blood of Christ, *and* through the living sacrifice of their own broken bodies as they stoop to wash feet.

Of course, this is a much different understanding of eucharistic sacrifice than the conventional view, which focuses on the elements of the bread and cup. Yet it should not be disregarded too quickly. Is it a coincidence that the understanding of the Eucharist as the "unbloody sacrifice" emerged at the end of the fourth century at precisely the same time that Christian feetwashing was fading out of practice? It makes perfect sense that the revolutionary submission embodied in the act of feetwashing could no longer be maintained after Constantine moved Christian worship to the basilicas and made legal changes that quickly enlarged the church. As the "otherness of the church" faded away and the church and world became fused, feetwashing was one of many early church practices that no longer held value in the imperial church. When Christian worship no longer included the washing of feet, which clearly demonstrated submission and sacrifice, the understanding of the sacrifice of the Mass began to emerge, focusing more intently on the substance of the elements than did the early church.

Understanding feetwashing as a eucharistic sacrifice is not limited to the Brethren or the Anabaptists. In his book *God's Companions*, Anglican theologian Samuel Wells also argues that feetwashing should be understood as sacrifice:

> [W]hen disciples wash one another's feet, they enact the most succinct summary of Jesus' whole career that the New Testament offers—a performance of the celebrated hymn of Philippians 2:5–11. Here, perhaps more distinctively than anywhere else in the liturgy, Christians may perceive the significance of sacrifice. Sacrifice is not primarily identified with offering—the "sacrifice" of time, possessions, money, firstfruits, for the sake of the worship of God. This would be a propitiatory reading of sacrifice. Neither is sacrifice primarily identified with the broken body of Christ (portrayed in the breaking of the bread), as a view of the atonement that strongly emphasized the death of Jesus would have it. . . .
>
> But footwashing denotes a third, perhaps most significant dimension of sacrifice. Sacrifice is focused on the moment when Jesus "got up from the table, took off his outer robe, and tied a towel around himself." It is the moment when Jesus relinquished the limitless range of options open to him, and chose a single path. It is more about Bethlehem than Calvary. Sacrifice is the

consequence of following a call: it is an accounting for the roads not yet taken. *Sacrifice is still an integral part of the Christian life, yet it is not a pyre on which a first-born creature burns to appease an angry potentate, but a sober estimate of the personal and corporate cost of following a distinct path and leaving the rest to God.* Temptation—the agony of Gethsemane—pleads that one can make a choice, follow a call, and still leave all the options open. Sacrifice names the discovery that the call to follow Christ still maps out a path via the way of the cross. God's sacrifice is the same as God's choice: never to be except to be for us in Christ. *Our sacrifice mirrors God's, when it is the commitment never to seek any god that is different from the God revealed in Christ. This is enacted every time the disciple leaves the Eucharistic table, lays aside a robe, and puts on a towel.*[25]

Would that the church could reclaim this understanding of eucharistic sacrifice! Would that we could reclaim the regular practice of washing feet! A final word from Wells is insightful: "The great mystery of contemporary liturgy is that the washing of feet is so seldom practiced. Once again, if God gives his people everything they need to follow him by giving them Jesus, the Church, and the Eucharist, *if they do not embrace the whole of what the Eucharist involves* they are in no position to complain that they have not been given everything they need."[26]

3. Learning to Receive

It is an act of submission to be able to receive a gift graciously without having to return the favor. This is one virtue that is extremely hard to practice, for people often feel compelled to reciprocate when someone else gives them a gift. This is not always bad, of course, but there are occasions when trying to give something back in return cheapens the gift first being offered. Many Brethren today wash feet in small groups arranged in a row or a circle, although some still wash feet at the Love Feast table. One member (often a deacon) begins the practice by washing and drying the feet of a neighboring brother or sister. After the service is offered, both members rise and embrace (sometimes a holy kiss is given), whereupon the member who received the washing then turns to wash the feet of the next person in the row or circle. This continues until the last member washes the feet of the person who started the ceremony.

25. Wells, *God's Companions*, 216–17.
26. Ibid., 216 (emphasis added).

The beauty of this practice is that even though all members both receive and give the service of feetwashing, it is not done in pairs, where the act is reciprocated. It is not a situation in which one says figuratively "I'll scratch your back if you scratch mine." Rather, each member graciously receives the act of service from one person, and then graciously offers the same service to a different person; a "pay it forward" system. Christians are to be people who can graciously receive gifts without having to feel the need to give something back in return. This is not done out of selfishness, but rather out of a desire to honor the giver and the service given. Foster concludes:

> It is an act of submission and service to allow others to serve us. It recognizes their "kingdom authority" over us. We graciously receive the service rendered, never feeling we must repay it. Those who, out of pride, refuse to be served are failing to submit to the divinely appointed leadership in the Kingdom of God.[27]

D. FEETWASHING AND THE LOVE FEAST

The practice of feetwashing is important to the celebration of the Love Feast because Jesus clearly links the action with his command for us to love one another. Paul Duke writes:

> Clean for what? For the New Mandate, at last. To his friends with the freshly scrubbed ankles and toes, Jesus, back in his place and reclothed, says, "Do as I have done to you . . ." (v. 15). "I give you a new commandment, that you love one another. Just as I have loved you, you also should love one another" (v. 34). It is worth noticing that in John's Gospel, this is the first positive use of the verb *agapao* for anyone but God and Jesus. In fact, the verb applied to humans has been used three times negatively (3:19; 8:42; 12:43) and the only use of the noun *agape* has been negative (5:42). It is as if human love had been impossible until now. Only after receiving the cleansing sign of Jesus' love for them are the disciples in position to love each other. In more ways than one, this commandment is "new."[28]

Earlier Duke explains: "This text [John 13], like Jesus, takes hold of our feet, then pulls us down a hard path of embarrassment, resistance, acquiescence, assurance—then commands us to get up and love like Christ.

27. Foster, *Celebration of Discipline*, 136–37.
28. Duke, "John 13:1–17, 31b–35," 400.

We may not rise to the mandate ["love one another" v. 34] without being taken down to the bath."[29] We would do well to meditate on that last sentence. *We may not rise to the mandate without being taken down to the bath.* Do we truly believe this? Is it truly necessary for us to wash feet in order to love one another? It is true that many acts of love have been performed by those who have not washed feet. And yet the question remains of whether the fullness of Christ's command to love one another as he loved us can be obeyed apart from the washing of feet. Some believe that the two commands are separate. Why not take the hard path of submission and feetwashing, rather than not doing so and finding out later that we were mistaken? Let us examine more closely a few aspects of practicing feetwashing today.

1. Feetwashing: For the Baptized or Open to All?

Should feetwashing be limited only to those who are baptized Christians, or should guests in the Love Feast be able to participate? In many ways this depends on how each local congregation understands the practice. If feetwashing is understood as simply an act of service, then there is no need to place any restrictions on who participates. There may be occasions when churches will celebrate the Love Feast in a homeless shelter or a nursing home, and in such a public setting (with both Christians and non-Christians) it may be a particularly powerful witness for members of the church to wash the feet of the poor, the infirm, and the stranger.[30] However, in most cases, particularly involving mutual feetwashing, it is probably best for feetwashing to be practiced by baptized Christians. This is because, as we have demonstrated, feetwashing is more than just an act of service. Feetwashing should be understood as sacramental in some sense, a mystery through which believers are cleansed and reconciled to

29. Ibid., 398.

30. Samuel Wells, *God's Companions*, 219, writes: "[I]f making the whole world a Eucharist is too broad or vague a commission, the place to start is by washing feet. Washing feet means beginning with human touch, and trusting the encounters that gentle touch may provoke. It means not fearing taboos, daring to accompany shunned people, and being willing to help people engage parts of themselves they would rather ignore. It means seeing the person through the soiled barriers, much as a parent or caregiver sees a child with love, rather than a full diaper with disgust. It means never seeing another person as beneath oneself, since they are never lower than Christ. Archbishop Oscar Romero famously said 'our task is to put feet on the Gospel': this task is never more appropriately performed than in washing feet."

Christ and his body, the church. Understood in this fashion, then, one must first receive the initial cleansing of baptism before one can participate in a ceremonial cleansing of post-baptismal sin. Moreover, following our theme of submission, it is unreasonable to ask people who have not already committed their lives to Christ and the church to participate in this practice that involves submitting to Christ and our brothers and sisters. Since feetwashing today is seen as an abnormal and uncomfortable practice, it is unlikely that many non-Christians will object to being asked simply to observe the service.

2. How Often Should Feetwashing Be Practiced?

How often should feetwashing be practiced with the Love Feast? According to the old Brethren, every time, although each congregation only celebrated the Love Feast one or two times a year. If congregations choose to celebrate the Love Feast only once or twice a year, then feetwashing should be an important element of these celebrations. However, I am of the mind that the Love Feast should be celebrated more than twice a year; perhaps monthly for congregations (and maybe more frequently for house churches or other groups that regularly gather around a table for worship). The Love Feast is simply too valuable a practice to celebrate it only twice a year. If churches experiment with celebrating the Love Feast more often, I do not see a problem with feetwashing being left out of some of these services, as long as it is practiced at other times. In fact, there may be some occasions when Love Feasts are held in settings that are not conducive to feetwashing. This seems to be a reasonable accommodation, especially since feetwashing is not a normal societal practice today.

3. Is Feetwashing Relevant?

There are some people who argue that feetwashing is no longer a relevant practice for the church. This challenge is summarized by Vernard Eller:

> Granted, there are some people (even among the Brethren, whose Supper has always included feetwashing) who [object] on the grounds that the very act of baring one's own feet or of washing another's is distasteful and impolite. Their argument is that feetwashing was an accepted custom in Jesus' day but one that is completely foreign to us. Nevertheless, it must be recalled that Jesus chose to wash the disciples' feet precisely *because* of

the offense and scandal involved. It is true that the offense was not related to delicate feelings about bare feet; it came at a much deeper, a much more scandalous level, and one we hardly are in [a] position to appreciate. Yes, feet were publicly washed in Jesus' day—but no one but slaves were expected to do it. Jesus washed feet as a way of demonstrating that he was willing to make himself a slave out of love for his brethren. It is certain that he did not do it for the sake of any pleasurable sensations involved. And Peter's response, "I will never let you wash my feet," indicates something of the shock he felt. *Thank God feetwashing is still somewhat distasteful; otherwise we would miss the point entirely.*[31]

The question of relevance completely misses the point. Submitting to Christ and to one another is not a question of relevance, but rather of discipleship. Christ's command to wash feet in John 13 is not limited to the original cultural setting, just as his command to love one another in the same chapter transcends cultural boundaries. In fact, over the last several decades the trend has been that Christian denominations that traditionally did not practice feetwashing are beginning to reclaim the practice, even in the face of its current cultural irrelevance. This does not mean that the practice cannot be adapted somewhat to reflect cultural values (e.g., many Brethren congregations today add Lysol to the feet-washing water to kill germs, even though such a product did not exist in biblical times). However, when the question of cultural relevance is raised with the goal of ceasing the practice of feetwashing, it should be rejected on the grounds of false reasoning.

4. What About Handwashing?

In recent years some congregations have instituted the practice of hand-washing for those members who have physical disabilities that prevent them from stooping to wash feet. On the whole there is no problem with handwashing, as long as it remains the exception rather than the rule. If churches prefer handwashing because it is less uncomfortable than feetwashing, then they have missed the mark entirely. Feetwashing and handwashing are not about comfort, they are about submission. The practices are also about communal obedience, and not just the obedience of the individual. This means that there is value in everyone who is able to participate together in the same act, rather than making prepara-

---

31. Eller, *In Place of Sacraments*, 112–13 (the second emphasis is mine).

tions for both handwashing and feetwashing and allowing members to choose which cleansing act in which to participate. By doing this the church prevents fickleness from becoming the norm (e.g., today I feel like washing hands, but next time I'll probably wash feet). Thus, for those who cannot physically bend down to wash feet, handwashing offers an appropriate alternative so that these members can still participate in the practice of cleansing and submission.

> After [Jesus] had washed their feet, had put on his robe, and had returned to the table, he said to them, "Do you know what I have done to you? You call me Teacher and Lord—and you are right, for that is what I am. So if I, your Lord and Teacher, have washed your feet, you also ought to wash one another's feet. For I have set you an example, that you also should do as I have done to you.
>
> —JOHN 13:12–15

> To wash the feet of a brother or sister in Christ, to allow someone to wash our feet, is a sign that together we want to follow Jesus, to take the downward path, to find Jesus' presence in the poor and the weak. Is it not a sign that we too want to live a heart-to-heart relationship with others, to meet them as a person and a friend, and to live in communion with them? Is it not a sign also that we yearn to be men and women of forgiveness, to be healed and cleansed and to heal and cleanse others and thus to live more fully in communion with Jesus?
>
> —JEAN VANIER[32]

---

32. Vanier, *The Scandal of Service*, 85–86.

8

Formed to Love

Eating With One Another, Strangers, and even Enemies

"You shall love the Lord your God with all your heart, and with all your soul, and with all your mind." This is the greatest and first commandment. And a second is like it: "You shall love your neighbor as yourself."

—MATT 22:37b–39

Let love (*agape*) be genuine; hate what is evil, hold fast to what is good; love (*philadelphia*) one another with mutual affection (*philostorgoi*); outdo one another in showing honor. Do not lag in zeal, be ardent in spirit, serve the Lord. Rejoice in hope, be patient in suffering, persevere in prayer. Contribute to the needs of the saints; extend hospitality (*philoxenia*) to strangers. . . .

Beloved, never avenge yourselves, but leave room for the wrath of God; for it is written, "Vengeance is mine, I will repay, says the Lord." No, "if your enemies are hungry, feed them; if they are thirsty, give them something to drink; for by doing this you will heap burning coals on their heads." Do not be overcome by evil, but overcome evil with good.

—ROM 12:9–13, 19–21

> Given the centrality of common meals in the early Church—
> in a substantial and not merely token form—perhaps the
> most obvious [liturgical] recovery [is] the *agape*. . . . Even
> if it need not be a feature of every communion service,
> *Eucharist in the context of a shared substantial meal should*
> *be a regular part of the Christian experience of worship.*
>
> —Robert Song[1]

It seems obvious that love should be a theme of the Love Feast. Yet too often the celebration of the Lord's Supper would not appear to an outsider to be either celebratory or love-filled. Rather, it is often a somber affair characterized by mournful or morbid thoughts connected with the death of Christ. Many eucharistic practices today barely resemble the earliest practices, when celebrating the Love Feast was undoubtedly a chief example of the Christian practice of loving one another. The breaking of bread brought together Jewish and Gentile Christians, poor and rich, women and men, slaves and masters—something that was quite noticeable in societies that rarely sought to bridge the gap between these different groups. Recovering the original practice of celebrating the Eucharist along with a fellowship meal will help the church to witness to God's love by sharing food together.

In this chapter we explore how the Love Feast is most fundamentally an expression of love to God. We also examine how the fellowship meal helps to form Christians to love members within the church, strangers outside the church, and even enemies, both personal and corporate. Lastly, we explore a few ideas of how the fellowship meal might be a vital part of the celebration of the Love Feast today.

A. LOVING GOD: A HOLY CELEBRATION

Expressing love toward God is the most fundamental love in the Love Feast. Jesus told his disciples that the greatest commandment is to "love the Lord your God with all your heart, and with all your soul, and with all your mind" (Matt 22:37b). This love is not self-initiated; rather, "We love because [God] first loved us" (1 John 4:19). Thus, at the most basic level the Love Feast is an expression of our love for God, love that is only possible because we have received love from God (most powerfully

1. Song, "Sharing Communion," 394 (emphasis added).

revealed through the person and work of Jesus Christ). No action that conflicts with loving God should be practiced in the Love Feast. This is what distinguished the Christian Love Feast from the so-called love feasts celebrated by groups like the Carpocratians.[2] Even though they were called *agapae*, these "love feasts" were displays of passionate love (*eros*) rather than actions based on the pure love (*agape*) of God. It will be helpful to discuss briefly the act of celebration.

It is important for the church to reclaim an understanding of celebration as a sacred act of worship. The word "celebrate" originally entered language as a description of how "to do" the Eucharist, that is, the church celebrates Communion (or the Eucharist or the Mass) on Sunday. The term now has a much wider meaning; we celebrate birthday parties and fourth-of-July picnics, and the finishing of large projects. Nothing is inherently wrong with calling these occasions "celebrations." There are many blessings in life for which we should give thanks to God! However, we should also be careful to distinguish between celebrating a birthday, for instance, and celebrating the Love Feast. For the church's eucharistic celebration is of much greater importance than celebrating the gift of another year of life for one individual. Put differently, we must remember that the *object* of our celebration is crucial to evaluating its relative worth. Vernard Eller writes that things went wrong when

> it was decided that "celebrate" could retain its religious value and overtones but drop any reference to an object (or settle for the vaguest sort of object: celebrate "life," "our being human," or "the celebrativity of celebration"). Now "celebration" is a religious value (even a *Christian* value) in and of itself, without regard for what is being celebrated, whether it merits celebration, or how it is to be celebrated.[3]

How we celebrate is important! Paul condemns the Corinthians for getting drunk at the Lord's Supper (1 Cor 11:21–22). Thus, not all celebrations are equal or appropriate.

Christian celebration comes in and through obedience to God. Richard Foster writes, "In the spiritual life there is only one thing that will produce genuine joy, and that is obedience. . . . Joy comes through obedience to Christ, and joy results from obedience to Christ. Without obedience, joy is hollow and artificial. To elicit genuine celebration,

2. See the discussion of the fellowship meal in chapter 4, specifically the section on Clement of Alexandria.

3. Eller, *In Place of Sacraments*, 17.

obedience must work itself into the ordinary fabric of our daily lives."[4]
There is no other way to be happy in Jesus, says the old hymn, than to
trust and obey. Our celebration of the Love Feast is rooted in loving
God and obeying his commands. It is necessary to emphasize this distinction today, for there are other "love feasts" in contemporary culture
that are not grounded in obedience to God. In doing research for this
book I discovered a recent film titled "The Feast of Love," which is rated
R for nudity and strong sexual content. I have no idea what the film
is about, but its existence demonstrates that even today celebrating a
Love Feast can still be confused with sexual love. Other examples of the
ambiguity of the word love are the "Love Parades," which were first held
in cities across Europe and later spawned the "LoveFest" parade held in
San Francisco.[5] Nudity is common in these parades (at least in Europe),
which do not celebrate Christian love but rather "celebrate" love that is
free from any moral restrictions. These two examples show that celebrating the Love Feast may still be confused with other cultural practices that
are antithetical to the love of God. This does not mean that we should
name our celebration differently (although churches in San Francisco or
Berlin might find it beneficial to use some other name, e.g., *agape* meal);
it just means that we have to be clear that our Love Feast is defined by
loving God and following the law of Christ. When we love God, this love
overflows in loving our brothers and sisters in Christ.

B. LOVING ONE ANOTHER: FEASTING IN THE CHURCH

While there are many ways in which we demonstrate love for one another, there is one in particular that has declined appreciably in many
Christian communities, and that is the sharing of food together, or feasting. Indeed, we have seen that Christian worship in the early church
was called a Love Feast, and yet many churches today do not emphasize
feasting, nor do they consider feasting to be a primary example of love

---

4. Foster, *Celebration of Discipline*, 192.

5. The first Love Parade was held in Berlin in 1989, a few months after the fall of
the Berlin Wall. Love Parades are held annually in Berlin and other European cities
and draw crowds numbering in the hundreds of thousands. The events are huge dance
parties, featuring electronic dance music, which afterwards spill over into clubs and dis-
cothèques. Love Parades are opportunities to "celebrate" publicly a variety of alternative
lifestyles. For more information, see www.loveparade.net and www.sflovefest.org.

within the church.[6] This should not be the case. The feast of the church, the fellowship meal, should be an expression of love within the community of faith, a practical way to love our brothers and sisters in Christ. At the same time, people in the world are welcomed in to share food and drink with members of the church, for, as is made clear in the title of John Koenig's book, the Eucharist is the feast of the world's redemption.[7] Shannon Jung makes a helpful distinction, namely, to talk of *sharing food* within the context of the church and *extending hospitality* to those outside the church.[8] Thus, in this section we address how the fellowship meal is an opportunity to share food with other members of the congregation, and in the next section we examine how we might also include strangers in our feasting.

1. The Importance of Feasting[9]

Humans are created with the need to celebrate and to feast. Feasting belongs to the deepest, most primitive level of human life and culture. Not surprisingly, the most important feature of early Christian worship was feasting together, celebrating the Love Feast, sharing the Lord's Supper, celebrating the Eucharist. Although over the centuries some aspects of this eucharistic feast have been neglected, it is still the case that feasting is an essential practice for the church. June Goudey states: "When Jesus calls us to abundant life, he calls us to experience life as a feast, a feast of meanings, a feast of opportunities, and a feast of possibilities. To be invited to such a feast is to make Eucharist, to offer thanks for divine and diverse epiphanies of love that nurture toward well-being. Would that more of us could welcome his invitation."[10] What would it look like for feasting to be once again a communal practice of the church? How does feasting form us to love one another? And what exactly is feasting, anyhow?

Feasting should not be understood as consuming massive quantities of food and drink, but rather as a communal practice of celebration. Shannon Jung writes:

6. Indeed, the word "feast" today usually means a meal eaten with a group during which we eat in excess, as at Thanksgiving.

7. Koenig, *Feast of the World's Redemption.*

8. See his chapter, "Sharing and Hospitality," in Jung, *Sharing Food*, 38–54.

9. See the chapter "Feasting in Community," in ibid., 55–69.

10. Goudey, *The Feast of Our Lives*, 172, quoted in Jung, *Sharing Food*, 55.

There is an essential truth underlying affluent people's sense that simply eating and drinking in excess does not constitute a feast. Rather, the act of feasting arises from the celebration of a community. Thus the broader issue concerns the strength of community and our ability to take delight, to celebrate together, to make community together.

In the post-9/11 climate of national security and war, we have become fearful as a people. Fear has a tendency to destroy social bonds and threaten relations of trust. In a culture where a sense of community was already attenuated, fear can heighten our individualism and render celebration even more problematic.[11]

In a culture characterized by consumerism, fear, and weak communal bonds, feasting is frequently misunderstood as individual indulgence and is limited to family or institutional settings, rather than open to the wider community. In contrast to this understanding, Jung outlines four elements of Christian feasting: (1) feasting is joy-full; (2) feasting is doxological; (3) feasting grows out of a sense of God's abundance and generosity; and (4) feasting is a communal celebration that transforms us.[12] This last characteristic is particularly relevant to our current discussion, for celebrating the fellowship meal is a primary way in which members of the church are formed and transformed to love one another.

Before moving on, it is important to mention a corresponding practice to feasting, and that is fasting. Feasting and fasting are essentially two sides of a coin representing Christian practices of eating. We cannot have one without the other, or else our understanding of food and communal celebration will become warped. Richard Foster describes the relationship in this way: "Fasting reminds us that we are sustained 'by every word that proceeds from the mouth of God' (Matt 4:4) . . . [I]n experiences of fasting we are not so much abstaining from food as we are feasting on the word of God. Fasting is feasting!"[13] Our fasting sharpens the joy of eating. When we have felt the pangs of hunger, we can appreciate more fully the experience of feasting. "If you never fast," writes pastor Mark Buchanan, "then the whole concept of being wholly nourished and sustained by God's word will be only a nice, sweet and totally irrelevant thought. You may pay the idea lip service, but you'll be too busy licking sauce off your lips to do any more. And worse: if you never fast, you may not stand when the day

11. Jung, *Sharing Food*, 57.

12. Ibid., 62–65.

13. Foster, *Celebration of Discipline*, 55.

of testing and temptation comes."[14] Thus, the discipline of fasting is important for the church, even—or perhaps especially—as we reclaim the importance of feasting in our common life and worship.

2. Sharing Food

In John's account of the Last Supper, Jesus says to his disciples: "I give you a new commandment, that you love one another. Just as I have loved you, you also should love one another" (13:34). In the previous chapter we observed that this command was related to the act of feetwashing; how submitting to one another and washing feet is an act of sacrificial love. Now we focus on the fact that this command came in the context of a meal. For Jesus, sharing food with people was demonstrating love, and he constantly went out of his way to eat with people who were rejected by the Jewish culture. Yet even as he pushed out the boundaries of the community of faith, he continued to emphasize the importance of loving one another within that community ("By this everyone will know that you are my disciples, if you have love for one another," 13:35).[15] The New Testament and the writings of the early church make it clear that breaking bread together bore witness to the revolutionary love in the church, love that made it possible for Jewish and Gentile believers, women and men, rich and poor, slaves and free people to eat together. It is no wonder that the meal became known as a Love Feast.[16] There are several ways that celebrating the fellowship meal today continues to show this love.

14. Buchanan, "Go Fast and Live," 16, quoted in Jung, *Food for Life*, 110.

15. Victor Furnish, *The Love Command*, 139, writes: "That the commandment to love one another forms Jesus' followers into a community and provides it its identity in the world is clearly indicated in 13:35: 'By this love you have for one another, everyone will know that you are my disciples' (JB). Not just the *possession* of the commandment (which in any case is not unique to the Christian community) but the manifest reality of the love it commands is to characterize Jesus' disciples."

16. We could also examine 1 Cor 11–14 to see how love was essential to the mealtime worship of the church. John Koenig comments on this passage: "All members are to welcome one another with a joyful expectation that mutual needs and ministries will converge during the eucharistic meal in such a way that everyone will be 'built up.' This is not an easy mind-set for selfish and impatient humans to adopt, even those baptized into Christ's body. That is why Paul inserts his now famous hymn to love into his discussion of worship. If we understand the following words primarily as instructions on how to treat one's neighbor in an exchange of spiritual gifts and ministries at table, they take on a new specificity [1 Cor 13]. Here we find Paul's exposition of the Lord's Supper as a love feast. The clear implication is that not only during the prescribed time of worship but also in daily life, a deep respect for neighbors that honors their value, contrary to any negative feelings one may have toward them, must become the community's norm.

A. POTLUCK MEALS

We show our love for one another by cooking food and sharing it with one another. There is a goodness experienced in eating food prepared by other people in the church. In my congregation, different members are known for their particularly good contributions to our meals: biscuits, pickles, Asian salad, chicken casserole, deviled eggs, and, of course, éclair cake and apple pie! Sharing potluck meals helps us to value equally the contributions of others in the church and allows us to taste foods that we may not normally eat.

B. ECONOMIC SOLIDARITY WITHIN THE CONGREGATION

Reclaiming regular fellowship meals, particularly potlucks, also helps to break down economic barriers in the church. It is an injustice when some members of the church have more than enough food and money, while others are skipping meals because they cannot afford to buy food. Yoder writes:

> It is not enough to say merely that in an act of "institution" or symbol-making, independent of ordinary meanings, God or the church would have said, "Let us say that 'bread' stands for daily sustenance." . . . It is that bread *is* daily sustenance. Bread eaten together *is* economic sharing. Not merely symbolically, but also in fact, eating together extends to a wider circle the economic solidarity normally obtained in the family. . . . In short, the Eucharist is an economic act. To do rightly the practice of breaking bread together is a matter of economic ethics.[17]

Sharing food in the church is but one example of how Christian love breaks down economic barriers. We may find that, in our current context of economic unrest, returning to the regular practice of eating together will not only more strongly unite the body of Christ in love, but also will be a powerful witness of love to those in the community who have economic need.

For Paul, growth in such love is most effectively stimulated during the celebration of the holy meal. Here, in the 'table manners' of the assembly, love becomes most visible—or most tragically absent. Once again we catch sight of the apocalyptic and missionary dimensions of the Lord's Supper in Paul's understanding. For him, each meal setting presents itself as a decisive moment in the progress of salvation; it is either a time of joyful upbuilding or a painful judgment upon believers by the risen Christ (11:29–32)," Koenig, *Feast of the World's Redemption*, 120–21.

17. Yoder, *Body Politics*, 20–21. (emphasis in original)

C. LOVING STRANGERS: EXTENDING HOSPITALITY

The Love Feast fellowship meal should not be thought of as primarily for the church, however; it is clear from the New Testament and from the early church writings that outsiders and strangers were welcome to eat and to participate. One of Paul's key reasons for instructing the Corinthian church to worship "decently and in order" (1 Cor 14:40) was so that outsiders and unbelievers would not be distracted, but rather meaningfully engaged and (hopefully) drawn into worship themselves.[18] Their worship was, of course, connected with their fellowship meal, and in Corinth, at least, outsiders were present. Moreover, Paul's instruction to the Romans to extend hospitality to strangers follows on the heels of his instructions describing the church's worship: "Let love (*agape*) be genuine; hate what is evil, hold fast to what is good; love (*philadelphia*) one another with mutual affection (*philostorgoi*); outdo one another in showing honor. Do not lag in zeal, be ardent in spirit, serve the Lord. Rejoice in hope, be patient in suffering, persevere in prayer. Contribute to the needs of the saints; extend hospitality (*philoxenia*) to strangers" (Rom 12:9–13). Both Tertullian and Augustine described the Love Feast as benefiting the needy in the community. Should not Love Feasts today be an opportunity for the poor and the stranger to be loved and to eat a good meal?

In her book *Making Room: Recovering Hospitality as a Christian Tradition*, Christine Pohl argues that the church today must do a better job of extending hospitality. She writes:

> Hospitality is not optional for Christians, nor is it limited to those who are specially gifted for it. It is, instead, a necessary practice in the community of faith. One of the key Greek words for hospitality, *philoxenia*, combines the general word for love or affection for people who are connected by kinship or faith (*phileo*), and the word for stranger (*xenos*). Thus, etymologically and practically, in the New Testament, hospitality is closely connected to love. Because *philoxenia* includes the word for stranger, hospitality's

---

18. "If, therefore, the whole church comes together and all speak in tongues, and outsiders or unbelievers enter, will they not say that you are out of your mind? But if all prophesy, an unbeliever or outsider who enters is reproved by all and called to account by all. After the secrets of the unbeliever's heart are disclosed, that person will bow down before God and worship him, declaring, 'God is really among you'" (1 Cor 14:23–25).

orientation toward strangers is also more apparent in Greek than in English.[19]

It is notable that the English word "hospitality" is, in Greek, a compound word that literally means loving strangers. While hospitality involves many actions, it almost always includes offering food and drink. Pohl continues:

> Eating together, ritualized in the Lord's Supper, continually re-enacts the center of the gospel. As we remember the cost of our welcome, Christ's broken body and shed blood, we also celebrate the reconciliation and relationship available to us because of his sacrifice and through his hospitality. The Eucharist most fundamentally connects hospitality with God because it anticipates and reveals the "heavenly table of the Lord." In that sacrament, we are nourished on our journey towards God's banquet table, even as we experience the present joy and welcome associated with sharing in that table. A shared meal is the activity most closely tied to the reality of God's Kingdom, just as it is the most basic expression of hospitality.[20]

There is hardly a more appropriate way for the church to love strangers than to invite them to share food with us in a fellowship meal. As David Kirk wonderfully puts it, *"Hospitality becomes, for the Christian community, a way of being the sacrament of God's love in the world."*[21]

D. LOVING ENEMIES

The Love Feast also helps to form members of the church to love their enemies. In the New Testament, the command to "love your enemies" is only found coming from the mouth of Jesus (Matt 5:44; Luke 6:27, 35).[22] However, in Rom 12, where Paul instructs the church on the proper

---

19. Pohl, *Making Room*, 31.

20. Ibid., 30.

21. Kirk, "Hospitality," 112 (emphasis added), quoted in Pohl, *Making Room*, 34.

22. The full quotation from Matthew reads: "You have heard that it was said, 'You shall love your neighbor and hate your enemy.' But I say to you, Love your enemies and pray for those who persecute you, so that you may be children of your Father in heaven; for he makes his sun rise on the evil and on the good, and sends rain on the righteous and on the unrighteous. For if you love those who love you, what reward do you have? Do not even the tax collectors do the same? And if you greet only your brothers and sisters, what more are you doing than others? Do not even the Gentiles do the same?" (Matt 5:43–47).

practices of mealtime worship, he also stresses the Christian duty to act lovingly toward enemies.[23] After describing how Christian brothers and sisters are to love one another and to show love to strangers, he states: "'if your enemies are hungry, feed them; if they are thirsty, give them something to drink; for by doing this you will heap burning coals on their heads [Prov 25:21–22].' Do not be overcome by evil, but overcome evil with good" (Rom 12:20–21). In the context of ch. 12, which speaks of believers offering their bodies to God as spiritual worship and extending hospitality to strangers, it is logical that when Paul instructs the church to give food and drink to enemies, he means during their worship meals, that is, during the Love Feast. If this is not the case, then why does Paul insert the quotation from Proverbs (mentioning food and drink) in the midst of his discussion on worship practices? Our celebration of the Love Feast today should also be an opportunity for us to demonstrate love for our enemies by welcoming them to the meal.

Before we examine the impact of loving our enemies more closely, it should be clearly stated what loving our enemies *does not entail.* Loving our enemies does not mean approving of their actions. It does not mean that our differences are unimportant. It does not mean that we have to like them. It is significant that only the verb *agapao* is used to name our love of the enemy. The *Complete Word Study Dictionary* states:

> *Agapao,* and never *phileo,* is used of love toward our enemies. The range of *phileo* is wider than that of *agapao,* which stands higher than *phileo* because of its moral import (i.e., love that expresses compassion). We are thus commanded to love (*agapao*) our enemies, to do what is necessary to turn them to Christ, but never to befriend them (*phileo*) by adopting their interests and becoming friends on their level.[24]

Of course, it is the hope of the Christian that our love will be used by God to transform our enemies so that it may indeed be possible for reconciliation, and perhaps even friendship.

---

23. Paul does not specifically say "love your enemies"; only Jesus does. However, when, in the context of instructing the church to love one another and to love strangers, he says to give enemies food and drink, it seems clear that this is an outward expression of love for one's enemies.

24. Zodhiates, *The Complete Word Study Dictionary: New Testament,* 66.

1. How Loving Our Enemies Can Transform Them

When we love our enemies by giving them food and drink, the author of Proverbs writes that we "heap coals of fire on their heads" (25:22). This is a poetic way of saying that we are used to bring the fire of God's judgment upon them, which hopefully leads them to repentance. Walter Wink explains how Jesus clarifies the purpose of God's judgment:

> Jesus . . . understood judgment not as an end but as a beginning. The penitential river of fire was not to consume but purify, not annihilate but redeem (Luke 15:1–32; 18:9–14). Divine judgment is intended not to destroy but to awaken people to the devastating truth about their lives. Jesus seizes the apocalyptic vision of impending doom and hurls it into the present time, into the present encounter with God's unexpected and unaccountable forgiveness. Judgment no longer is the last crushing word on a failed life, but the first word of a new creation.
>
> Jesus lived this new creation out in his table fellowship with those whom the religious establishment had branded outcasts, sinners, renegades: the enemies of God. He did not wait for them to repent, become respectable, and do works of restitution in hope of gaining divine forgiveness and human restoration. Instead, he audaciously burst upon these sinners with the declaration that their sins had been forgiven, prior to their repentance, prior to their having done any acts of restitution or reconciliation. Everything is reversed: you are forgiven; now you can repent! God loves you; now you can lift your eyes to God! The enmity is over. You were enemies and yet God accepts you! There is nothing you must do to earn this. You need only to accept it.[25]

While Jesus' love for enemies is most *powerfully* demonstrated on the cross, it is most *frequently* demonstrated in his table fellowship with prostitutes, tax collectors, and other sinners. Time and again we find Jesus eating with people who have done nothing to deserve an audience with the Son of God.[26] Will we do the same today? Will our Love Feasts include our enemies? For by sharing food with our enemies, walls of

25. Wink, *The Powers that Be*, 163–64. Wink observes, "Jesus' understanding is scarcely reflected in most Christian worship services, which make forgiveness conditional on repentance," p. 164.

26. Conrad Gempf, *Mealtime Habits of the Messiah*, 133, notes the absurdity of this mealtime fellowship when he writes: "For a first century Jew, having dinner with someone was making a statement about acceptance and about religious fellowship. Supper was not just sustenance; supper was spirituality. Doing lunch was doing theology."

hostility are (at least temporarily) breached, and God's love and forgiveness are made manifest.

2. How Loving Our Enemies Can Transform Us

Loving our enemies is a two-way affair; it can transform us as well as them. Walter Wink calls this "the gift of the enemy." He explains:

> [T]he gift our enemy brings us [is] *to see aspects of ourselves that we cannot discover any other way.* Our friends are not good sources of information about these things; they often overlook or ignore these parts of us. The enemy is thus not merely a hurdle to be leapt on the way to God. The enemy *can be* the way to God. We cannot come to terms with our shadow except through our enemy, for we have no better access to those unacceptable parts of ourselves that need redeeming than through the mirror that our enemies hold up to us. . . . How wonderfully humiliating: we not only may have a role in transforming our enemies, but our enemies can play a role in transforming us![27]

It could very well be that our avoidance of loving our enemies may be holding us back from the transformation that God desires to awaken within us. Yet "God's forgiving love can burst like a flare even in the night of our grief and hatred and free us to love," writes Wink. "There is a subtle pride in clinging to our hatreds as justified, as if our enemies had passed beyond even God's capacity to love and forgive, as if no one in human history had known sufferings greater than ours, as if Jesus' sufferings were inadequate and puny alongside what we have faced."[28] By choosing to love our enemies, rather than hate them, we loose ourselves from this pride and open ourselves to the possibility that God might use our enemies to reveal other areas of sin in our lives. Loving our enemies is a way of "living in expectation of miracles. . . . People can, and do, change, and their change can make a fundamental difference. We must pray for our enemies [and ourselves], because God is already at work in their depths [and in our depths], stirring up the desire to be just."[29]

27. Wink, *The Powers that Be*, 170–71 (emphasis in original).
28. Ibid., 176.
29. Ibid., 178–79.

E. THE FELLOWSHIP MEAL AND THE LOVE FEAST

What does this mean for the celebration of the Love Feast? Let us consider a few suggestions.

1. A Meal of Love and Celebration

The fellowship meal is an occasion for Christian love to be embodied. It is a reflection of our love of God and our obedience to God's Word. This love is also expressed to our brothers and sisters in the church as we gather to eat together. The world should know we are Christians by our love, especially as demonstrated in our occasions of eating together. The fellowship meal should stand out from cultural feasts in the way that it includes strangers and possibly even enemies. The fellowship meal celebrates the presence of the resurrected Christ among and within his church. Accordingly, it should be a joyful feast, not a solemn occasion. Songs and confessions of praise are appropriate before, during, or after the meal. The meal should not be eaten in silence, for this detracts from the celebratory mood.[30]

2. The Menu Matters

Marshall McLuhan famously stated, "The medium is the message."[31] Applying this maxim to the fellowship meal, if the food tastes bad, so does the message. Since the meal is to be characterized by celebration, the food should reflect this. In my view, the traditional Brethren meal of dipping bread into sop should be discontinued. Overall, the practice of having a potluck fellowship meal is much more commendable. In this way, every person or family has the opportunity (and the responsibility) to contribute something to the common meal (even if it is only five loaves and two fish!). Homemade dishes are to be preferred over

---

30. Brethren congregations that still eat the meal in silence should recognize that this practice is based on the *Apostolic Tradition* and not on the practice of the early church. Moreover, when the Brethren celebrated a two-day Love Feast, the Saturday lunch fellowship meal was a time of joyful reacquaintance with friends and relatives from around the region, while the evening meal was eaten in silence. When the celebration was condensed into a single evening, some congregations seem to have held on to the practice of eating in silence. This is lamentable. Have we completely forgotten the joyful celebration of the risen Lord in our midst? Can we truly eat a celebratory meal in silence?

31. McLuhan, *Understanding Media*, 7.

processed foods and packaged items. Care should be taken to avoid the overconsumption of fattening or unhealthy foods (perhaps churches could provide some basic instruction on nutrition?).[32]

3. How Often Should We Celebrate the Love Feast?

While there should be no standard set in stone, a good principle would be to celebrate the Love Feast as often as is reasonably possible, depending on the contexts of each specific church. This is a significant difference from the contemporary Brethren practice of celebrating the Love Feast twice a year. However, if the celebration of the Love Feast is to have any meaningful impact on the formation of character within the Christian community, it must be practiced more frequently. For some churches, especially those that meet in homes, it may be possible to celebrate the Love Feast weekly. Other congregations might find it more appropriate to have a fellowship meal monthly. While both feetwashing and the fellowship meal are important practices, it is more important to celebrate the fellowship meal frequently. Accordingly, it may be the case that the actual act of washing feet is only observed quarterly or twice a year, with the other fellowship meals including some other form of submission in the place of feetwashing.

4. Who Should Participate in the Fellowship Meal?

Everyone. All are welcome at the table of the Lord. Everyone can eat and drink in the meal of the church. This means not only those who are members of a particular church, but also non-members. It means that we should welcome the poor, those who we do not know, and even those who are our enemies, to eat with us. It may also mean that we may need to take our fellowship meal out to other people rather than expecting them to come inside the walls of our church buildings. Perhaps a recovery of the Love Feast celebration can alleviate some of the division that currently exists in the Christian body concerning open and close communion. If our communion service is connected to a meal in

---

32. Since America is in the midst of an obesity epidemic, we in the church should do our part to help those who struggle with overeating or eating unhealthy foods. Is this not a direct application of the Apostle Paul's teaching to the church in Rome: "Do not, for the sake of food, destroy the work of God. Everything is indeed clean, but it is wrong for you to make others fall by what you eat; it is good not to eat meat or drink wine or do anything that makes your brother or sister stumble" (Rom 14:20–21).

which everyone can participate, then perhaps it will not come across as exclusivistic if some churches prefer to limit the celebration of the Eucharist to those who have been baptized. If those who are not a part of the church have the opportunity to eat Aunt Judy's chicken and Steve's macaroni and cheese, and the opportunity to share in spiritual conversation with Chris and Rebecca, all in a context where Christ is honored, then it should not be too great a problem if they are asked to refrain from participating in one aspect of the celebration reserved for those who have been baptized.

5. Should Communion Accompany the Fellowship Meal?

Yes. We recall that the Eucharist was originally a part of a fellowship meal. It is entirely appropriate for our contemporary celebration of Communion to be in the context of a meal. It does not seem to be of great importance whether the meal precedes Communion or follows after it; some churches may prefer to start the meal with the Eucharist, while others may wish to end the meal with the bread and cup. Or some might even choose to do both, beginning the meal with the Eucharist and ending with a cup of blessing.[33] Some churches use homemade bread and/or locally-made wine (or grape juice), rather than store-bought products.

How will the world recognize Christians today? Perhaps a new worship song will emerge with a chorus that goes: "And they'll know we are Christians by our Love Feast, by our Love Feast, yes they'll know we are Christians by our Love Feast?"

The eucharistic feast Christians share is believed to anticipate the heavenly peace. . . . Christian peace is one that makes them friends of God, one another, and the stranger. Christians, therefore, were and are obligated to offer hospitality to the stranger, a stranger they hope may become a friend, having learned from their Lord that he will continue to make himself known in the face of the hungry and despised. Christian witness will continue to be identified not by those to whom Christians give money, but by those with whom Christians take time to eat.

—STANLEY HAUERWAS AND SAMUEL WELLS[34]

33. See Luke's account of the Last Supper, 22:14–23. Also see Eller, *In Place of Sacraments*, 132–44.

34. Hauerwas and Wells, "How the Church Managed before there Was Ethics," 42.

The mystery which sets the Lord's table apart is that it is a common table of humanity, but transformed through acted memory by Christ's own presence and love. If churches reclaim real meals as the setting for communion services, if they replace (or supplement) the ceremonial table with the dining table, surprising things might happen. The enormous symbolic power in the table, with its rituals of hospitality, conviviality, blessing, and shared food might once again enable congregations corporately and radically to imitate Christ and to be more attractively recognized as his very own people.

—ELEANOR KREIDER[35]

35. Kreider, *Communion Shapes Character*, 27.

9

Formed to Confess

Reclaiming a Broad Understanding of Confession

If you confess with your lips that Jesus is Lord and believe
in your heart that God raised him from the dead, you will
be saved. For one believes with the heart and so is justified, and one confesses with the mouth and so is saved.

—ROM 10:9–10

A threefold confession is commended by the Scriptures.
One is the confession of matters of faith, and this is
a proper act of faith, since it is referred to the end of
faith . . . Another is the confession of thanksgiving or
praise, and this is an act of adoration, for its purpose is to
give outward honour to God, which is the end of adoration. The third is the confession of sins, which is ordained
to the blotting out of sins, which is the end of penance, to
which virtue it therefore belongs.

—THOMAS AQUINAS[1]

THE CELEBRATION OF THE Love Feast should help the church to
confess faith, confess praise, and confess sins. Rightly practiced, the
Love Feast can help the church to understand both the corporate and
the individual dimensions of confession. The current chapter begins by
defining confession, noting that it is broader than just confessing sins. In
the next several sections we examine the confession of faith, the confes-

---

1. Aquinas, *Summa Theologica*, Part II-II, q.3.1, 400–401.

sion of praise, and the confession of sin. The chapter concludes with a reflection on the importance of practicing confession during the Love Feast.

A. BROADENING OUR UNDERSTANDING OF CONFESSION

1. Common Understandings of Confession

When one hears the word "confession" today, it is most commonly understood to mean an acknowledgment of wrongdoing (or sin, in Christian terms). *Merriam-Webster's Collegiate Dictionary* defines "confess" as follows: "1) to tell or make known (as something wrong or damaging to oneself): ADMIT; 2) to acknowledge (sin) to God or to a priest; 3) to declare faith in or adherence to: PROFESS; 4) to give evidence of; 5) to disclose one's faults; *specif:* to unburden one's sins or the state of one's conscience to God or to a priest."[2] Although the primary meanings of confession and confess are general in nature, in contemporary English, both words are primarily understood to indicate acknowledging fault.

2. Confession in the Old Testament

Unlike contemporary usage, in the Old Testament to "confess" generally meant to confess praise and thanksgiving to God, not to confess sin. A simple search using an electronic Bible program reveals that the Hebrew word *yadah*—which can be translated "to praise," "to give thanks," "to confess," or "to throw down"—appears 111 times in the Old Testament. In the vast majority of these instances, the word is translated in English as "to praise" or "to give thanks." In the NRSV, only 19 times is the word translated by some form of "confess." Thus, one can make a solid argument that confession in the Old Testament does not primarily refer to confessing sin, but rather is generally understood as confessing praise and giving thanks to God.

3. Confession in the New Testament

In the New Testament, confession is also used in a broad sense, encompassing confession of faith in Jesus, confession of praise to God, and confession of sin. In fact, of the 32 instances where confess/confessing

---

2. Mish, ed. *Merriam-Webster's Collegiate Dictionary*, 241.

(*exomologeo, homologeo*) appears in the New Testament, only four examples deal with confessing sin.[3] The primary meaning of confession in the New Testament has to do with confessing faith in Jesus as Lord. For instance, in the opening quotation of this chapter we see that the verbal confession that Jesus is Lord was crucial to salvation (Rom 10:9–10). In Philippians, Paul quotes an early Christian hymn, which ends with a reference to Isa 45:23: "Therefore God also highly exalted him and gave him the name that is above every name, so that at the name of Jesus every knee should bend . . . and every tongue should confess that Jesus Christ is Lord, to the glory of God the Father" (Phil 2:9–11).[4] John Koenig explains how the confession "Jesus is Lord" fits in with the mealtime worship setting:

> [T]he most primal confession of the early church [was] Kyrios Jesous (1 Cor 12:3; literally "Lord Jesus"), which should be taken in this meal context as a greeting and welcome, an acknowledging of Christ's presence in the assembly [note the appearance of "Lord Jesus" in the institutional narrative found in the previous chapter, 11:23].[5]

During the New Testament era the practice of confession expanded so that the confession of faith in Jesus as Lord became the primary definition of the word, even though its earlier understanding regarding sin was still practiced in the church. However, during the Constantinian shift, as the government began to support Christianity, the *confessores* in the church decreased in number; that is, there were fewer church members who had suffered persecution for confessing their faith. Gradually, confessing sins became the primary understanding of confession.

---

3. Examples of confession (*exomologeo, homologeo*) as general forth telling (including examples of the confession "Jesus is Lord") are found in the following verses: Matt 7:23, 10:32, 11:25, 14:7; Luke 10:21; 12:8; 22:6; John 1:20; 9:22; 12:42; Acts 19:18; 23:8; 24:14; Rom 10:9, 10; 14:11; 15:9; Phil 2:11; 1 Tim 6:12; Titus 1:16; Heb 11:13; 13:15; 1 John 2:23; 4:2, 3, 15; 2 John 1:7; Rev 3:5. Examples of confession of sin appear much less frequently: Matt 3:6; Mark 1:5; Jas 5:16; 1 John 1:9.

4. For additional references to confessing Jesus as Messiah or Lord, see John 9:22; 12:42; 1 Tim 6:12–13; 1 John 2:23; 4:2, 3, 15; 2 John 1:7.

5. Koenig, *Feast of the World's Redemption*, 118 (emphasis added). Also recall the discussion in chapter 2 about the dedication of the libation to a god, or gods, or the emperor. The Christian confession "Jesus is Lord" in this context was likely very subversive. See Taussig, *In the Beginning Was the Meal*, 115–43.

4. Reclaiming a Broad Understanding of Confession

As we try to reclaim the Love Feast in the church today, it is vital to understand eucharistic confession in its broadest sense, and not simply as the confession of sins prior to partaking of the bread and cup. Thomas Aquinas describes this full-orbed confession in his *Summa Theologica*:

> A threefold confession is commended by the Scriptures. One is the confession of matters of faith, and this is a proper act of faith, since it is referred to the end of faith . . . Another is the confession of thanksgiving or praise, and this is an act of adoration, for its purpose is to give outward honour to God, which is the end of adoration. The third is the confession of sins, which is ordained to the blotting out of sins, which is the end of penance.[6]

Churches today would benefit from a renewed focus on these *three* forms of confession. In addition to broadening the understanding of the content of confession, it is also important to examine who makes confession, who hears confession, and where and when confession is made. The table below demonstrates various ways confession can be expressed:

6. Aquinas, *Summa Theologica*, Part II-II, q.3.1, 400–401. Jaroslav Pelikan states the following concerning Aquinas's threefold definition of confession: "In the use of *homologia* and *homologein* in the New Testament, this 'confession of matters of faith' seems to be seen consistently as an individual act, which it is proper to describe by a verb that is in the singular, as in the words of the apostle Paul: 'if thou shalt confess [*ean homologeseis*] with thy mouth the Lord Jesus' [Rom 10:9 AV]. Therefore it is apparently not . . . the sort of formal 'creed, known to the faithful and committed to memory' of which Augustine speaks, but a spontaneous and individual act. The second and third forms of 'confession' in Thomas's catalog, 'the confession of thanksgiving or praise' and 'the confession of sins,' while continuing to be individual as well, also acquired collective form and corporate language. The second, 'the confession of thanksgiving or praise,' flowered into the eucharistic liturgies of East and West: *eucharistia* means 'thanksgiving,' and the liturgies all contain 'confessional' expressions of thanksgiving. The third, 'the confession of sins,' grew into the elaborate penitential systems of both the Eastern and the Western church. As a result of this, at least in common parlance, the word *confess* refers primarily to penitential confession . . . and the noun *confessional* stands for the booth in which penitent sinners make their confession to a priest and are absolved by him. In the usage of the Protestant churches and confessions of faith, reaction against the medieval penitential system . . . [leads] to a definition of confession in this third sense as 'this sincere confession which is made to God alone, either privately between God and the sinner, or publicly in the church where the general confession of sins is said' [*Second Helvetic Confession* 14.6]," Pelikan, *Credo*, 55–56.

Who makes confession?	An individual ↔ The worshiping community
Who hears confession?	(*Private*)→ Only God (prayer), a brother/sister, a priest, the entire congregation, the world ←(*Public*)
What is confessed?	Sin ↔ Praise ↔ Lord Jesus (Christian faith)
Where is confession made?	In the church ↔ In the world
When is confession made?	Before Communion ↔ During worship ↔ Anytime
Why is confession made?	Obtain forgiveness ↔ Praise God ↔ Share faith

The above table helps to expand our concept of confession so that we see many possibilities for confession in the life of the church. Confession may be made by an individual or by the congregation. Not only is it important for the congregation to confess praise to God, but the church should also explore ways of confessing both Christian faith and sin to the surrounding community. Individuals can practice the discipline of confession by learning to praise God throughout the day and by sharing their faith while working. Celebrating the Love Feast can help to form these practices of confession in the congregation and in the individual believer.

B. CONFESSING JESUS AS LORD

Confessing the faith begins with confessing "Jesus is Lord." Contemporary celebrations of the Love Feast should confess the Lordship of Jesus Christ. Douglas John Hall writes: "Confessing the faith is not an option for the disciple community; *confessio* (from the Latin *com* [together] + *fateri* [to acknowledge]) is inherent in faith as such. It would be as unthinkable for faith to refrain from expressing itself as for the heart to suppress its own pulsations."[7] Recall the passage in Matt 10 when Jesus tells his disciples:

> So have no fear of [persecutors]; for nothing is covered up that will not be uncovered, and nothing secret that will not become known. What I say to you in the dark, tell in the light; and what you hear whispered, proclaim from the housetops. Do not fear those who kill the body but cannot kill the soul; rather fear him who can destroy both soul and body in hell. . . . "Everyone therefore who [confesses] me before others, I also will [confess] before my Father in heaven; but whoever denies me before others, I also will deny before my Father in heaven." (Matt 10:26–28, 32–33).[8]

7. Hall, *Confessing the Faith*, 35.

8. Although in v. 32 the NRSV translates *homologesei* as "acknowledges," it is better

Confessing faith in Christ is crucial, for if disciples fail to confess their faith, then, they will be denied by Jesus before the Father in heaven.

Historically, the Brethren Love Feast provided the opportunity for members to confess their faith publicly. As previously stated, until the early twentieth century, every Love Feast was preceded by an annual visit in which pairs of deacons visited the entire membership of a congregation. The purpose of this "deacon visit" was to discern the spiritual health and unity of the congregation. The first of the three questions the deacons asked members was: "Are you still in the faith of the Gospel, as you declared when you were baptized?"[9] Thus, each year every member of the church had the opportunity to confess and reaffirm their faith in Christ. As the deacon visit declined and was later replaced with a short service of examination at the beginning of the Love Feast, the practice of individual members confessing their faith was often neglected. However, the *primary* purpose of the Love Feast is not to make the *individual* right with God, but rather to celebrate God's love in a *community* of Christians who are committed to confession, both the confession of sin and the confession of faith! Perhaps the Brethren and others who celebrate the Love Feast today can explore ways of recovering the earlier practice of confessing faith that was a part of the deacon visit.

1. The Language of Confession

Confessing the faith requires Christians to use the language of the church and of the world. First, the church's confession necessarily involves the use of language that is scriptural and theological. Karl Barth calls this the language of Canaan:

> When the Christian confesses his [or her] faith, when we have to let the light that is kindled in us shine, no one can avoid speaking in [the language of Canaan, i.e., the language of the Church and the Bible]. For . . . if the things of Christian faith, if our trust in God and His Word is to be expressed precisely . . . —then *it is in-*

---

rendered using "confess." Jaroslav Pelikan writes, "This relation between the disciple's 'confessing' and the 'confessing' by the Son of man before his Father is obscured when practically all modern versions of the English Bible render the Greek verb *homologein* there with some other English verb than 'confess,' with which they usually translate that verb at other places, including the clear parallel to these passages in the words of Christ . . . 'I will confess his name before my Father and before his angels' [Rev 3:5]," Pelikan, *Credo*, 59.

9. See "The Emergence of the Deacon's Visit Preceding Love Feast" in chapter 6.

*evitable that all undaunted the language of Canaan should sound
forth.* For certain lights and indications and heartening warnings
can be uttered directly in this language alone. To anyone rather
too sensitive in his desires and too tender about dealing with his
soul—"I believe, but my faith is so deep and inward that I cannot
bring myself to utter the words of the Bible, that it is difficult
for me to pronounce God's name, let alone the name of Christ
or the blood of Jesus Christ or the Holy Spirit"—to anyone who
should speak in this strain, I would say: "Dear friend, you may
be a very spiritual man, but see to it that you are deemed worthy
to be publicly responsible for your faith. And is your alleged shyness not shyness about emerging from your uncommitted private
world? Ask yourself! *One thing is certain, that where the Christian
Church does not venture to confess in its own language, it usually
does not confess at all.* Then it becomes the fellowship of the quiet,
whereby it is much to be hoped for that it does not become a
community of dumb dogs.[10]

As Barth wonderfully puts it, the confession of faith must use the language of the Scriptures, the language of the community of faith, the
church. Stanley Hauerwas has similarly argued that the church is God's
language to the world, that through the church God communicates the
gospel to the world.[11] Thus it is essential that as members of the church
confess the faith, they use words such as "salvation" and "sin" and "forgiveness," all of which are theological in nature. This is the language of
confession that occurs in the context of the church community.

The confession of faith does not only occur in the confines of the
church community. In fact, it is essential that the confession of faith be
made publicly. When the confession of faith moves into the public realm,
however, it is important for the language of confession to be translated
into terms the world can understand. Barth explains:

Where confession is serious and clear, it must be fundamentally
translatable into the speech of . . . the man and woman in the
street, into the language of those who are not accustomed to
reading Scripture and singing hymns, but who possess a quite
different vocabulary and quite different spheres of interest. . . .
For the Confession of Faith claims to be fulfilled in its application
to the life we all live, to the problems of our actual existence in

---

10. Barth, "Faith as Confession," 126 (emphasis added).
11. Hauerwas, "The Church as God's New Language."

the theoretical and practical questions of our everyday life. If our faith is real, it must encroach upon our life.[12]

The church's confession must be understandable in the world because the church exists to glorify God. Some terms will need to be translated to be understood, and the community of faith, or the individual Christian, must learn how to confess their faith so that the confession addresses the "practical questions of our everyday life." Put differently, the confession of faith must be relevant to the times, not functionally obsolete.

2. The Timeliness of Confessing the Faith

As the church celebrates the Love Feast and confesses faith in Jesus Christ, the confession should be timely and relevant, not merely the recitation of an ancient creed. Douglas Hall writes: "Confessing the faith does not mean saying everything. It means 'saying'—whether with words, or deeds, or sighs too deep for either—*the one thing that needs to be said, then and there*." In order for a confession of faith to be meaningful, it must have some relevance to the situation at hand. Hall continues:

> That is why it represents a certain misappropriation of the tradition when congregational recitations of creeds, however hallowed by time, are labeled "confessions of faith"; they are in reality summaries of what Christians *profess*. No community of Christians ever arrives at the place of *confession* apart from an ongoing and disciplined struggle to comprehend the whole substance of what Christians *profess*. But when faith's profession is substituted for confession, the means have assumed the position of the end, and saying "everything" has become, in all likelihood, an excuse for saying nothing in particular.[13]

---

12. Barth, "Faith as Confession," 127.

13. Hall, *Confessing the Faith*, 11 (emphasis added). This notion that in saying everything in a creed, the church is likely saying nothing in particular is in large part why the Brethren have rejected a formal creed, instead claiming "the New Testament as [their] rule of faith and practice," see the 1998 Annual Conference Statement, "The New Testament as our Rule of Faith and Practice." Formed in an era when Christians were persecuting and even killing other Christians over differences in creeds, the Brethren rejected the notion that they needed a confession of faith in document form; a summary of their Christian belief. While this position was valuable at the time of their formation, Brethren may need to reexamine their non-creedal stance to some degree in the current century in order to combat some of the relativism that has become increasingly prevalent.

Both Christian communities and individuals need to be ready to articulate the specifics of their faith at the moment when it is needed, not simply possess the ability to recite from memory certain points from a confession/profession of faith.

Karl Barth, the chief author of the *Barmen Declaration* (which outlined the beliefs and mission of the Confessing Church in mid-1930s Nazi Germany), had much to say about the importance of the church's confession being applicable to current events in the world. He writes:

> In relation to the world and to the error within its own ranks [the church] will necessarily be a *confessing* Church, making its own confession along with the [forerunners] in the faith, but, for the very reason that it confesses with them, *making its own confession*, and that also *in the present.* In other words, in obedience to its Lord and therefore in obedience to the Scriptures, it *answers clearly and consistently and fearlessly the questions put to it from moment to moment.*[14]

Of course, Barth's concern was strongly rooted in the events of Europe in the 1930s and '40s. He knew that the church could not afford to recite mindlessly the confessions of old without speaking out and acting against the insidious doctrines of the Nazi Party. He states this clearly:

> Let us beware of remaining stuck where we are and *refusing to advance to meet worldly attitudes.* For instance, in 1933 in Germany there was plenty of serious, profound and living Christianity and confession—God be praised and thanked! But unfortunately *this faith and confession of the German Church remained embedded in the language of the Church*, and did not translate what was being excellently said in the language of the Church into the political attitude demanded at the time; in which it would have become clear that the Evangelical Church had to say "No" to National Socialism, "No" from its very roots. The confession of Christianity did not at the time become clear in this form. *Think what would have happened, had the Evangelical Church at that time expressed its Church knowledge in the form of a worldly, political attitude.*[15]

Again, not only is it important for the church to translate its message into the language of the world—this must also be done *at the appropriate time.* While there were some—like Barth, Bonhoeffer, and other mem-

14. Barth, *Credo,* 145, quoted in Hall, *Confessing the Faith,* 36–37 (emphasis added).

15. Barth, "Faith as Confession," 128 (emphasis added).

bers of the Confessing Church—who realized the idolatrous nature of Nazi propaganda, most churches in Germany allowed the Nazis to exert influence over their leadership and teaching. Hopefully we can learn from Barth that the clarity and timeliness of our individual and communal confessions of faith can have a significant impact on the world.

Overall we have seen that a chief purpose of the church's confession is the confession of faith. Both individual members and the church community are to grow in their abilities to confess the faith. When confession occurs in the context of the church it is important that biblical and theological language is used. However, when faith is confessed publicly, Christians should use language that is understandable to common people. In addition to using understandable language, the confession of faith must be relevant to the practical concerns of people in the world. As the author of 1 Peter states: "[I]n your hearts sanctify Christ as Lord. Always be ready to make your defense to anyone who demands from you an accounting for the hope that is in you; yet do it with gentleness and reverence" (1 Pet 3:15–16).

C. CONFESSING PRAISES TO GOD

In addition to proclaiming the truth of the gospel, confession is also an aspect of the worship of God. In the context of worship, Christians confess praises to God. Since the earliest Christians were Jews who believed that Jesus was the Messiah, it is not surprising that Christian worship continued the Jewish tradition of confessing praises to God in worship: "I will give to the LORD the thanks due to his righteousness, and sing praise to the name of the LORD, the Most High" (Ps 7:17); "Sing praises to the LORD, who dwells in Zion. Declare his deeds among the peoples" (Ps 9:11). Thus, in the New Testament we see similar references to confessing praise to God:

> Welcome one another, therefore, just as Christ has welcomed you, for the glory of God. For I tell you that Christ has become a servant of the circumcised on behalf of the truth of God . . . in order that the Gentiles might glorify God for his mercy. As it is written, "Therefore I will confess (*exomologesomai*) you among the Gentiles, and sing praises to your name." (Rom 15:7–9)

> Through [Jesus], then, let us continually offer a sacrifice of praise to God, that is, the fruit of lips that confess (*homologounton*) his name. (Heb 13:15)

> And from the throne came a voice saying, "Praise our God, all you
> his servants, and all who fear him, small and great." (Rev 19:5)

Confessing praises to God was a central part of worship in both the Old
and New Testaments.

Confessing praise to God during worship can be done in both
song and the spoken word. Confessions can be offered individually or
corporately. They can come from pastors and lay people. In fact, many
congregations would do well to encourage lay members to grow more
comfortable with confessing praise to God. Too often churches unof-
ficially designate their pastor as "confessor-in-chief," thus allowing most
worship participants to be unconcerned with offering individual confessions of praise to God. While there are certainly some Christians who
are less comfortable making a public confession of praise, confessing
praise is required of all Christians, not just Christian leaders: "Praise our
God, *all you his servants*, and all who fear him, *small* and great" (Rev
19:5, emphasis added). Many congregations can grow in their understanding and practice of confession as a spiritual discipline, encouraging
one another to confess our faith and our praises. A fitting conclusion
and transition is found in the epistle of James:

> Are any among you suffering? They should pray. Are any cheer-
> ful? *They should sing songs of praise.* Are any among you sick?
> They should call for the elders of the church and have them pray
> over them, anointing them with oil in the name of the Lord. The
> prayer of faith will save the sick, and the Lord will raise them up;
> and anyone who has committed sins will be forgiven. Therefore
> *confess your sins to one another*, and pray for one another, so that
> you may be healed. (Jas 5:13–16, emphasis added)

D. CONFESSING OUR SINS TO GOD

We come now to the most recognized aspect of confession: the confession of sins. Ever since the Reformation, when various groups did away
with the sacrament of Penance, many churches have struggled to understand and incorporate the practice of confessing sins. This is surely
one of the disgraces of the Reformation, for even though the reformers
were right to challenge the widespread abuses of Penance, the resulting
rejection of the practice of individual confession surely was not ideal.
Thus, the reality for many churches is that there is a lack of confessional

practices in their tradition upon which to build. Moreover, reintroduc-
ing practices of confession is bound to be difficult, for most people are
not eager to reveal the sins with which they are currently struggling.
Nevertheless, it will be important for the authentic confession of sin to
have a place in the life of the church today, especially during the celebration of the Love Feast.

In the *Celebration of Discipline*, Richard Foster devotes a chapter
to the discipline of confession, in which he specifically focuses on the
confession of sin. He acknowledges that

> Confession is a difficult discipline for us because we all too often
> view the believing community as a fellowship of saints before we
> see it as a fellowship of sinners. We feel that everyone else has
> advanced so far into holiness that we are isolated and alone in
> our sin. We cannot bear to reveal our failures and shortcomings
> to others. . . . But if we know that the people of God are first a
> fellowship of sinners, we are freed to hear the unconditional call
> of God's love and to confess our needs openly before our brothers
> and sisters. We know we are not alone in our sin. The fear and
> pride that cling to us like barnacles cling to others also. We are
> sinners together. *In acts of mutual confession we release the power
> that heals.* Our humanity is no longer denied, but transformed.[16]

In this section we will not describe in detail how practices of confession
can occur within congregational practice; Foster already has done this in
the *Celebration of Discipline*. Instead, we will focus on the way in which
the confession of sin is a communal discipline.

1. Reclaiming Communal Eucharistic Confession

In chapter 3 it was shown that the scriptural basis for confession prior
to the Eucharist comes from 1 Cor 11, where Paul instructs church
members to examine themselves before partaking of the bread and cup.
Paul is not asking them to examine their consciences introspectively
and to confess their sin to God. Rather, he wants them to "discern the
body," to examine the unity of their community, and to make whatever
corrections are necessary so that their celebration of the Lord's Supper
honors Christ and does not serve to propagate injustice (which God will
judge). Stanley Hauerwas notes the importance of confession for the
faith community:

---

16. Foster, *Celebration of Discipline*, 145–46 (emphasis added).

The necessity of confession and repentance was the church's way of maintaining communal corrections necessary to be the kind of community capable of receiving the Eucharist. Confession, which required people to learn to name their sins, was necessary for the church to deal with sin after baptisms. Though private penitential practice developed . . . it was never "private" in the sense that penitents could think of themselves as individuals. Their confession was necessary for the good of the church so that the whole church could come to the table as a reconciled community.[17]

In many churches in which I have worshiped, little emphasis is given to the importance of confession for the health of the church. Most often the focus is on the individual benefits of confession. Those who refuse to confess their own sin to another Christian, or refuse to hear another's confession, detract from the unity of the church. They impede the grace of God for themselves and their fellow believer. Thus, the discipline of confession ought to be practiced, not only for the personal benefit, but also for the overall strengthening of the church community.

2. Confessing Sin Privately

Church history is rife with examples of mishandled public confession. In fact, the system of private penance developed in large part as a reaction against overly harsh penitential practices in the early church. In the case of the Brethren Love Feast, the disappearance of the deacon visit is related in some degree to instances where the church forced individual members to confess sins publicly before the congregation, sometimes "sins" that were quite trivial.[18] While there are occasions when it is ap-

17. Hauerwas, "Casuistry in Context," 279.

18. Carl Bowman interviewed a retired Brethren elder who told him that some youth were forced to confess the "sin" of attending the Hill Church picnic, an exciting non-Brethren social event: "How the Official Board ever discovered the names of the young people who went there is beyond me, but I tell you, there was a lot of tattling going on, a lot of tattling . . . and they would report this to some deacon or some minister, and many times the individual would be visited. 'Is this true that you were there?' And if they admitted that it was true, then they would say, 'Well, we ask you to appear at the next Council Meeting to make a confession.' Sometimes you had a whole row of [youth who] would confess that they had gone. The time came when they wouldn't admit that they were sorry; they would simply say, 'We're sorry we offended the church.' . . . I just felt that many times the older Brethren asked questions and went into areas in which they had absolutely no business," Bowman, *Brethren Society*, 287.

propriate for a public confession of sin to be made in the church,[19] many times the best intentions for public confession backfire and end up causing more harm than good. As Dietrich Bonhoeffer writes:

> A confession of sin in the presence of all the members of the congregation is not required to restore one to community with the entire congregation. In the one other Christian to whom I confess my sins and by whom my sins are declared forgiven, I meet the whole congregation. Community with the whole congregation is given to me in the community which I experience with this one other believer. For here it is not a matter of acting according to one's own orders and authority, but according to the command of Jesus Christ, which is intended for the whole congregation, on whose behalf the individual is called merely to carry it out. So long as Christians are in such a community of confession of sins to one another, they are no longer alone anywhere.[20]

Thus, in most cases it is best for individuals to confess their sins privately to another trustworthy brother or sister.

19. "There certainly is an appropriateness for the public restoration of one who has previously and publicly turned entirely away from Christ . . . Similarly, it may be appropriate for any 'open' sin to be openly confessed and for a public declaration of absolution and restoration to be made. But there is no merit in the public confession of the 'private' sins, frailties, and temptations with which we all struggle—indeed, there may be great harm in such potential self-indulgence. And here, to one for whom (as a Baptist) the Catholic rite of private penance is entirely foreign, the rite of private penance seems both appropriate and helpful," Colwell, *Promise and Presence*, 186.

20. Bonhoeffer, *Life Together*, 110–11. Earlier Bonhoeffer describes the authority each Christian has been given by Christ to forgive his sister's or brother's sin: "Jesus gave his followers the authority to hear the confession of sin and to forgive sin in Christ's name. 'If you forgive the sins of any, they are forgiven them; if you retain the sins of any, they are retained' (John 20:23). When he did that, Christ made us into the community of faith, and in that community Christ made the other Christian to be grace for us. Now each stands in Christ's place. In the presence of another Christian I no longer need to pretend. . . . I am permitted to be the sinner that I am, for there alone in all the world the truth and mercy of Jesus Christ rule. Christ became our brother in order to help us; through Christ other Christians have become Christ for us in the power and authority of Christ's commandment. Other Christians stand before us as the sign of God's truth and grace. They have been given to us to help us. Another Christian hears our confession of sin in Christ's place, forgives our sins in Christ's name. Another Christian keeps the secret of our confession as God keeps it. When I go to another believer to confess, I am going to God. Thus the call within the Christian community to mutual confession and forgiveness goes out as a call to the great grace of God in the congregation," Bonhoeffer, *Life Together*, 109.

Because many congregations in America do not have structures in place for the private confession of sin, it follows that some thoughtful work will need to be done to help facilitate this process. Perhaps Bible study groups or Sunday School classes could organize times of confession for their members throughout the year. Some churches have cell groups, home groups, or other small group structures within which members could find a person to whom they would confess their sins. Or maybe the deacons, elders, pastors, and other leaders of a congregation could serve as hearers of confession. Since the confession of sins prior to celebrating Communion goes back to the second-century, it would make sense for congregations to encourage the private confession of sin before Communion celebrations. Regardless of the specific structure that is used, it would be beneficial for some sort of confessional structure to take root in Protestant churches.

3. Confessing Sin Publicly

When sin is confessed publicly in the church, it is often best for it to be a general confession. While there may be occasions when it is appropriate and helpful for a congregation to hear a personal confession of sin (along with an assurance of pardon), on the whole it is better for a church not to parade its sinful members in front of the congregation. Accordingly, the public confession of sin should be a general confession of the ways in which members of the congregation have sinned against God. John Colwell writes:

> An insistence upon a detailed and comprehensive private [or public] confession inevitably issues in legalism, selectivity and artificiality: inevitably we focus on specific "commands" that have been broken; inevitably we omit to itemize the dispositions and the struggles that are continuous and, often, apparently trivial. But more pertinently, we tend to focus on that which ought not to have been done rather than on that which ought to have been done . . . [i.e., the Greatest Commandment, Matt 22:37–40] *A general confession is comprehensive by its very nature but it need not thereby be insincere or cursory.* Rather, by identifying the essence of sin—that we have not done that which we ought to have done—*a general confession identifies that which can too easily be overlooked within private confession* and yet which lies at the root of all that there is confessed.[21]

21. Colwell, *Promise and Presence*, 187–88 (emphasis added).

General confession is appropriate because it helps us to name the sin of omission—the failure to do what we should have done—in addition to sins of commission. Naming sins of omission is important because too frequently our churches are racially segregated, comprised of only one or two social classes, and restrictive of women in leadership. This is an affront to the gospel that in the past brought reconciliation to Jewish and Gentile Christians, to the rich and the poor, to slaves and masters, to men and women, and that continues to bring reconciliation today. A general confession names our complacency in these areas (and many others), and asks God to forgive us and to help us overcome our sin.

In sum, the confession of sin is an under-celebrated discipline in the church that, when practiced appropriately, can help the church and its members to experience healing and spiritual growth. While it may be difficult to practice confession, the Christian life is not one of comfort but one of discipleship and obedience. "The discipline of confession brings an end to pretense. God is calling into being a church that can openly confess its frail humanity and knows the forgiving and empowering graces of Christ. Honesty leads to confession, and *confession leads to change*. May God give grace to the church once again to recover the discipline of confession."[22] Again, it is fitting to conclude with Scripture: "If we say that we have no sin, we deceive ourselves, and the truth is not in us. If we confess our sins, he who is faithful and just will forgive us our sins and cleanse us from all unrighteousness" (1 John 1:8–9).

E. CONFESSION AND THE LOVE FEAST

So how does all of this relate to the Love Feast? After all, much of this chapter does not sound anything like a Brethren Love Feast. That may be a good thing, for although the Brethren have contributed much to reclaiming the Love Feast, they do not "own" the celebration. The Love Feast is a practice for the entire Christian church, and confession—the confession of faith in Jesus, the confession of praises to God, and the confession of sin—should be a crucial element of that celebration. It is important for the church to rediscover a three-dimensional understanding of confession that is based on the Scriptures and the practice of the early church.

22. Foster, *Celebration of Discipline*, 157 (emphasis added).

1. Confessing Faith in the Love Feast

The Love Feast should not be so rooted in tradition that it becomes irrelevant in contemporary society. This is a challenge for many Brethren communities, because many congregations treat the Love Feast as a sacred object received from their ancestors in the faith—a practice that is timeless and unchangeable. Yet, if we understand the celebration of the Love Feast to be an opportunity for the confession of Christian faith to be made—which it most definitely is—then we must also realize that in order for this confession to be understood, it must be timely and relevant. Every celebration of the Love Feast should not be a carbon copy of the previous celebration; rather, each Love Feast should be characterized by a confession of Christian faith that is relevant to each local community. In times of economic prosperity or economic hardship, the church should confess that Jesus is Lord, and not money (while taking hardship seriously). In times of war, the church should confess that Christ calls us to love the people we are told are our enemies. We should confess that God cares deeply for the poor and the oppressed, both in our own land and across the globe, and that the church has an important role in feeding the hungry and in calling on leaders to combat injustice. These are but three examples of how a Love Feast could be characterized by a specific confession of faith that is relevant to the contemporary world.

Serious attention also needs to be given to the location of the Love Feast, especially as it relates to the setting of the church's confession of faith. If the church is looking for ways to confess the faith during the Love Feast, it matters where such a confession is made. If the Love Feast is held in a church fellowship hall with only a faithful remnant of the congregation present, the confession of faith has not reached the ears of those in the community who need to hear the good news. Both the early church and the early Brethren celebrated the Love Feast in homes, not church fellowship halls. Perhaps it would be good to explore ways of celebrating the Love Feast in homes once again. After all, the home setting is much more welcoming for friends and neighbors who may never have attended a Love Feast before, and this broadening of participation enables the confession of faith to reach more individuals. Or maybe churches could experiment by renting out local community centers or restaurant dining rooms in which to hold Love Feasts. When we celebrate the Love Feast outside the church building it takes on a more missional character and becomes an opportunity to confess the Lordship of Christ in the world.

2. Confessing Praise in the Love Feast

The early church worship meals were joyous celebrations. Although there are times of serious reflection during the Love Feast (i.e., confessing sin and remembering the cross), overall the service should be an occasion of praise and thanksgiving. The confession of praise will most often be offered during congregational singing, but in addition to this, other avenues of praising God should be explored. We should remember that the Methodist love-feast was primarily known as a service of testimony about God's grace, power, provision and salvation. These services were very moving. Both individual and communal confession of praise should be encouraged in the celebration of the Love Feast.

3. Confessing Sin in the Love Feast

It is important to understand that confessing sin is both a communal discipline and an individual practice. While the early Brethren practice of the deacon's visit had its difficulties, it did recognize the importance of reconciliation and common unity among members as they prepared to share Communion. The current Brethren practice of examination and preparation before the Love Feast is often an inadequate replacement of the deacon's visit, primarily because it makes confession of sin into an introspective, individual experience. In addition to asking members to examine their lives before taking the Eucharist, congregations should explore ways for members to confess sin privately *to one another* before taking Communion. This will probably need to happen in the days and weeks prior to the Love Feast, although it may be possible in some instances to devote a block of time to this at the beginning of the Love Feast. This exercise also allows for individuals in the church to approach other members with whom they have a conflict and to make amends prior to celebrating the Lord's Supper. In this way the members of the church are "discerning the body" before breaking bread together, that is, they are examining their relationships within the body of Christ. Lastly, during the Love Feast time should be devoted to the general confession of sin, reminding the congregation of both the sins of commission *and* omission. Such confessions should be followed by words of assurance, reminding the church of the power of Christ to forgive sins.

> To what do we bear witness at the table of the Lord? . . .
> Is it not the reality of the holy Trinity, the one God who
> is Father, Son, and Holy Spirit? Is it not the person and
> work of Jesus Christ, the eternal Son of God, who in the
> fullness of time was conceived by the Holy Spirit, born of
> the Virgin Mary, suffered under Pontius Pilate, was buried,
> raised again from the dead, ascended into heaven, and one
> day is coming again in power and glory? This is a common
> Christian faith, to which we too bear witness. Often we've
> done it in formal confessions, some of us; others have been
> more reluctant to express those commitments and beliefs
> in formal confessional documents, claiming the Bible only
> as our creed. But whether we do that in formal confes-
> sional documents or in other ways, that is a part of the
> common faith we share. *The Lord's Supper is a place where
> [confession] is given visible expression.*
>
> —TIMOTHY GEORGE[23]

---

23. George, "Reflections," 267 (emphasis added).

10

Formed to Reconcile

Experiencing Reconciliation with God and One Another

So if anyone is in Christ, there is a new creation: everything
old has passed away; see, everything has become new! All
this is from God, who reconciled us to himself through
Christ, and has given us the ministry of reconciliation;
that is, in Christ God was reconciling the world to himself,
not counting their trespasses against them, and entrusting
the message of reconciliation to us. So we are ambassadors
for Christ, since God is making his appeal through us; we
entreat you on behalf of Christ, be reconciled to God.

—2 COR 5:17–20

The ministry of reconciliation stands as the key for relating to "the other" that the Corinthian (or any other) community can identify within and outside its fold. It leaves
no room for engaging in any type of divisive activity or
nourishing a divisive or prejudiced attitude towards others. More comprehensively, the ministry invites one to see
the entire creation and everything as one's own (since the
entire earth and all its peoples belong to God, Ps 24:1), to
be cherished and nourished into fullness of life.

—TERESA OKURE[1]

R ECONCILIATION SHOULD BE AN important focus of the Love Feast. In
the worship of the early church, one of the ways that reconciliation
was expressed was in the kiss of peace, the holy kiss. This sign of peace

1. Okure, "The Ministry of Reconciliation," 116.

functioned as a greeting and soon became a part of the liturgy, preceding the Eucharist. When we look back at groups that recovered the Love Feast, many of them also reclaimed the holy kiss as a concurrent practice: for example, some Pietists, the Brethren, the Moravians, and the Glasites. And in recent decades, the Roman Catholic Church and the Anglican Church have revised their liturgies to include the sign of peace. Whether through the holy kiss, the holy handshake, the holy hug, or the holy washing of feet, it is crucial that the Love Feast explicitly communicate the message of reconciliation to those who participate in it.

It will be helpful briefly to define reconciliation.[2] Reconciliation is a process in which something is changed or adjusted and brought into agreement with a standard. When you balance your checkbook, you compare your own records to the bank statement. This is called reconciling your checkbook. Or when you adjust your watch to a standard time, you are performing a reconciliation, so to speak. When we look in the Bible, we see two types of reconciliation. First, the scriptures talk about reconciliation between God and the world. Sin has damaged humankind's relationship with the God who created all things. The biblical witness reveals that God takes the initiative to reconcile humanity and creation to himself; to restore to wholeness the relationship damaged by sin. This is the vertical dimension of reconciliation. Secondly, the New Testament, emphasizes that followers of Jesus are to seek reconciliation with one another. As people who have been forgiven by God and reconciled into right relationship, we are to imitate God by working toward reconciliation in our congregations and in the world. This is the horizontal dimension of reconciliation. Let us briefly explore these two dimensions of reconciliation and their relationship to the Love Feast.

A. RECONCILED TO GOD

1. God's Initiative.

Reconciliation begins with God. God has taken the initiative to reconcile the world to himself through Jesus Christ. In 2 Cor 5, quoted at the beginning of the present chapter, Paul writes that the new creation begins

2. It is ironic that as I write this chapter, the United States Senate is using the reconciliation procedure to usher through changes to a significant health care reform bill that recently passed through both houses of Congress. Reconciliation is the talk of Washington, DC this week, although not the type of reconciliation we are discussing.

with God's work of reconciling the world (*kosmon*) to himself through Jesus. We see the same message in several other Pauline epistles:

> But God demonstrates his own love for us in this: While we were still sinners, Christ died for us. . . . For if, when we were God's enemies, we were reconciled to him through the death of his Son, how much more, having been reconciled, shall we be saved through his life! Not only is this so, but we also rejoice in God through our Lord Jesus Christ, through whom we have now received reconciliation. (Rom 5:8, 10–11)

> [In Christ] all the fullness of God was pleased to dwell, and through him God was pleased to reconcile to himself all things, whether on earth or in heaven, by making peace through the blood of his cross. And you who were once estranged and hostile in mind, doing evil deeds, he has now reconciled in his fleshly body through death, so as to present you holy and blameless and irreproachable before him. (Col 1:19–22)

Thus, reconciliation is the gift of God, initiated by God while humanity was estranged and hostile in mind. Because of the cross of Christ, God has reconciled us to himself.

2. Humanity's Role in Reconciliation

Although we did not initiate reconciliation with God, it is clear that we have a role in being reconciled to God. Through the cross of Jesus, God has made reconciliation available to all people. Paul Sampley writes: "People have value because Christ has died for them. People, whoever they are, whether they have responded to Christ or not—Christ died for everyone—are treasured by God. From the moment of Christ's death, everyone, everyone, has value."[3] Of course, the gospel of Jesus Christ is not an ancient story, it is still good news today, and the good news is realized as individuals respond to the gift of God through repentance and commitment. In 2 Cor 5 Paul writes that the church has been given the ministry of reconciliation, and he entreats his listeners to "be reconciled to God!" A response is required. God does not force reconciliation on people. They must desire to be reconciled to God and must act on that desire.

In previous chapters we have discussed some of the actions involved in reconciliation with God. One key response is confession, and in particular, confession of sin. The author of 1 John writes: "If we say that we

---

3. Sampley, "The Second Letter to the Corinthians," 98.

have no sin, we deceive ourselves, and the truth is not in us. If we confess our sins, he who is faithful and just will forgive us our sins and cleanse us from all unrighteousness" (1:8–9). Here we see that confession precedes forgiveness and reconciliation. As we confess our sins of commission and omission, God forgives us and cleanses us. In the chapter on submission we saw that feetwashing can be a powerful demonstration of this cleansing. When we see feetwashing as more than humble service and also recognize its relationship to the sacrament of cleansing (to use John Colwell's language),[4] we see that feetwashing can be a repeated sign of our reconciliation with God. Thus, the practice of feetwashing can be an occasional ceremony that calls to mind the believer's baptism and serves as an outward demonstration of the renewed reconciliation that they experience with God. Of course, God continues to reconcile us to himself, whether or not we wash feet, but there is hardly a more powerful demonstration of this cleansing than feetwashing.

3. Reconciling the Cosmos

The message of the gospel is that God is reconciling the world, the cosmos, to himself. Sometimes we need to be reminded of this bigger picture of reconciliation. God so loved the *cosmos* that he sent Jesus to reconcile the *cosmos* to himself (John 3:16; 2 Cor 5:19). Clearly humans are an important part of the world; we are, after all, created in God's image (Gen 1:26–27). Yet God's reconciliation also includes the rest of the created world. "God was pleased to reconcile to himself all things, whether on earth or in heaven, by making peace through the blood of his cross" (Col 1:20). It is the purpose of God to redeem the earth so that heaven and earth may be one. This is the marriage of heaven and earth, as N. T. Wright explains:

> Heaven and earth, it seems, are not after all poles apart, needing to be separated forever when all the children of heaven have been rescued from this wicked earth. . . . No, they are different, radically different, but they are made for each other in the same way (Revelation is suggesting) as male and female. And when they finally come together, that will be a cause for rejoicing in the same way that a wedding is: a creational sign that God's project is going forward; that opposite poles within creation are made for union [or reconciliation], not competition; that love and not

4. Colwell, *Promise and Presence*, 177–96.

hate have the last word in the universe; that fruitfulness and not sterility is God's will for creation.[5]

So, God's reconciliation has an eschatological dimension as well. God's mission is to redeem all of creation, and the culmination of this will be the wedding feast of the Lamb celebrating the marriage of Christ to his bride, the church. Let us also consider how we are called to be ministers of reconciliation with those around us.

B. RECONCILING WITH ONE ANOTHER

1. Ambassadors for Christ

Before the Gospels were written, the Apostle Paul wrote to the believers in Jesus at Corinth that he and they were to be "ambassadors for Christ" (2 Cor 5:20). Paul uses governmental language here. An ambassador is someone who lives in a foreign land and who serves as a representative of his or her homeland and its leader. The instruction to be Christ's ambassadors is still relevant today; we are to represent Christ to the world. Just as we have been reconciled to God, we also have been given the responsibility to ask others, on Christ's behalf, to be reconciled to God. What a task! This is a task of Christian mission. As followers of Jesus, we are "agents" of God's kingdom who wish for those in the world to experience reconciliation with God; to settle up their account with God, so to speak, and to begin living the new, abundant life available to those who are in Christ Jesus (John 10:10; 2 Cor 5:17). We should be open to making this appeal for reconciliation at any time, and not merely during evangelistic services. When we celebrate the Love Feast today, we should be mindful that there may be some in our midst who have never been reconciled to God. The first part of reconciliation in the human dimension is for Christians to be open to being used by God in order to bring others into a reconciled relationship with him.

2. The Holy Kiss and Reconciliation

When we look at the scriptures and the witness of the early church, it is clear that the holy kiss was a practice that expressed peace and reconciliation in the Christian community. It really is quite amazing to think about

5. Wright, *Surprised by Hope*, 105.

how the gospel of Jesus Christ spread from the first Jewish disciples to the Gentile world of the Mediterranean and then to the farthest reaches of the globe, especially when we consider the tenacity with which groups usually hold on to their religious beliefs. Michael Penn has argued that the holy kiss was a powerful ritual in the early church that helped to redefine or reconstruct kinship.[6] Thus, as Christians shared the kiss of peace, they were being reformed into the family of God as brothers and sisters, united not by the blood in their own veins, but rather through the blood of Christ, shed on the cross (Col 1:20). We see a wonderful description of this reconciliation in Ephesians:

> Remember that [formerly you Gentiles were] without Christ, be-
> ing aliens from the commonwealth of Israel, and strangers to the
> covenants of promise, having no hope and without God in the
> world. But now in Christ Jesus you who once were far off have
> been brought near by the blood of Christ. For he is our peace;
> in his flesh he has made both groups into one and has broken
> down the dividing wall, that is, the hostility between us. He has
> abolished the law with its commandments and ordinances, that
> he might create in himself one new humanity in place of the two,
> thus making peace, and might reconcile both groups to God in
> one body through the cross, thus putting to death that hostility
> through it. So he came and proclaimed peace to you who were far
> off and peace to those who were near; for through him both of us
> have access in one Spirit to the Father. So then you are no longer
> strangers and aliens, but you are citizens with the saints and also
> members of the household of God. (Eph 2:12–19)

He is our peace. What a beautiful phrase. And these are not just words on a page; they become embodied as we continue the ministry of recon- ciliation inaugurated by Jesus. How do we embody reconciliation today in the Love Feast? Will we share the holy kiss? Will we shake hands? Wash feet? Hold hands in prayer? It seems clear to me that there must be physical ways in which we appropriately touch other people in the midst of our worship, because we need these physical actions to remind and encourage us to be reconciled with our brothers and sisters.

---

6. Penn, "Performing Family."

3. Reconciliation in the Sermon on the Mount

There are two passages in the Sermon on the Mount that show that Jesus was passionate about reconciliation in the church. First, after telling his disciples that God sees our hearts and considers anger toward a brother to be like murder, he says: "Therefore, if you are offering your gift at the altar and there remember that your brother has something against you, leave your gift there in front of the altar. First go and be reconciled to your brother; then come and offer your gift" (Matt 5:23–24). Human reconciliation is clearly important to Jesus. When someone recalls a conflict they have with another person, he wants them to drop everything and go to seek reconciliation with that person, even if it means running out of the Temple and leaving their (live animal?) offering there before the altar (to wander off?)![7] It is almost as if Jesus is saying that reconciliation is more important than worship, although clearly worship is vitally important. He uses this story to drive home the point that God deeply cares about our relationships with one another and that God does not want us to go through the motions of worship when we are not reconciled to our brother or sister: "Those who say, 'I love God,' and hate their brothers or sisters, are liars; for those who do not love a brother or sister whom they have seen, cannot love God whom they have not seen" (1 John 4:20).

Perhaps Jesus' most recognizable teaching on reconciliation is found in the Lord's Prayer, more specifically in the only petition of the prayer that is conditional (and the only petition on which Jesus provides further commentary): "Forgive us our debts (*opheilemata*), as we also have forgiven our debtors. . . . For if you forgive others their trespasses (*paraptomata*), your heavenly Father will also forgive you; but if you do not forgive others, neither will your Father forgive your trespasses" (Matt 6:12, 14–15). Again we see the connection between our relationships on earth and our relationship with God. The connection between forgiveness and reconciliation is evident in the usage of monetary language (*opheilemata*, lit. "what is owed"). When we pray, we are to ask God to forgive our debts and trespasses in the same way that we forgive those who are indebted to us, those who have sinned against us. Jesus connects our reconciliation to God with our reconciliation to those around us. In other words, if we fail to forgive those who have sinned against us, we should not count on God to forgive us.

7. Jewish Temple offerings included live animals, grain, oil, and wine. The passage takes on a humorous, yet powerful, note when we imagine a person leaving their sheep or dove before the altar to go and make reconciliation.

4. Reconciliation in Matthew 18

Lastly, in Matt 18 Jesus outlines the process of reconciliation. Among Anabaptists, this passage has been referred to as the "Rule of Christ":

> [Jesus said:] "If another member of the church sins against you, go and point out the fault when the two of you are alone. If the member listens to you, you have regained that one. But if you are not listened to, take one or two others along with you, so that every word may be confirmed by the evidence of two or three witnesses. If the member refuses to listen to them, tell it to the church; and if the offender refuses to listen even to the church, let such a one be to you as a Gentile and a tax collector. Truly I tell you, whatever you bind on earth will be bound in heaven, and whatever you loose on earth will be loosed in heaven. Again, truly I tell you, if two of you agree on earth about anything you ask, it will be done for you by my Father in heaven. For where two or three are gathered in my name, I am there among them."
>
> Then Peter came and said to him, "Lord, if another member of the church sins against me, how often should I forgive? As many as seven times?" Jesus said to him, "Not seven times, but, I tell you, seventy-seven times. (Matt 18:15–22)

Here we see that Jesus gives the church a method for members to deal with sin and at the same time instructs them to be liberal with forgiveness. It would go beyond the current scope to provide an in-depth analysis of this passage; the best I can do is point the reader to three significant essays by John Howard Yoder.[8] In "The Hermeneutics of Peoplehood," Yoder comments on several strengths of the Matt 18 procedure:

> The context is *conversation*, not the jurist's simple deductive application of universally valid rules. The conversation takes place in a context of commitment to forgive (the theme of the entire chapter 18 of Matthew's Gospel). The deliberative process begins with only the two parties to the conflict being involved. The conflict is broadened only gradually, and only so far as is needed to achieve reconciliation. The tests of the validity of the process are procedural, having to do with the hearing of several witnesses, subject to correction and change over time. We have here then a kind of situation ethics, i.e., a procedure for doing practical moral reasoning, in a context of conflict, right in the situation where divergent views are being lived out in such a way as to cause offense.

8. Yoder, "Binding and Loosing (1992)," 1–13; "Binding and Loosing (1998)," 323–58; and "The Hermeneutics of Peoplehood," especially 26–28.

230 RECOVERING THE LOVE FEAST

This rejects a rigid or automatic casuistic deduction on one hand and *individualism* or *pluralism* on the other. The obedience of the brother or sister is my business. There is no hesitancy in using the word "sin"; yet *the intention of the procedure is reconciliation, not exclusion or even reprimand.* Out of this utterly personal exchange comes the confirmation (or perchance the modification) of the rules of the community, which can therefore be spoken of, with the technical language of the rabbis, as having "bound" or "loosed" [the brother or sister].[9]

This procedure outlined by Jesus is a real gift to the church. By nature of being a *process* rather than a *pronouncement*, it allows the church to make corrections when it has failed to embody the Kingdom of God (like, for instance, its past acceptance of slavery, the evils of the Crusades, the labeling of brilliant thinkers such as Galileo as "heretics," and the wrongful killing of other "heretics" such as John Hus, Michael Sattler, and hundreds of other Anabaptist martyrs). Yet this process is also grounded by its ability to name sin as sin, with the understanding that the Holy Spirit empowers the community to maintain biblical and theological faithfulness.[10]

So we see that reconciliation and forgiveness are emphasized by Jesus, who calls the church community to help one another to live in faithfulness. This mutual concern and desire for reconciliation in the church are similar to the Apostle Paul's concern that the "leaven" of sin might spread throughout the church (1 Cor 5:6–8). Yoder writes:

> [T]he church is the lump of dough, all of which will be caused to ferment by the presence of a few yeast cells within it. Paul thus says that there is a kind of moral solidarity linking all the members of the body so that if individuals persist in disobedience within the fellowship, their guilt is no longer the moral responsibility of those individuals alone but becomes a kind of collective blame shared by the whole body. I should deal with my fellow believer's sin because that person and I are members of one another; unless I am the agent of that person's sharing in restoration, he or she is the agent of my sharing guilt.[11]

Thus, for the good of the individual who has sinned, and for the good of the community, members of the church should initiate the process of

9. Yoder, "The Hermeneutics of Peoplehood," 27 (emphasis added).
10. See Yoder, "Binding and Loosing (1992)," 9.
11. Yoder, "Binding and Loosing (1998)," 336.

reconciliation, first going privately to the one who has committed the offense. If this step fails to bring reconciliation, then several others are brought along to try to resolve the conflict. Only after these steps have failed is the person brought before the church. And if the offender refuses to turn away from their sin and to be reconciled to their brothers and sisters, they are set back from the community, not to be treated with contempt, but rather to be treated with love, like the Gentiles and tax collectors who have yet to be reconciled to God.

The consequences for neglecting reconciliation are several: we are not faithful as the church, we impair our witness to the world, and we cause members to look toward secular resources to find some type of fix for their unforgiven sin. However, Yoder writes that the real tragedy

> is not that individuals within the larger society are without guidance and without forgiveness; it is that as *church* we have come to respect as a sign of maturity the willingness to live with directionlessness and with unreconciled divisions and conflicts. We reject as immature or impatient those who would argue that something definitely must or must not be done. We make a virtue of the "acceptance" of intolerable situations rather than of the obedience in openness and forgiveness that could transform situations.[12]

Thus we see the critical importance for the church to practice the ministry of reconciliation. Just as God has forgiven us, so we too are called to forgive one another and to initiate the process of reconciliation. We can sum up this discussion with the words of Paul in Gal 6:1–2: "My friends, if anyone is detected in a transgression, you who have received the Spirit should restore such a one in a spirit of gentleness. Take care that you yourselves are not tempted. Bear one another's burdens, and in this way you will fulfill the law of Christ."

C. RECONCILIATION AND THE LOVE FEAST

1. Reconciliation Prior to the Love Feast

Ideally, there should be opportunities for reconciliation to occur between members of a congregation in the days and weeks before the Love Feast is celebrated. This was the pattern in the early Brethren Love Feast, when the deacons would visit members of the congregation in their homes for

---

12. Ibid., 350 (emphasis in original).

the purpose of members reaffirming their faith and confessing conflict or sin. There were times when a congregation's Love Feast was put off for weeks or months until a certain conflict could be resolved among members. I believe that this was a healthy benefit of the deacon's visit. There were also times when church leaders abused their authority, or were legalistic, or caused more harm than good when they dealt with members who had fallen from grace. Ultimately, these negative stories contributed to the decline of the deacon's visit.[13] But something like the deacon's visit or the process of Matt 18 can happen in churches today. Pastors can provide instruction to members of the congregation on how to take the initiative to work for reconciliation in their personal lives. Assuming that the Love Feast does not happen weekly, churches can focus on reconciliation during the week or two prior to the Love Feast. Such efforts will help the congregation to experience greater unity and will make the experience of the Love Feast a richer one.

2. Reconciliation During the Love Feast: The Sign of Peace

In addition to emphasizing reconciliation prior to the Love Feast, reconciliation should also be a theme during the celebration of the Love Feast. Most often, reconciliation is expressed in the sign of peace: a kiss, a hug, or a handshake. It is not practical to insist on a common expression or practice of reconciliation in churches that celebrate the Love Feast. The reality is that the cultural environment of each church has a significant impact on how expressions of reconciliation are interpreted in the church and in the broader community. Churches that attempt to recover the holy kiss will likely find the task difficult, but in the right community, with the right congregation, leadership, and guidance, I believe that it could be accomplished. A kiss on the cheek should suffice. Certainly the task would prove easier if there were church members who were already accustomed to greeting family members with a kiss. There are several German Baptist Brethren districts (congregations) in southwest Virginia (near where I live) that continue to greet one another with the kiss of peace before and after their worship services and during their Love Feasts (during feetwashing and prior to Communion). It is a strange yet beautiful thing. I recently visited one district, and although it was a bit

13. Another factor in the decline was the emerging role of paid pastors in Brethren churches. As churches began to hire paid pastors, the ministry role of the deacons in the congregation gradually waned.

awkward to see men kissing men, and women kissing women, it was also obvious that this was a familial practice, a social custom. The kiss was shared with a closed mouth, and it was in no way erotic. It seemed clear to me that these brothers and sisters in Christ had deep and strong relationships with one another. I came away from the experience wishing that my own church had that kind of closeness, although I doubt that we would reclaim the actual holy kiss as a Christian greeting.

The reality is that most churches will not reclaim the holy kiss. Yet, as this chapter should make clear, if we find it culturally inappropriate to share the kiss of peace, some other expression of reconciliation should be substituted. Perhaps it will be shaking hands. Perhaps it will be side-hugging.[14] A fist-bump might be more appropriate or meaningful than a handshake in an urban congregation. And feetwashing certainly serves as a powerful physical expression of reconciliation. It requires much forethought and preparation for the sign of reconciliation to be deep and authentic, and not merely a quick handshake or kiss. Based on the history of the church, it seems appropriate for the sign of peace to precede the Eucharist. In the context of the Love Feast, the sign of peace can function as a transition between the fellowship meal and celebration of Communion. In the traditional Brethren Love Feast, the kiss of peace was also shared between members after one had washed the feet of another. As those who have been reconciled to God through Christ, and who have been given the ministry of reconciliation, we need to embody that reconciliation when we celebrate the Love Feast.

> God reconciling the world through Christ is the central story of God's interaction with creation in the Christian tradition. That great story of God drawing us back into the circle of divine love lies also at the very heart of our understanding of the liturgy—that ritual action that both recalls what God has done, makes it present for us now, and points us toward the final consummation and fulfillment.
>
> —ROBERT J. SCHREITER[15]

Forgiveness is the boundary between exclusion and em-

---

14. Many women and men would find side-hugging, as opposed to front-hugging, to be a more appropriate form of hug in a church community, since it is more of a friendly hug (and less of a romantic hug).

15. Schreiter, "Liturgy as Reconciling," 139.

brace. It heals the wounds that the power-acts of exclusion have inflicted and breaks down the dividing wall of hostility. Yet it leaves a distance between people, an empty space of neutrality, that allows them either to go their separate ways in what is sometimes called "peace" or to fall into each other's arms and restore broken communion. . . . But a parting of the ways is clearly not yet peace. Much more than just the absence of hostility sustained by the absence of contact, *peace is communion between former enemies.* Beyond offering forgiveness, Christ's passion aims at restoring such communion—even with the enemies who persistently refuse to be reconciled.

—MIROSLAV VOLF[16]

---

16. Volf, *Exclusion and Embrace*, 125–26 (emphasis in original).

11

Formed to Give Thanks

Past, Present, and Future

Rejoice always, pray without ceasing, give thanks in all
circumstances; for this is the will of God in Christ Jesus
for you.

—1 Thess 5:16–18

Now thank we all our God, with heart and hands and voices,
Who wondrous things has done, in whom this world rejoices,
Who, from our mother's arms, has blessed us on our way,
With countless gifts of love, and still is ours today. . . .
All praise and thanks to God the Father now be given,
The Son, and him who reigns with them in highest heaven;
The one eternal God, whom earth and heaven adore,
For thus it was, is now, and shall be evermore.

—Martin Rinckard[1]

"THE LORD'S SUPPER IN most of our churches . . . is a solemn affair marked by sad, mournful, even morbid thoughts associated
with death," writes Arthur Cochrane. "It is more like a fast than a feast.
It bears little resemblance to the banquet which the father prepared for
his lost son. It seems that we can no longer partake of food with glad and
generous hearts."[2] In chapter 8 we examined ways in which reclaiming
the fellowship meal can help the church more fully to *celebrate* the Lord's
Supper. In this chapter we examine the final element of the Love Feast,
Communion, and how our practices using the bread and cup might
form us more fully to give thanks to God.

1. English translation by Catherine Winkworth (1856), in Slough, ed., *Hymnal: A
Worship Book*, 85.

2. Cochrane, *Eating and Drinking with Jesus*, 74, quoted in Jung, *Sharing Food*, 60.

John Koenig notes that one characteristic of early eucharistic cel-ebration is the way in which it "collapses the past, present, and future sal-vation history into what worshipers may experience as a single visionary moment."[3] This panoramic view of eucharistic worship is evident in the hymn that Paul quotes in Phil 2, in which present worshipers remember the past death of Christ and the future judgment, when every person will confess that Jesus is Lord. In my experience, such a panoramic view is often lacking in our eucharistic worship today. We seem to focus pri-marily on Christ's death on the cross, and perhaps to a slightly lesser extent on Christ's presence to the believer and the community. Rarely in my experience has the celebration of Communion been connected to the hopeful expectation of the return of Christ. Thus, in this chapter we reexamine our practices of Holy Communion, focusing in particular on how our celebration forms us to be a thankful people. First, we look at ways in which we give thanks for past events—most importantly the death and resurrection of Jesus Christ. Next we explore ways in which we are formed to give thanks for our present blessings—especially the continued presence of the risen Christ in the church. Third, we examine how celebrating the Eucharist helps us to be thankful for the future re-turn of the Lord. Finally, we explore a few practical ways for churches to celebrate Communion in the Love Feast.

A. GIVING THANKS FOR THE PAST

1. Thanking God for Jesus Christ

Of all the aspects of thanksgiving associated with Communion, churches are most familiar with remembering the past actions of Jesus Christ. Indeed, this is necessary, for the church would not exist without the historical Jesus of Nazareth, who was executed on a Roman cross in Palestine during the rule of Pontius Pilate. Yet death could not conquer Jesus, being at the same time fully God and fully human. Christians can celebrate Christ's death because we know that he was raised on the third day. It is Christ's resurrection, perhaps more than his death, that redefines Christian worship. Easter, and not Good Friday, is the chief celebration of the church. The church even moved the day of corporate worship from

---

3. Koenig, *Feast of the World's Redemption*, 139. See Koenig's n. 9 for a list of works that support this view.

Saturday to Sunday in order to celebrate the resurrection—which was no small task considering how hard religious traditions die. Of course, because our eucharistic worship uses the bread and cup, which Jesus refers to as his body and blood, it is good and right to focus on the cross, where his body was broken and his blood was shed for the forgiveness of sin. Yet our focus also extends beyond the cross to the resurrection, for the glorious mystery of our faith is that Christ is risen! Thus we are thankful to God for Christ's broken body and shed blood, but also for his resurrected body and blood, which are a sign of the resurrected bodies which we shall receive when the Lord returns.

2. *Thanking God for our Spiritual Ancestors*

We also look to the past to give thanks to God for those who have faithfully passed on the good news of Jesus. We would not be Christians today without those in the past who confessed and lived out faith in Christ. This includes both the "giants of the faith" (like Augustine, Aquinas, Luther, Calvin, Menno, and Mack), but also mothers, fathers, grandparents, pastors, teachers, and spiritual friends who have passed on the faith. In many ways, it is these "lesser giants" who have been more instrumental in our own coming to faith. It is entirely appropriate for churches to take time to remember and give thanks for these individuals during eucharistic worship. This does not mean that we are equating their service with Christ's; it is simply recognition of the fact that we have faith because of their faithfulness and the grace of God.

3. *Thanking God for Our Past Blessings*

We also ought to thank God for our past blessings, both personal and corporate. God is not an absent watchmaker but rather a God who is actively involved in the details of life. Our eucharistic worship should provide opportunities to express thanksgiving for the ways that God has helped us in the past. We offer thanks for moments of spiritual insight, baptismal cleansing, the healing of disease, the restoration of broken relationships, "divine coincidences" that opened doors for both church and personal ministry, and many other blessings. The celebration of Communion becomes more robust as we remember these occasions and return thanks for God's gracious presence and action.

B. GIVING THANKS IN THE PRESENT

1. Thanking God for Christ's Continual Presence

When the church celebrates Communion it is an occasion to offer thanks to God for the miracle of Christ's continual presence in the church. Throughout history there has been much debate over the presence of Christ in the Eucharist, much of which has detracted from Christian unity. Regardless of how we understand Christ's presence in Communion, we must thank God that he is indeed present! The one who knelt to wash feet and who was nailed to a cross is present with us at the table! The resurrected Christ is no longer limited by time and space, and Christ is thus truly and mysteriously present when the church gathers in his name to celebrate the Lord's Supper.

There are two passages in Matthew that help us to understand this presence of Christ. In Matthew's Great Commission, Jesus tells the disciples: "All authority in heaven and on earth has been given to me. Go therefore and make disciples of all nations, baptizing them in the name of the Father and of the Son and of the Holy Spirit, and teaching them to obey everything that I have commanded you. *And remember, I am with you always, to the end of the age*" (Matt 28:18–20, emphasis added). What a reassurance for the disciples to hear that their once-crucified-but-now-resurrected Lord has been given all authority, *and* that he will be with them always as they go out to make disciples of all nations. Only the miracle of the resurrection could make such a magnificent claim believable. And earlier in Matthew we find a similar passage that also addresses both authority and presence: "Truly I tell you [plural],[4] whatever you bind on earth will be bound in heaven, and whatever you loose on earth will be loosed in heaven. Again, truly I tell you, if two of you agree on earth about anything you ask, it will be done for you by my Father in heaven. *For where two or three are gathered in my name, I am there among them*" (Matt 18:18–20, emphasis added). From the context it is clear that Christ is present among his followers, even—and especially—when they are working through conflict. Jesus, the one who has received all authority, shares the authority to forgive sins with the church. We should recall the earlier discussion on feetwashing and spiritual cleans-

---

4. Every "you" is plural in these verses, indicating that Jesus is giving instruction to the church community.

ing (chapter 7), noting that it is the present-yet-invisible Christ who cleanses our brother or sister of sin when we wash their feet. And it is to that same Christ—in the form of our brother or sister—that we must submit, allowing him to cleanse and heal our spirits and minds.

But what about the presence of Christ in the bread and cup? We would do well to avoid the scholastic and philosophical debate over the real presence of Christ in the elements. Catholic theologian Gary Macy argues that modern science and psychology have increasingly narrowed the gap between mind/spirit and body, which may help the church to move beyond the spiritual vs. bodily presence argument. We must have a worldview that allows the ordinary things of life, like bread and wine, to be instrumental in salvation. Then, according to Macy:

> The question whether the risen Lord is present spiritually or bodily would become irrelevant, since both categories are inadequate descriptions of reality (Remember what Christians have always tried to say about the experience of the Lord in the liturgy is that it is real). Irrelevant as well would be questions about when, where, and how long the Lord is present. These questions depend on an understanding of reality that stresses the material as the only real. In any case, the risen Lord is present in our whole lives; that is the point of the eucharistic celebration. It seems rather stingy to begin to debate whether Christ is more or less present here or there, which actually brings us back to the issue of whether we (or a small group of us) can control where the Lord is present.
>
> To give just one example of how one can speak of presence that is real, but not physical, I might simply point out this book. I am not physically present to you, but I certainly am present. I am directing the flow of the words and the presentation of the material. . . . By using the first person, I am not even trying to hide my presence. There is an offer here to share part of my life, my ideas, my life work. You can accept it by reading the book (or at least buying it), or reject it by heaving it across the room (or by at least setting it down). You could go further, and agree with the book (or parts of the book). We would then share at least a small portion of our lives. Now, would you say I was present in, under, or with the book; or present only where the book was, or present to a mouse who nibbled the book? Seem like pretty silly questions, don't they? . . . People (persons) can be present to us when they are not physically present, and actually can be absent to us when their bodies are present. Say, for instance, you find out that a very

good friend of yours was sitting at the table next to you at the restaurant last week, and you never noticed each other. You would
be physically in the same place, but not present to each other.
Worse yet, your friend could have seen you at the restaurant and
you could have seen her, and you both could have snubbed the
other. Presence was offered and presence was rejected. Presence,
then, is a more complex issue than mere proximity.[5]

We can learn from history that it is best to avoid the extremes of speaking
of Christ's presence in the celebration of Communion as purely spiritual
or purely material. In fact, often the best way to do this is to abandon the
distinction itself.

2. Thanking God for the Unity of the Church

We also give thanks to God for the way that God makes the many members of the church into one body; the body of Christ. It does not take
long to realize, in any church gathering, that there are people present
who have different views on a number of subjects, including theology,
politics, and ministry. Yet in the midst of this diversity, God calls the
church to be united under the authority of Christ. Paul writes in 1 Cor
12 that we are members of the body of Christ, and that each of us has
an important function in the life of the church. In order for the body to
work properly, though, each member must be submitted to Christ, the
head of the body. We are also called to yield to one another, not so much
out of duty, but rather out of love. It is cause for thanksgiving when the
church is united thus. And because our congregations are most always
"located" somewhere in between discord and harmony, and rarely in
full communion, we give thanks for the present level of unity and for the
presence of Christ, who is helping us to reach a fuller communion.

3. Really Celebrating!

The celebration of the Eucharist should really feel and look and sound
like a celebration, not a funeral. Many of our experiences of celebration are artificial. When we free ourselves from the perceived need to
look and act respectable (according to society) and allow the joy of the
Lord to be expressed, we move from artificial to authentic celebration.
In fact, it is likely that by putting restraints on godly celebration, we are

5. Macy, *The Banquet's Wisdom*, 252–53.

also limiting our ability to practice the other disciplines of the Christian life. Foster explains: "Celebration gives us the strength to live in all the other disciplines. When faithfully pursued, the other Disciplines bring us deliverance from those things that have made our lives miserable for years which, in turn, evokes increased celebration. Thus an unbroken circle of life and power is formed."[6]

What might it take for us more fully to give thanks and celebrate the Lord's Supper? It may mean increasing the volume of our corporate worship. The Scriptures say "Clap your hands, all you peoples; shout to God with loud songs of joy" (Ps 47:1). Yet too often our celebration of Communion is quiet. How many people do you know who, when learning of great, life-changing news, would go about telling their friends *quietly*? Not many. Instead, with thanksgiving, they share their good news in a loud voice, barely able to contain themselves. Can you not recall someone in a shopping mall or a restaurant blabbing loudly on a cell phone, telling some wonderful story to the person on the other end (who is probably holding the phone several inches away from their ear)? Should not our celebration of the Eucharist be at least this joyful and loud, if not more? For "we've a story to tell to the nations, that shall turn their hearts to the right; a story of truth and sweetness, a story of peace and light."[7] It is a story so good that it should be almost impossible to tell it quietly.[8]

It may also mean that we might find ourselves laughing in worship! Foster writes, "It is an occupational hazard of devout folk to become stuffy bores. This should not be. Of all people, we should be the most free, alive, interesting. Celebration adds a note of gaiety, festivity, hilarity to our lives."[9] And not only to our lives, but to our worship as well. Some of the parables of Jesus are downright funny, and yet they are often read in a boring and monotone fashion. Christ was constantly challenging the Pharisees to understand that God cares about the heart of our worship, and not the outward appearance. If he were physically present today, I have a feeling he would tell us to take ourselves less seriously and to laugh more.

6. Foster, *Celebration of Discipline*, 201.

7. Hymn by Colin Sterne, in *The Broadman Hymnal*, 379.

8. There are, however, appropriate and powerful times of silence and meditation in worship. Many churches seem to do silence well, while worshipers may feel ashamed to get overly excited in worship.

9. Foster, *Celebration of Discipline*, 196.

There are many other ways in which our worship might become more celebratory: dancing, creating art, performing dramas, and feasting. We need not explore each of these here. What is necessary, however, is for us to "get serious" about really celebrating Communion.

4. Avoiding Fatalism

Paul wrote to the Thessalonians that they were to give thanks in all circumstances (1 Thess 5:18). However, this does not mean that we are supposed to consider it good or God's will when evil things happen. Richard Foster explains: "A popular teaching today instructs us to praise God for the various difficulties that come into our lives, asserting that there is great transforming power in thus praising God. In its best form such a teaching is a way of encouraging us to look up the road a bit through the eye of faith and see what will be. It affirms in our hearts the joyful assurance that God takes all things and works them for the good of those who love him. In its worst form this teaching denies the vileness of evil and baptizes the most horrible tragedies as the will of God."[10] There is a difference between fostering an attitude of thanksgiving, even in the midst of the worst circumstances, and celebrating the presence of evil. Scripture commands us to do the first but not the second.

C. GIVING THANKS FOR THE FUTURE

Celebrating Communion today, in the context of the Love Feast, should also focus our attention on the future, the time when Christ will return to the earth in glory. In my experience, celebrating Communion least often has this future-looking focus. Yet the institution narratives of the Lord's Supper in all three synoptic Gospels have Jesus looking forward to the future when he will drink the fruit of the vine (with the disciples) at the banquet table in the Kingdom of God. In 1 Corinthians Paul emphasizes that "as often as you eat this bread and drink the cup, you proclaim the Lord's death *until he comes*" (11:26, emphasis added). The eucharistic prayers in the *Didache* also focus on the end of the present world: "Remember, Lord, your Church, to save it from all evil and to make it perfect by your love. Make it holy, '*and gather*' it 'together from the four winds' *into your Kingdom which you have made ready for it.* . . . Let Grace [i.e., Jesus] come and let this world pass away. Hosanna to the God of

10. Ibid., 194.

David! If anyone is holy, let him come. If not, let him repent. Our Lord, come (*Marana tha*)!" (10:5–6, emphasis added) The future focus of the Eucharist has two facets: the forward movement of the church into the Kingdom of God, and the prayerful expectation of the coming of the Lord. It will help to examine these two aspects in more detail.

First, it is important for our celebration of Communion to emphasize the future-ward movement of the church. The image is one of Christ gathering together the church and pulling it forward into the Kingdom of God; helping the church to ascend heavenward just as Christ has ascended.[11] We can learn something from our Orthodox brothers and sisters on this matter. Theologian Alexander Schmemann writes:

> [U]nder the influence of the western understanding of the eucharist, we usually perceive the liturgy not in the key of *ascent* but of *descent*. The entire western eucharistic mystique is thoroughly imbued with the image of Christ *descending* onto our altars. Meanwhile, the original eucharistic experience . . . speaks of our *ascent* to that place where Christ ascended, of the heavenly nature of the eucharistic celebration. The eucharist is always a going out from 'this world' and an ascent to heaven.[12]

The eucharistic celebration is to remind the church of the *telos* of our faith, the goal of our faith. For we are not forever and always relegated to life on "this world," a world struggling with corruption and death; rather, we are strengthened by the hope of our future resurrection when we will live with Christ in a new heaven and new earth. Communion is a foretaste of this ascension, reminding us to look forward.

---

11. This *does not* mean that Christians are fleeing the earth, for when Christ returns, heaven and earth will be made whole. See Wright, *Surprised by Hope*.

12. Schmemann, *The Eucharist*, 60–61, quoted in Paul, *Feast of Faith*, 47–48. Schmemann continues by describing the importance of understanding the symbolic nature of the altar: "[T]he altar is a symbol of the reality of this ascent, of its very 'possibility.' For Christ has ascended to heaven, and his altar is 'sacred and spiritual.' In 'this world' there *is not and cannot be an altar*, for the kingdom of God is 'not of this world.' And that is why it is so important to understand that we regard the altar with reverence—we kiss it, we bow before it, etc.—not because it is 'sanctified' and has become, so to speak, a 'sacred object,' but because its very sanctification consists in its *referral* to the reality of the kingdom, in its conversion into a symbol of the kingdom. Our reverence and veneration is never related to 'matter,' but always to that which it reveals, of which it is an *epiphany*, i.e., a manifestation and presence." Of course, there are some who would disagree on the importance of using a physical altar in worship, although Schmemann's emphasis on its symbolic nature may help to tone down the disagreement somewhat.

Second, our eucharistic celebration shapes us to be thankful because the church, with fortitude, holds to the promise that Christ will return, at which time the Kingdom of God will be fully established. In my experience, there are many churches in which the Lord's return is either muted in, or absent from, the celebration of the Lord's Supper. Yet both the New Testament and the writings of the early church demonstrate that the petition for Christ's return was central to eucharistic worship. We see this in the frequent use of the early Christian prayer *marana tha* ("Our Lord, come!"). This petition likely had a double meaning; it was both a prayer for the final appearance (*parousia*) of Christ and for his immediate coming to be with the church in the eucharistic celebration.[13] It is likely that, because of our relative prosperity in recent years, many individuals and congregations have felt less of a need to look to the future for God to make things right; for the most part, things are going just fine. Or so we think. If we have neglected regular prayer for the return of the Lord in our eucharistic worship, it is crucial to recover this. Not only will it form us to give thanks for God's ultimate victory, but it can also remind us of the call to increasing holiness, which can be ignored when the *telos* of faith is forgotten.

D. COMMUNION AND THE LOVE FEAST

Celebrating Communion forms us to give thanks to God for the work of Christ in the past, his continued presence with us here and now, and his anticipated return at the end of this age. We now address several practical matters related to the eucharistic celebration during the Love Feast.

1. Who Should Participate in Communion?

I believe that only those who have committed their lives to Christ and have been baptized should partake of the bread and the cup. This has been the tradition of the church, if not from the very beginning, then from the second century onward. When we celebrate Communion, we celebrate the church's unity with the Lord and the unity of members with one another. We must not minimize the otherness of the church, the biblical witness that the church is a holy nation, a people who live in the world but are not of the world. While the fellowship meal should be open to everyone, the celebration of the Eucharist proper (the bread and

---

13. Wainwright, *Eucharist and Eschatology*, 68–70.

the cup) is a unique practice of the family of God, and non-Christians should politely be asked to observe. This does not mean they are of lower value or second class. It is merely a way of maintaining the familial identity of the church, much like the way a guest on a cross-cultural visit might be welcomed to eat with a family, yet would not fully participate in certain rituals connected with the meal (like a prayer), because of differences in language, culture, or religion.

Beyond the distinction of baptism, the Communion table should be open to Christians of all denominations. N. T. Wright observes:

> From the first generation of the Church, eating together was a sign of the breaking down of boundaries between Christians of different groups: Jew and Greek (Galatians 2), rich and poor (1 Corinthians 11), and so on. This was a sign of God's saving justice going out into all the world. When this caused difficulties, Paul was adamant, in the name of Jesus who had included everyone at his table, that unity there was not negotiable. "We, who are many, are one bread, one body—for we all partake of the one bread" (1 Corinthians 10:17). Sharing Communion together between Christians of different denominations ought not to be the goal at the end of a long process of unity negotiations. It ought to be the means, the thing we already do, that will create a context in which we will be able to understand and respect one another, and grow towards richer unity.[14]

In the last decades, progress has been made in helping churches to be open to sharing Communion among other Christians, with whom they once were not open to communing. Let us pray this will continue, so that the Eucharist can more fully be a celebration of Communion for the universal church, and not just a particular congregation.

2. The Breaking of Bread

When we celebrate the Eucharist, we should literally break bread together. This was always the case in the early church, when the Eucharist was a part of a full meal. The breaking of the bread, accompanied with prayers of thanksgiving, was a ritual beginning for the meal, signifying the companionship of the participants. Dale Brown explains that "emphasis is not as much on eating bread as on breaking it. Bread already broken in many places constitutes a privatized symbol of chewing and

---

14. Wright, *The Meal Jesus Gave Us*, 81–82.

swallowing, of individual possession. The breaking of bread signifies the intention to share it, to give it to others, thus portraying the character of Christ's body."[15] We most fully embody the breaking of bread when we share the Eucharist in the context of a fellowship meal. However, on occasions when Communion is celebrated apart from a meal, if we maintain the act of breaking bread together with other members of the church, it helps to counteract the ideas of individualism that can creep into the church (i.e., partaking of Communion is primarily about my personal relationship with God).

3. Celebrating Communion with a Meal

It is important for the church to celebrate Communion with a fellowship meal. This need not be the case for every eucharistic celebration, particularly for those churches that wish to celebrate the Eucharist weekly in a large group setting. While there are logistical challenges inherent in the practice of sharing meals together, this should not diminish the importance of celebrating the Lord's Supper as a substantial meal, rather than a token meal. Groups that want to continue their liturgical practices involving only the bread and cup might explore ways for small groups of church members to celebrate a Love Feast in homes after the large group worship service. Thus, the token meal shared in corporate worship could be a symbol of the full meal shared later in homes. As our postmodern culture increasingly demands authenticity from individuals and communities, it will be important for Communion to be a part of a genuine meal, and not just celebrated as a symbolic meal.

4. How Frequently Should We Celebrate Communion?

Often enough that it characterizes our worship and forms our character. It is sad that some groups in the Reformation encouraged the *limited* practice of the Lord's Supper (i.e., one, two, or four times a year). This only contributed to the view that the Eucharist was a super-sacred supper, at least when compared to ordinary meals. We should consider that Christ can (and often does) indwell the ordinary moments of life, enabling every moment to be sacred and worshipful. When we begin to see our entire lives as a living sacrifice to God, then we realize that eucharistic worship can happen in a house or in a cathedral; among many people

15. Brown, "An Anabaptist Theology of the Sacraments," 17.

or a few; with or without a clergyperson officiating; with or without a full meal. We need to be reminded often that our own denominational tradition does not "own" the only authentic practice of the Lord's Supper. There is much that we can learn from our Christian brothers and sisters concerning ways in which we might more faithfully give thanks to God as we celebrate Communion.

Thankfulness works in the Christian community as it usually does in the Christian life. Only those who give thanks for little things receive the great things as well. We prevent God from giving us the great spiritual gifts prepared for us because we do not give thanks for daily gifts. . . . If we do not give thanks daily for the Christian community in which we have been placed, even when there are no great experiences, no noticeable riches, but much weakness, difficulty, and little faith—and if, on the contrary, we only keep complaining to God that everything is so miserable and so insignificant and does not at all live up to our expectations—then we hinder God from letting our community grow according to the measure and riches that are there for us all in Jesus Christ.

—Dietrich Bonhoeffer[16]

12

Conclusion

Embodying Submission, Love, Confession, Reconciliation, and Thanksgiving

How THEN SHALL WE celebrate the Love Feast today? Will we be open to broadening our eucharistic celebrations by incorporating aspects of the Love Feast, or will we continue to celebrate the Eucharist in the same way? *Why* will we celebrate the Love Feast? Will we celebrate it out of a desire to be historically accurate, or because of our denominational tradition, or because it places the bread and cup celebration in the context of an actual meal? *What will it look like* to celebrate the Love Feast? *What will it sound like*? What sign of peace will we use? Will it always include feetwashing and a fellowship meal? Will it truly be a celebration, or will it be an occasion of mournful remembrance? *Where* will we celebrate the Love Feast? In homes, in churches, in restaurants or community centers? Will it help us to build ecumenical relationships? Will it help us to be missional? *When* will we celebrate the Love Feast? Will the celebration always be at suppertime, or will we celebrate it at lunch or breakfast? *How often* will we celebrate the Love Feast? Monthly? Quarterly? Once or twice a year? *Who will participate* in our Love Feasts? Will we include our neighbors, the poor, and our enemies, or will the Love Feast be celebrated by the faithful few? These are but a few questions that we must wrestle with as we consider how to recover the Love Feast celebration today. And these questions will be answered differently by various groups within the body of Christ.

A. REFLECTING ON THE LOVE FEAST'S HISTORY

The historical evidence is clear that the Love Feast was an important celebration of the early church in some locations, although because the church's worship was pluriform in the early stages, we cannot claim that *all* churches celebrated the Love Feast. We can, however, claim with certainty that the worship of the early church was connected to an evening meal. In chapter 2 we examined the banqueting practices of the Greco-Roman world, which gave us the historical context to understand better the development of the Christian Love Feast. In chapters 3 and 4 we explored the evidence for the Love Feast in the early church. It is probable that the term "Love Feast" originated from the ministry of Jesus. In the Last Supper in John's Gospel, after Jesus washes his disciples feet he gives them a new commandment to love one another (13:34), and after his resurrection, Jesus ate a meal of bread and fish with seven disciples on the shores of Lake Galilee; a meal in which love was the central topic of conversation (John 21). These two meals likely were instrumental in the development of the term "Love Feast" for the Christian worship meal. The only scriptural evidence for the term Love Feast is in Jude 12, although it seems evident that Paul's discussion of Corinthian worship (1 Cor 11–14) is a Love Feast (see ch. 13).

That the fellowship meal was important to the early church is clear from passages in Acts, 1 Corinthians, Galatians, and Jude. The ritual high point of this worship meal soon became the celebration of the bread and the cup, the Eucharist, the Communion. In the early church this remembrance of the body and blood of Christ would likely have occurred during the transition from the meal into the symposium, when a ceremonial libation would have typically been made. The early Christians, instead of dedicating the libation to a pagan god or the emperor, celebrated the cup in honor of and remembrance of their crucified and risen Lord Jesus. It is no wonder that in some locations this evening meal was thought to be seditious, since Jesus, and not Caesar, was honored as Lord. By the end of the first century, the *Didache* makes clear that confessing sins and congregational reconciliation were to be done prior to celebrating the Eucharist. Also, only those who were baptized were permitted to partake of Communion.

The worship activities that followed the meal included offering prayers, singing hymns, reading epistles and the Hebrew scriptures, and listening to instruction. The holy kiss was the greeting given between all

Christians, men and women, a greeting that served to emphasize their new relationship as brothers and sisters in the household of God. Some congregations practiced feetwashing after the command of Christ, either at the beginning of the meal, as was the custom of the day, or during the symposium. Early on the *agape* also seems to have been celebrated as a funerary meal in cemeteries and as a ministry to the poor and those imprisoned.

In the second century, some churches began to celebrate the Eucharist on Sunday morning. In some places the *agape* meal also continued to be celebrated, while other cities seem to have left it behind. Clement of Alexandria indicates that one of the challenges to the Christian Love Feast was the so-called love feast of the Carpocratians, a Gnostic sect whose meal gatherings were notorious for their licentiousness. Of course, the sporadic persecution of Christians throughout the Roman Empire and the restrictions on *collegia* also seem to have negatively impacted the celebration of the Love Feast. Although the Love Feast was still being practiced in some locations in the fourth century, the Constantinian shift sounded the death knell of the practice. As Christian worship moved from homes and cemeteries into basilicas and cathedrals, the "primitive" mealtime worship of the early church was replaced with the formal worship of the church in the empire. The canons of several fourth- and fifth-century church councils make it clear that the celebration of the Love Feast was to be prohibited, and that the Eucharist should only be celebrated apart from a meal.

Beginning in the early 1500s and continuing on into the 1700s, various groups of Christian reformers sought to reclaim the eucharistic practices of the early church. In 1708, the Schwarzenau Brethren celebrated their first Love Feast, which included several practices of the early church that had been recovered by the Anabaptists and Pietists. After migrating to the new world, the Brethren celebrated the first Love Feast in America in 1723. As the Brethren grew in numbers, they began to build meetinghouses, sometimes called "Love Feast houses," which were likely the first American church buildings to contain kitchens. In addition to the Brethren, the Moravians, the Glasites, and the Methodists also reclaimed the celebration of the Love Feast. An important task for the church today is to reflect on the history of eucharistic worship and to consider how well our own eucharistic celebrations embody and communicate the themes of Christian worship.

B. CELEBRATING THE LOVE FEAST TODAY

A central purpose of this book is to clearly articulate that the Love Feast is not just a practice of several fringe groups, but instead is a vital eucharistic celebration for the entire church. It is possible for a wide range of Christian denominations to incorporate aspects of the Love Feast celebration into their current eucharistic practices. It is important to recognize that there is not one authentic, divinely instituted celebration of the Love Feast; rather, there can be a multitude of expressions of the Love Feast, just like there are a variety of forms of baptismal rituals and other worship services across the globe. At the same time, not all Love Feasts are "created equal." Just as Clement of Alexandria had to distinguish the Christian Love Feast from the Carpocratian love feast, so today we too may have to differentiate between competing forms of the Love Feast, using the Scriptures and the witness of church tradition to help us make distinctions. Celebrating the Love Feast can be a powerful practice of Christian discipleship through which God shapes and reforms the church to embody the disciplines of submission, love, confession, reconciliation, and thanksgiving.

1. Submission

Submission is a central biblical theme. As Christians, we are to submit to God and to submit to one another in love. Because of our cultural context and because of past failures in the church, it is often difficult to commend the discipline of submission to church members. Nevertheless, the faithful church will not disregard submission but will instead provide helpful teaching on godly submission. The Love Feast should help to form members of the church to submit to God and to one another. In particular, the practice of feetwashing is a powerful expression of submission. Washing feet reminds us that we must submit to God in Christ, who desires to cleanse us from the filth of our sin. When we stoop to wash the feet of another, we are also practicing submission as we sacrifice our own pride to perform the act of a servant in obedience to the command of Christ. Celebrating the Love Feast forms us to submit.

2. Love

Love is a central biblical theme. Jesus said that all of the Jewish Law and the Prophets can be summed up in the Greatest Commandment: Love the Lord with all of your being and love your neighbor as yourself

(Matt 22:37–39 and parallels). When we celebrate the Love Feast today, we have many opportunities to express love. We express love to God as we worship God during the Love Feast. We practice loving one another in the church as we share a fellowship meal together. We look for opportunities to invite strangers and even enemies to join us in eating, so that we might show them the love of God. Celebrating the Love Feast forms us to love.

3. Confession

Confession is a central biblical theme. Biblical confession is a three-fold task involving the confession of faith, the confession of praise to God, and the confession of sin. We should consider these three types of confession as we celebrate the Love Feast. During the Love Feast, members should have the opportunity to confess their faith in God to one another and, depending on the setting, perhaps to those in the broader community. The church's confession of praises in word and song is also a key element of the Love Feast. The Love Feast also involves the confession of sin, either corporately or individually, or perhaps in both forms. Following Christian tradition, this confession of sin should precede the celebration of the Eucharist. Celebrating the Love Feast forms us to confess.

4. Reconciliation

Reconciliation is a central biblical theme. The Bible tells both of God's actions to reconcile the world to himself and of God's commissioning of Christ-followers to be agents of God's reconciliation in the world. The Love Feast can be an expression of both types of reconciliation. During the Love Feast we remember the atoning death of Christ on the cross, which has reconciled us to God. Congregations would also do well to focus on reconciliation between members in the days prior to the celebration of the Love Feast. And during the Love Feast itself, the sign of peace serves as a physical demonstration of the unity and reconciliation within the body of Christ. Celebrating the Love Feast forms us to reconcile.

5. Thanksgiving

Thanksgiving is a central biblical theme. Christians are to give thanks for God's acts of salvation in the past, the presence of the Holy Spirit in the church today, and the future return of Jesus at the end of the age. These thanksgivings are expressed throughout the Love Feast, but perhaps most especially during the celebration of the Eucharist. Celebrating the Love Feast forms us to give thanks.

In sum, celebrating the Love Feast is an expression of worship to God and an occasion to practice submission, love, confession, reconciliation, and thanksgiving. These disciplines are interrelated and are emphasized throughout the Love Feast. It is not essential that they flow in a particular order, although since they are often connected with certain practices of the Love Feast, it does make sense for some to come before others; for example, confession before sharing the Eucharist. May it be said of us—the members of Christ's body on earth, the church—that our celebration of the Love Feast bears witness to the Kingdom of God. As we glorify God in the Love Feast, may we also experience the sanctifying power of the Holy Spirit forming us to be individuals and communities that embody submission, love, confession, reconciliation, and thanksgiving. Amen.

∾ ∾ ∾

In essentials unity, in non-essentials liberty,
in all things charity.

—Rupertus Meldenius[1]

---

1. Schaff, *History of the Christian Church*, 6:650. Sometimes falsely attributed to Augustine, this maxim was written during the 30 Years War, when Christians were killing one another over religious and political differences.

Bibliography

Aland, Barbara, Kurt Aland, Johannes Karavidopoulos, Carlo M. Martini, and Bruce M. Metzger, eds. *The Greek New Testament.* 4th rev. ed. Stuttgart: Deutsche Bibelgesellschaft, 2001.

Allen, Ronald J. *Wholly Scripture: Preaching Biblical Themes.* St. Louis: Chalice, 2004.

Allison, Richard E. "Feetwashing." In *The Brethren Encyclopedia*, edited by Donald F. Durnbaugh, 481–82. Oak Brook, IL: The Brethren Encyclopedia, Inc., 1983.

———. "Foot Washing." In *The Encyclopedia of Christianity*, edited by Erwin Fahlbusch, 322–23. Grand Rapids: Eerdmans, 2001.

Ambrose. *Ambrose: Select Works and Letters.* Edited by Philip Schaff and Henry Wace. Nicene and Post-Nicene Fathers, 2nd ser., 10. Grand Rapids: Eerdmans, 1955.

———. *On the Holy Spirit*, in *Saint Ambrose: Theological and Dogmatic Works.* 31–216. Washington, D.C.: Catholic University of America Press, 1963.

———. *The Sacraments*, in *Saint Ambrose: Theological and Dogmatic Works.* 265–328. Washington, D.C.: Catholic University of America Press, 1963.

———. *St. Ambrose "on the Mysteries" and the Treatise "on the Sacraments".* Translated by T. Thompson. London: SPCK, 1919.

Apostolic Constitutions, in *Ante-Nicene Fathers*, edited by Alexander Roberts, James Donaldson and A. Cleveland Coxe, 385–508. Grand Rapids: Eerdmans, 1956.

Aquinas, Thomas. *Thomas Aquinas II: The Summa Theologica of Saint Thomas Aquinas.* Vol. 2. Translated by Fathers of the English Dominican Province. Edited by Robert Maynard Hutchins. Great Books of the Western World 20. Chicago: Encyclopædia Britannica, Inc., 1952.

Augustine. *Letters*, in *Nicene and Post-Nicene Fathers*, vol. 1, edited by Philip Schaff, 209–594. Grand Rapids: Eerdmans, 1952.

———. *Lectures or Tractates on the Gospel According to St. John*, in *Nicene and Post-Nicene Fathers*, vol. 7, edited by Philip Schaff, 1–452. Grand Rapids: Eerdmans, 1956.

———. *Reply to Faustus the Manichaean*, in *Nicene and Post-Nicene Fathers*, vol. 4, edited by Philip Schaff, 151–345. New York: Christian Literature Publishing Co., 1890.

———. *Sermons on the Liturgical Seasons.* Translated by Mary Sarah Muldowney. Edited by R. J. Deferrari. The Fathers of the Church 38. New York: Fathers of the Church, 1959.

Bach, Jeff. "The Agape in the Brethren Tradition." In *The Lord's Supper: Believers Church Perspectives*, edited by Dale R. Stoffer, 161–68. Scottdale, PA: Herald, 1997.

Bader-Saye, Scott. "Listening: Authority and Obedience." In *The Blackwell Companion to Christian Ethics*, edited by Stanley Hauerwas and Samuel Wells, 156–68. Malden, MA: Blackwell, 2006.

Bahr, Gordon J. "The Seder of Passover and the Eucharistic Words." *Novum Testamentum* 12, no. 2 (1970) 181–202.

Baker, Frank. *Methodism and the Love-Feast.* London: Epworth, 1957.

Barrett, C. K. *A Critical and Exegetical Commentary on the Acts of the Apostles.* International Critical Commentary. Edinburgh: T. & T. Clark, 1992.

Barth, Karl. *Credo.* Translated by Robert McAfee Brown. New York: Charles Scribner's Sons, 1962.

———. "Faith as Confession: Excerpts from *Dogmatics in Outline.*" In *The World Treasury of Modern Religious Thought*, edited by Jaroslav Pelikan, 123–29. Boston: Little, Brown & Company, 1990.

Bender, Harold S. "The Discipline Adopted by the Strasbourg Conference of 1568." *Mennonite Quarterly Review* 1, no. 1 (1927) 57–66.

Benko, Stephen. "The Kiss." In *Pagan Rome and the Early Christians*, 79–102. Bloomington, IN: Indiana University Press, 1986.

Boismard, M.-E. "Le lavement des pieds (Jn XIII, 1–17)." *Revue Biblique* 71 (1964) 5–24.

Bonhoeffer, Dietrich. *Discipleship.* Translated by Barbara Green and Reinhard Krauss. Edited by Wayne Whitson Floyd, Jr. 16 vols. Dietrich Bonhoeffer Works 4. Minneapolis: Fortress, 2001.

———. *Life Together: Prayerbook of the Bible.* Edited by Wayne Whitson Floyd, Jr. Dietrich Bonhoeffer Works 5. Minneapolis: Augsburg Fortress, 1996.

Bowman, Carl F. *Brethren Society: The Cultural Transformation of a "Peculiar People".* Baltimore: The John's Hopkins University Press, 1995.

Bradshaw, Paul F. "The Reception of Communion in Early Christianity." *Studia Liturgica* 37, no. 2 (2007) 164–80.

———. *The Search for the Origins of Christian Worship.* 2nd ed. New York: Oxford University Press, 2002.

Brown, Dale W. "An Anabaptist Theology of the Sacraments." Presidential address presented at the Midwest Section of the American Theological Society, April 25, 1986.

———. *Another Way of Believing.* Elgin, IL: Brethren, 2005.

Brown, Raymond E. *The Gospel According to John (XIII–XXI).* Anchor Bible 29A. Garden City, NY: Doubleday, 1970.

Brumbaugh, Henry B. *The Brethren's Church Manual.* Huntingdon, PA: Brethren's Publishing, 1887.

Brumbaugh, Martin Grove. *A History of the German Baptist Brethren in Europe and America.* Mount Morris, IL: Brethren Publishing House, 1899.

Buchanan, Mark. "Go Fast and Live: Hunger as Spiritual Discipline." *Christian Century* 118, no. 7 (February 28, 2001) 16–20.

Bultmann, Rudolf. *The Gospel of John: A Commentary.* Translated by George R. Beasley-Murray, R. W. N. Hoare and J. K. Riches. Philadelphia: Westminster, 1971.

Burchard, Christoph. "Joseph and Aseneth." In *Outside the Old Testament*, edited by Marinus de Jonge, 92–110. Cambridge: Cambridge University Press, 1985.

The Canons of Athanasius of Alexandria. Edited by W. Riedeland and W. E. Crum. London: Williams & Norgate, 1904.

Chilton, Bruce D. *A Feast of Meanings: Eucharistic Theologies from Jesus through Johannine Circles*, Nov. Test. Sup. 72. Leiden: E. J. Brill, 1994.

Chrysostom, John. *Saint John Chrysostom: Commentary on Saint John the Apostle and Evangelist, Homilies 44–88.* Edited by T. A. Goggin. New York: Fathers of the Church, 1960.

Clement of Alexandria. *The Instructor,* in *Ante-Nicene Fathers,* vol. 2, edited by Alexander Roberts, James Donaldson and A. Cleveland Coxe, 207–98. Grand Rapids: Eerdmans, 1951.

———. *The Stromata,* in *Ante-Nicene Fathers,* edited by A. Cleveland Coxe, 299–588. Grand Rapids: Eerdmans, 1951.

Cochrane, Arthur C. *Eating and Drinking with Jesus: An Ethical and Biblical Inquiry.* Philadelphia: Westminster, 1974.

Cole, R. Lee. *Love-Feasts: A History of the Christian Agape.* London: Charles H. Kelly, 1916.

Coloe, Mary L. "Sources in the Shadows: John 13 and the Johannine Community." In *New Currents Through John: A Global Perspective,* edited by Francisco Lozada and Tom Thatcher, 69–82. Atlanta: Society of Biblical Literature, 2006.

Colwell, John E. *Promise and Presence: An Exploration of Sacramental Theology.* Milton Keynes, UK: Paternoster, 2005.

Conybeare, Fred C. "The Survival of Animal Sacrifices Inside the Christian Church." *The American Journal of Theology* 7, no. 1 (1903) 62–90.

Corley, Kathleen E. *Private Women, Public Meals: Social Conflict in the Synoptic Tradition.* Peabody, MA: Hendrickson, 1993.

———. "Were the Women Around Jesus Really Prostitutes? Women in the Context of Greco-Roman Meals." In *SBL 1989 Seminar Papers,* edited by D. J. Lull, 487–521. Atlanta: Scholars, 1989.

Cotter, Wendy. "The Collegia and Roman Law: State Restrictions on Voluntary Associations, 64 BCE–200 CE." In *Voluntary Associations in the Graeco-Roman World,* edited by John S. Kloppenborg and Stephen G. Wilson, 74–89. London: Routledge, 1996.

Coxe, A. Cleveland, ed. *Fathers of the Second Century.* Edited by Alexander Roberts and James Donaldson. American ed. Ante-Nicene Fathers 2. Grand Rapids: Eerdmans, 1951.

Cranmer, Thomas. "Of Ceremonies." In *The First and Second Prayer Books of Edward VI.* London: Dent, 1964.

Crossan, John Dominic. *Jesus: A Revolutionary Biography.* San Francisco: Harper San Francisco, 1994.

Cuming, Geoffrey J. "Service-Endings in the Epistles." *New Testament Studies* 22 (1975/6) 110–13.

Cyprian. "The Treatises of Cyprian." In *Ante-Nicene Fathers* 5, edited by Alexander Roberts, James Donaldson and A. Cleveland Coxe, 421–564. Grand Rapids: Eerdmans, 1953.

Daube, David. *The New Testament and Rabbinic Judaism.* New York: Arno, 1973.

Duke, Paul D. "John 13:1–17, 31b–35." *Interpretation* 49, no. 4 (1995) 398–492.

Dupont, Florence. *Daily Life in Ancient Rome.* Oxford: Blackwell, 1992.

Durnbaugh, Donald F. *The Believers' Church: The History and Character of Radical Protestantism.* New York: Macmillan, 1968.

———, ed. *The Brethren Encyclopedia.* Vol. 1. Elgin, IL: Brethren, 1983.

———. *The Brethren in Colonial America.* Elgin, IL: Brethren, 1967.

———. *European Origins of the Brethren: A Source Book on the Beginnings of the Church of the Brethren in the Early Eighteenth Century.* Elgin, IL: Brethren, 1958.

———. *Fruit of the Vine: A History of the Brethren, 1708–1995.* Elgin, IL: Brethren, 1997.

Easton, B. S. *The Apostolic Tradition of Hippolytus*. Cambridge: Cambridge University Press, 1934.

Eller, Vernard. *In Place of Sacraments: A Study of Baptism and the Lord's Supper*. Grand Rapids: Eerdmans, 1972.

Erb, Peter C. "Arnold, Gottfried." In *The Brethren Encyclopedia*, edited by Donald F. Durnbaugh, 57. Oak Brook, IL: The Brethren Encyclopedia, Inc., 1983.

Eshbach, Warren M. "Another Look at John 13:1–20." *Brethren Life and Thought* 14, no. 2 (1969) 117–25.

Ferguson, Everett. *Baptism in the Early Church: History, Theology, and Liturgy in the First Five Centuries*. Grand Rapids: Eerdmans, 2009.

———. "The Lord's Supper in Church History: The Early Church Through the Medieval Period." In *The Lord's Supper: Believers Church Perspectives*, edited by Dale R. Stoffer, 21–45. Scottdale, PA: Herald, 1997.

Finger, Reta Halteman. *Of Widows and Meals: Communal Meals in the Book of Acts*. Grand Rapids: Eerdmans, 2007.

Fitzmyer, Joseph A. *The Gospel According to Luke X-XXIV*. The Anchor Bible 28. Garden City, NY: Doubleday, 1981.

Foster, Richard J. *Celebration of Discipline: The Path to Spiritual Growth*. 25th Anniversary ed. New York: HarperSanFrancisco, 1998.

Freed, Edwin D. *The New Testament: A Critical Introduction*. 2nd ed. Belmont, CA: Wadsworth Publishing, 1991.

Fremantle, Anne Jackson, ed. *A Treasury of Early Christianity*. New York: Viking, 1953.

Frijhoff, Willem. "The Kiss Sacred and Profane: Reflections on a Cross-Cultural Confrontation." In *A Cultural History of Gesture: From Antiquity to the Present Day*, edited by Jan Bremmer and Herman Roodenburg, 210–36. Cambridge: Polity, 1991.

Furnish, Victor Paul. *The Love Command in the New Testament*. Nashville: Abingdon, 1972.

Gager, John G. *Reinventing Paul*. New York: Oxford University Press, 2000.

Gempf, Conrad. *Mealtime Habits of the Messiah: 40 Encounters with Jesus*. Grand Rapids: Zondervan, 2005.

George, Timothy. "Reflections on the Conference." In *The Lord's Supper: Believers Church Perspectives*, edited by Dale R. Stoffer, 266–70. Scottdale, PA: Herald, 1997.

———. *Theology of the Reformers*. Nashville: Broadman, 1988.

Gergen, Kenneth J. *The Saturated Self: Dilemmas of Identity in Contemporary Life*. New York: Basic, 2000.

Goehring, James E. "Withdrawing from the Desert: Pachomius and the Development of Village Monasticism in Upper Egypt." *The Harvard Theological Review* 89, no. 3 (1996) 267–85.

Gonzalez, Justo L. *The Story of Christianity: The Early Church to the Dawn of the Reformation*. Prince Press ed. San Francisco: Harper & Row, 1984.

Goudey, June Christine. *The Feast of Our Lives: Re-imaging Communion*. Cleveland: Pilgrim, 2002.

Graber-Miller, Keith. "Mennonite Footwashing: Identity Reflections and Altered Meanings." *Worship* 66 (March 1992) 148–69.

Hall, Douglas John. *Confessing the Faith: Christian Theology in a North American Context*. Minneapolis: Fortress, 1996.

Harland, Philip. *Associations, Synagogues, and Congregations: Claiming a Place in Ancient Mediterranean Society.* Minneapolis: Fortress, 2003.

Hauerwas, Stanley. *After Christendom? How the Church is to Behave if Freedom, Justice, and Christian Nation are Bad Ideas.* Nashville: Abingdon, 1991.

———. "Casuistry in Context: The Need for Tradition." In *The Hauerwas Reader*, edited by John Berkman and Michael Cartwright, 267–84. Durham: Duke University Press, 2001.

———. "The Church as God's New Language." In *The Hauerwas Reader*, edited by John Berkman and Michael Cartwright, 142–62. Durham: Duke University Press, 2001.

Hauerwas, Stanley, and Samuel Wells. "How the Church Managed Before There Was Ethics." In *The Blackwell Companion to Christian Ethics*, edited by Stanley Hauerwas and Samuel Wells, 39–50. Malden, MA: Blackwell, 2006.

Hays, Richard B. *First Corinthians*, Interpretation: A Bible Commentary for Teaching and Preaching. Louisville, KY: John Knox, 1997.

———. *The Moral Vision of the New Testament: Community, Cross, New Creation.* New York: HarperCollins, 1996.

Hippolytus. *On the Apostolic Tradition.* Edited by Alistair Stewart-Sykes. Popular Patristics Series 22. Crestwood, NY: St. Vladimir's Seminary Press, 2001.

Holsinger, Henry R. *History of the Tunkers and the Brethren Church.* Lathrop, CA: privately printed, 1901.

Jeremias, Joachim. *The Eucharistic Words of Jesus.* Translated by Norman Perrin. Philadelphia: Fortress, 1966.

Jewett, Robert. "Tenement Churches and Pauline Love Feasts." *Quarterly Review* 14, no. 1 (1994) 43–58.

Johnson, Luke Timothy. *Religious Experience in Earliest Christianity: A Missing Dimension in New Testament Studies.* Minneapolis: Fortress, 1998.

Joncas, Jan Michael. "Tasting the Kingdom of God: The Meal Ministry of Jesus and Its Implications for Contemporary Worship and Life." *Worship* 74, no. 4 (2000) 329–65.

Jung, L. Shannon. *Food for Life: The Spirituality and Ethics of Eating.* Minneapolis: Fortress, 2004.

———. *Sharing Food: Christian Practices for Enjoyment.* Minneapolis: Fortress, 2006.

Justin Martyr. "First Apology." In *Early Christian Fathers*, edited by Cyril C. Richardson, 225–89. Philadelphia: Westminster, 1953.

Kant, Immanuel. "What is Enlightenment?" In *Foundations of the Metaphysics of Morals and What is Enlightenment?* Indianapolis: Bobbs-Merrill, 1959.

Keating, J. F. *The Agape and the Eucharist in the Early Church: Studies in the History of the Christian Love-Feasts.* 2009 BiblioLife ed. London: Methuen, 1901.

Kettering, Denise D. "'Greet One Another with a Holy Kiss': The Evolution of the Holy Kiss in the Church of the Brethren." In *Lines, Places, and Heritage: Essays Commenorating the 300th Anniversary of the Church of the Brethren*, edited by Stephen L. Longenecker and Jeff Bach, 197–211. Bridgewater, VA: Penobscot, 2008.

Key, Newton E. "The Political Culture and Political Rhetoric of County Feasts and Feast Sermons, 1654–1714." *The Journal of British Studies* 33, no. 3 (1994) 223–56.

Kirk, David. "Hospitality: Essence of Eastern Christian Lifestyle." *Diakonia* 16, no. 2 (1981) 104–17.

"Kiss of Peace." In *Concise Dictionary of the Christian Church*, edited by E. A. Livingstone, 325. Oxford: Oxford University Press, 2000.

Klaassen, Walter. *Anabaptism in Outline*. Scottdale, PA: Herald, 1981.

Kloppenborg, John S., and Stephen G. Wilson, eds. *Voluntary Associations in the Graeco-Roman World*. London: Routledge, 1996.

Koenig, John. *The Feast of the World's Redemption: Eucharistic Origins and Christian Mission*. Harrisburg, PA: Trinity Press International, 2000.

Kreider, Alan. *The Change of Conversion and the Origin of Christendom*. Harrisburg, PA: Trinity Press International, 1999.

———. "Peacemaking in Worship in the Syrian Church Orders." *Studia Liturgica* 34 (2004) 177–90.

Kreider, Eleanor. *Communion Shapes Character*. Scottdale, PA: Herald, 1997.

———. "Let the Faithful Greet each Other: The Kiss of Peace." *Conrad Grebel Review* 5, no. 1 (1987) 29–49.

Lehman, James H. *The Old Brethren*. Elgin, IL: Brethren, 1976.

Leon-Dufour, Xavier. *Sharing the Eucharistic Bread: The Witness of the New Testament*. New York: Paulist, 1987.

Lietzmann, Hans. *Mass and the Lord's Supper: A Study in the History of the Liturgy*. Translated by D. H. G. Reave. Leiden: E. J. Brill, 1926, 1979.

Livingstone, E. A. *The Concise Oxford Dictionary of the Christian Church*. 2nd ed. Oxford: Oxford University Press, 2000.

Lucian. *Lucian: Demonax*. Translated by A. M. Harmon. London: Heinemann, 1913.

Mack, Alexander. "Rights and Ordinances." In *European Origins of the Brethren*, edited by Donald F. Durnbaugh, 344–404. Elgin, IL: Brethren, 1958.

Mack, Alexander, Sr. *The Complete Writings of Alexander Mack*. Edited by William R. Eberly. Winona Lake, IN: BMH, 1991.

Mack, Burton. *A Myth of Innocence: Mark and Christian Origins*. Philadelphia: Fortress, 1988.

Macy, Gary. *The Banquet's Wisdom: A Short History of the Theologies of the Lord's Supper*. Akron, OH: OSL Publications, 2005.

Marpeck, Pilgram. *The Writings of Pilgram Marpeck*. Translated by William Klassen and Walter Klaassen. Edited by William Klassen and Walter Klaassen. Scottdale, PA: Herald, 1978.

Martin, Ralph P. *A Hymn of Christ: Philippians 2:5–11 in Recent Interpretation and in the Setting of Early Christian Worship*. Westmont: InterVarsity, 1997.

———. *New Testament Foundations*. Vol. 1. Exeter: Paternoster, 1975.

McGowan, Andrew. "Rethinking Agape and Eucharist in Early North-African Christianity." *Studia Liturgica* 34 (2004) 165–76.

McKinnell, James C. "The Lord's Supper: Its Relevance for Faith and Worship." *Brethren Life and Thought* 7, no. 2 (1962) 44–59.

McKinney, B. B., ed. *The Broadman Hymnal*. Nashville: Broadman, 1940.

McLuhan, Marshall. *Understanding Media: The Extensions of Man*. 1st MIT Press ed. Cambridge, MA: MIT, 1994.

McMillon, Lynn A. "Discovery of the Earliest Extant Scottish Restoration Congregation." *Restoration Quarterly* 30, no. 1 (1988) 43–52.

Meier, Marcus. "Eberhard Ludwig Gruber's *Basic Questions*: Report of a Discovery." *Brethren Life and Thought* 43, no. 3 & 4 (1997) 64–67.

———. *The Origin of the Schwarzenau Brethren*. Translated by Dennis L. Slabaugh. Edited by William R. Eberly. Brethren Encyclopedia Monograph Series 7. Philadelphia: Brethren Encyclopedia, 2008.

Metzger, Bruce M. *A Textual Commentary on the Greek New Testament*. New York: United Bible Societies, 1975.

Minucius Felix. *The Octavius of Minucius Felix*, in *The Ante-Nicene Fathers*, vol. 4, edited by Alexander Roberts, James Donaldson and A. Cleveland Coxe, 173–98. Grand Rapids: Eerdmans, 1951.

Mish, Frederick C., ed. *Merriam-Webster's Collegiate Dictionary*. 10th ed. Springfield, MA: Merriam Webster, Inc., 2001.

Moloney, Francis J. *A Body Broken for a Broken People: Eucharist in the New Testament*. Rev. ed. Peabody, MA: Hendrickson Publishers, 1997.

———. "A Sacramental Reading of John 13:1–38." *Catholic Biblical Quarterly* 53 (1991) 242–48.

Morse, Kenneth I. "Lessons Learned at the Love Feast." In *The Brethren Encyclopedia*, edited by Donald F. Durnbaugh, 765. Oak Brook, IL: The Brethren Encyclopedia, Inc., 1983.

Nation, Mark Thiessen. "Washing Feet: Preparation for Service." In *The Blackwell Companion to Christian Ethics*, edited by Stanley Hauerwas and Samuel Wells, 441–51. Oxford: Blackwell, 2004.

Nead, Peter. *Primitive Christianity, or A Vindication of the Word of God*. Staunton, VA: Kenton Harper, 1834.

"The New Testament as our Rule of Faith and Practice." Paper presented at the Church of the Brethren Annual Conference, Orlando, FL, 1998.

Neyrey, Jerome H. "Meals, Food and Table Fellowship." In *The Social Sciences and New Testament Interpretation*, edited by Richard Rohrbaugh, 159–82. Peabody, MA: Hendrickson Publishers, 1996.

O'Day, Gail R. "The Gospel of John." In *The New Interpreter's Bible*, edited by Leander E. Keck, 491–865. Nashville: Abingdon, 1995.

Okure, Teresa. "'The Ministry of Reconciliation' (2 Cor 5:14–21): Paul's Key to the Problem of 'the Other' in Corinth." *Mission Studies* 23, no. 1 (2006) 105–21.

Oulton, John Ernest Leonard, and Henry Chadwick, eds. *Alexandrian Christianity: Selected Translations of Clement and Origen*. Library of Christian Classics 2. Philadelphia: Westminster, 1954.

Packer, James E. "Housing and Population in Imperial Ostia and Rome." *The Journal of Roman Studies* 57, no. 1 (1967) 80–95.

Parkes, William. "Watchnight, Covenant Service, and the Love-Feast in Early British Methodism." *Wesleyan Theological Journal* 32, no. 2 (1997) 35–58.

Paul, Archbishop of Finland. *Feast of Faith: An Invitation to the Love Feast of the Kingdom of God*. Crestwood, NY: St. Vladimir's Seminary Press, 1988.

Pelikan, Jaroslav. *Credo: Historical and Theological Guide to Creeds and Confessions in the Christian Tradition*. New Haven: Yale University Press, 2003.

Penn, Michael. "Performing Family: Ritual Kissing and the Construction of Early Christian Kinship." *Journal of Early Christian Studies* 10, no. 2 (2002) 151–74.

———. "Review of *Ascetic Eucharists*." *Church History* 69, no. 2 (2000) 403–4.

———. "Ritual Kissing, Heresy and the Emergence of Early Christian Orthodoxy." *Journal of Ecclesiastical History* 54, no. 4 (2003) 625–40.

Percival, Henry R., ed. *The Seven Ecumenical Councils*. Edited by Philip Schaff and Henry Wace. Nicene and Post-Nicene Fathers, 2nd ser., 14. Grand Rapids: Eerdmans, 1965.

Perella, Nicolas J. *The Kiss Sacred and Profane: An Interpretive History of Kiss Symbolism and Related Religio-Erotic Themes.* Berkeley, CA: University of California Press, 1969.

Perkins, William Rufus, and Barthinius L. Wick. *History of the Amana Society or Community of True Inspiration.* Iowa City: University of Iowa Press, 1891.

Phillips, L. Edward. "The Kiss of Peace and the Opening Greeeting of the Pre-anaphoral Dialogue." *Studia Liturgica* 23 (1993) 177–86.

———. *The Ritual Kiss in Early Christian Worship.* Cambridge: Grove, 1996.

Plumptre, Edward Hayes. "Agapae." In *A Dictionary of Christian Antiquities*, edited by William Smith and Samuel Cheetham, 39–41. London: John Murray, 1893.

Pohl, Christine D. *Making Room: Recovering Hospitality as a Christian Tradition.* Grand Rapids: Eerdmans, 1999.

Pope Pius X. "*Tra le sollecitudini*." In *The New Liturgy*, edited by Kevin Seasoltz, O.S.B. New York: Herder & Herder, 1966.

Ramirez, Frank. *The Love Feast.* Elgin, IL: Brethren, 2000.

Ramsay, William. *A Manual of Roman Antiquities.* 17th ed. London: Charles Griffin & Company, 1901.

Ratzinger, Cardinal Joseph, ed. *Catechism of the Catholic Church.* San Francisco: Ignatius, 1994.

Richardson, Cyril C. *Early Christian Fathers.* The Library of Christian Classics 1. Philadelphia: Westminster, 1953.

Richey, Russell E. "Family Meal, Holy Communion, and Love Feast: Three Ecumenical Perspectives." In *Ecumenical and Interreligious Perspectives: Globalization in Theological Education*, edited by Russell E. Richey, 17–29. Nashville: QR, 1992.

Richter, Georg. *Die Fusswaschung im Johannesevangelium.* Regensburg: Pustet, 1967.

Roth, Leland M. *Understanding Architecture: Its Elements, History and Meaning.* Boulder, CO: Westview, 2007.

Ruth, Lester. "A Little Heaven Below: The Love Feast and Lord's Supper in Early American Methodism." *Wesleyan Theological Journal* 32, no. 2 (1997).

Sampley, J. Paul. "The Second Letter to the Corinthians." In *The New Interpreter's Bible.* Vol. 11, edited by Leander E. Keck, 1–180. Nashville: Abingdon, 2000.

Sappington, Roger E. *The Brethren in Industrial America: A Source Book on the Development of the Church of the Brethren, 1865–1915.* Elgin, IL: Brethren, 1985.

Schaff, David S. *The Middle Ages: Part I (1049–1294).* Edited by Philip Schaff. History of the Christian Church 5. New York: Charles Scribner's Sons, 1916.

Schaff, Philip. *Ante-Nicene Christianity (A.D. 100–325).* 8th ed. History of the Christian Church 2. New York: Charles Scribner's Sons, 1908.

———. *History of the Christian Church: Modern Christianity and the German Reformation.* Vol. 6. 2nd rev. ed. New York: Charles Scribner's Sons, 1911.

———. *Nicene and Post-Nicene Christianity (A.D. 311–600).* History of the Christian Church 3. New York: Charles Scribner's Sons, 1910.

Schlosser, Eric. *Fast Food Nation: The Dark Side of the All-American Meal.* New York: Perennial, 2002.

Schmemann, Alexander. *The Eucharist: Sacrament of the Kingdom.* Crestwood, NY: St. Vladimir's Seminary Press, 1988.

Schneider, Hans. "'Basic Questions on Water Baptism': An Early Anti-Brethren Pamphlet." *Brethren Life and Thought* 43, no. 3 & 4 (1997) 31–63.

Schreiter, Robert J. "Liturgy as Reconciling." *Liturgical Ministry* 17, no. 3 (2008) 139–45.

Segovia, Fernando F. "John 13:1–20: The Footwashing in the Johannine Tradition." *Zeitschrift für die Neutestamentliche Wissenschaft* 73 (1982) 31–51.

Shepherd, Massey H., Jr. "Smyrna in the Ignatian Letters: A Study in Church Order." *The Journal of Religion* 20, no. 2 (1940) 141–59.

Shuman, L. Herman. "Kiss, Holy." In *The Brethren Encyclopedia*, edited by Donald F. Durnbaugh, 698–99. Oak Brook, IL: The Brethren Encyclopedia, Inc., 1983.

Slough, Rebecca, ed. *Hymnal: A Worship Book*. Elgin, IL: Brethren, 1992.

Smith, Dennis E. *From Symposium to Eucharist: The Banquet in the Early Christian World*. Minneapolis: Fortress, 2003.

Smith, Jonathan Z. *Drudgery Divine: On the Comparisons of Early Christianities and the Religions of Late Antiquity*. Jordan Lectures in Comparative Religion 14. Chicago Studies in the History of Judaism. Chicago: University of Chicago Press, 1990.

Snyder, C. Arnold. *Following in the Footsteps of Christ: The Anabaptist Tradition*. Edited by Philip Sheldrake. Traditions of Christian Spirituality. Maryknoll, NY: Orbis, 2004.

———. *From Anabaptist Seed: The Historical Core of Anabaptist-Related Identity*. Kitchener, ON: Pandora, 1999.

———, ed. *Sources of South German/Austrian Anabaptism*. Kitchener, ON: Pandora, 2001.

Snyder, Graydon F. *Ante Pacem: Archaeological Evidence of Church Life before Constantine*. Macon, GA: Mercer University Press, 1985.

———. *First Corinthians: A Faith Community Commentary*. Macon, GA: Mercer University Press, 1992.

———. *Inculturation of the Jesus Tradition: The Impact of Jesus on Jewish and Roman Cultures*. Harrisburg, PA: Trinity Press International, 1999.

———. "Love Feast." In *The Brethren Encyclopedia*, edited by Donald F. Durnbaugh, 762–65. Oak Brook, IL: The Brethren Encyclopedia, Inc., 1983.

Socrates Scholasticus. *Ecclesiastical History*. NPNF, 2nd ser., 2. New York: Christian Literature Publishing Co., 1886.

Song, Robert. "Sharing Communion: Hunger, Food, and Genetically Modified Foods." In *The Blackwell Companion to Christian Ethics*, edited by Stanley Hauerwas and Samuel Wells, 388–400. Oxford: Blackwell, 2004.

Stendahl, Krister. "The Apostle Paul and the Introspective Conscience of the West." In *Paul among Jews and Gentiles, and Other Essays*, 78–96. Philadelphia: Fortress, 1976.

Stewart-Sykes, Alistair. "Commentary on the Apostolic Tradition." In *On the Apostolic Tradition*, edited by Alistair Stewart-Sykes, 53–205. Crestwood, NY: St. Vladimir's Seminary Press, 2001.

Stoffer, Dale R., ed. *The Lord's Supper: Believers Church Perspectives*. Scottdale, PA: Herald, 1997.

Stowers, Stanley K. *A Rereading of Romans: Justice, Jews, and Gentiles*. New York: Yale University Press, 1994.

Taussig, Hal. *In the Beginning was the Meal: Social Experimentation and Early Christian Identity*. Minneapolis: Fortress, 2009.

Taussig, Hal, and Catherine T. Nerney. *Re-Imagining Life Together in America: A New Gospel of Community*. Lanham, MD: Sheed & Ward, 2002.

Tertullian. *Anti-Marcion*, in *Ante-Nicene Fathers*, vol. 3, edited by Alexander Roberts, James Donaldson and Allan Menzies, 237–654. Grand Rapids: Eerdmans, 1951.

———. *Apology*, in *Ante-Nicene Fathers*, vol. 3, edited by Allan Menzies, 17–60. Grand Rapids: Eerdmans, 1951.

———. *De Corona*, in *Ante-Nicene Fathers*, vol. 3, edited by Allan Menzies, 93–104. Grand Rapids: Eerdmans, 1951.

———. *On Prayer*, in *Ante-Nicene Fathers*, vol. 3, edited by Allan Menzies, 681–92. Grand Rapids: Eerdmans, 1951.

———. *On Repentance*, in *Ante-Nicene Fathers*, vol. 3, edited by Allan Menzies, 657–68. Grand Rapids: Eerdmans, 1951.

———. *To His Wife*, in *Ante-Nicene Fathers*, vol. 4, edited by Alexander Roberts and James Donaldson, 39–49. Grand Rapids: Eerdmans, 1951.

Thomas, John Christopher. *Footwashing in John 13 and the Johannine Community*. Journal for the Study of the New Testament Supplement Series 61. Sheffield: JSOT, 1993.

———. "Footwashing Within the Context of the Lord's Supper." In *The Lord's Supper: Believers Church Perspectives*, edited by Dale R. Stoffer. Scottdale, PA: Herald, 1997.

Thurston, Herbert. "Washing of Feet and Hands." In *The Catholic Encyclopedia*. New York: Robert Appleton, 1912. www.newadvent.org/cathen/15557b.htm.

Townsend, Michael J. "Exit the Agape?" *The Expository Times* 90 (September 1979) 356–61.

Vanier, Jean. *The Scandal of Service: Jesus Washes our Feet*. New York: Continuum, 1998.

Vedder, Henry C. *Balthasar Hubmaier: The Leader of the Anabaptists*. New York: AMS, 1971.

Visser, Margaret. *The Rituals of Dinner: The Origins, Evolution, Eccentricities, and Meaning of Table Manners*. New York: Penguin, 1991.

Volf, Miroslav. *Exclusion and Embrace: A Theological Exploration of Identity, Otherness, and Reconciliation*. Nashville: Abingdon, 1996.

Wainwright, Geoffrey. *Eucharist and Eschatology*. American ed. New York: Oxford University Press, 1981.

Watson, Duane F. "The Letter of Jude." In *The New Interpreter's Bible*. Vol. 10, edited by Leander E. Keck, 473–500. Nashville: Abingdon, 1998.

WCC. "Baptism, Eucharist and Ministry." Paper presented at the Faith and Order Conference of the World Council of Churches, Paper No. 111, Lima, 1982.

Weiser, A. "Joh 13, 12–20: Zufügung eines späteren Herausgebers?" *Biblische Zeitschrift* 12 (1968) 252–57.

Wells, Samuel. *God's Companions: Reimagining Christian Ethics*. Oxford: Blackwell, 2006.

Wenger, J. C., ed. *The Complete Writings of Menno Simons*. Scottdale, PA: Herald, 1956.

Wesley, John. *The Journal of the Rev. John Wesley*. Edited by Nehemiah Curnock. London: Epworth, 1909.

White, James F. *Documents of Christian Worship: Descriptive and Interpretive Sources*. Louisville: Westminster John Knox, 1992.

———. *Introduction to Christian Worship*. 3rd ed. Nashville: Abingdon, 2000.

Wilken, Robert Louis. *The Christians as the Romans Saw Them*. 2nd ed. New Haven: Yale University Press, 2003.

Williams, George H., and Angel M. Mergal, eds. *Spiritual and Anabaptist Writers*. Ichthus ed. The Library of Christian Classics 25. Philadelphia: Westminster, 1957.

Wink, Walter. *The Powers That Be: Theology for a New Millennium*. New York: Doubleday, 1998.

Witherington III, Ben. "'Making a Meal of It': The Lord's Supper in Its First-Century Social Setting." In *The Lord's Supper: Believers Church Perspectives*, edited by Dale R. Stoffer, 81–113. Scottdale, PA: Herald, 1997.

———. *Making a Meal of It: Rethinking the Theology of the Lord's Supper*. Waco: Baylor University Press, 2007.

Woolfenden, Graham. "'Let Us Offer Each Other the Sign of Peace'—An Enquiry." *Worship* 67, no. 3 (1993) 239–52.

Wright, N. T. *Surprised by Hope: Rethinking Heaven, the Resurrection, and the Mission of the Church*. New York: HarperOne, 2008.

Wright, Tom. *The Meal Jesus Gave Us: Understanding Holy Communion*. Louisville, KY: Westminster John Knox, 1999.

Yoder, John Howard. "Binding and Loosing." In *The Royal Priesthood: Essays Ecclesiological and Ecumenical*, edited by Michael G. Cartwright, 323–58. Scottdale, PA: Herald, 1998.

———. "Binding and Loosing." In *Body Politics: Five Practices of the Christian Community Before the Watching World*, 1–13. Nashville: Discipleship Resources, 1992.

———. *Body Politics: Five Practices of the Christian Community before the Watching World*. Scottdale, PA: Herald, 1992.

———. "The Constantinian Sources of Western Social Ethics." In *The Priestly Kingdom: Social Ethics as Gospel*, 135–47. Notre Dame: University of Notre Dame Press, 1984.

———. "The Hermeneutics of Peoplehood." In *The Priestly Kingdom: Social Ethics as Gospel*, 15–45. Notre Dame: University of Notre Dame Press, 1984.

———. "The Hermeneutics of Peoplehood: A Protestant Perspective." In *The Priestly Kingdom: Social Ethics as Gospel*, 15–45. Notre Dame: University of Notre Dame Press, 1984.

———. "The Otherness of the Church." In *The Royal Priesthood: Essays Ecclesiological and Ecumenical*, edited by Michael G. Cartwright, 53–64. Scottdale, PA: Herald, 1998.

———. *The Politics of Jesus*. 2nd ed. Grand Rapids: Eerdmans, 1994.

Zodhiates, Spiros. *The Complete Word Study Dictionary: New Testament*. Iowa Falls, IA: World Bible Publishers, Inc., 1992.

Scripture Index

Ancient Documents Index

Subject/Name Index

A

agape, agapais, 30–34, 42–44, 65, 66, 72n4, 75, 77–83, 90, 105, 114–16, 119–21, 145, 149, 157, 187–89
Allen, Ronald J., 54
Allison, Richard E., 55, 153
Amana Society, 156–57
Anabaptist(s), 138, 140–45, 179, 229
anamnesis, 31, 33, 49n46, 85
Aquinas, Thomas, 203, 206
Armenian Church, 114n9
Arnold, Gottfreid, 146, 147, 160

B

Bach, Jeff, 31, 146
Bader-Saye, Scott, 169, 170
Bahr, Gordon J., 24–26
ban, 140n4, 141–43
baptism, 56, 59, 60, 112, 129, 130, 136n55, 148, 175, 225
Barth, Karl, 208–212
basilica, 101, 117, 118
Benko, Stephen, 52, 53, 93
Bonhoeffer, Dietrich, 216, 247
Bowman, Carl, 151–154, 215
breaking of bread, 31–34, 39–41, 49, 142n8, 153n43, 178, 245, 246
Brethren, 134n53, 135, 147–156, 161, 162, 176, 179, 199, 210n13, 215n18, 232
Brown, Dale W., 41, 246
Brumbaugh, H. B., 150
Brumbaugh, M. G., 147, 149

C

Carpocrates, Carpocratian, 81, 82, 95, 109, 188
Cassian, John, 133
catacombs, 77, 86, 124
catechumens, 95, 102, 103, 111, 112n4, 126
Chilton, Bruce D., 31, 32
Cole, R. Lee, 6, 19, 32, 44, 77, 116, 157, 158
collegia, 17–21, 74, 76, 77
Colwell, John, 59–61, 176, 216, 217, 225
Communion, 30, 32, 44, 47, 72, 86, 88, 94, 102, 104, 107, 115, 119n23, 137, 139, 149n32, 150–55, 187, 188, 200–2, 217, 236–38, 241–49. *See also* Eucharist; Lord's Supper.
confession, 28, 60n82, 103–7, 135, 136, 139, 142, 203–21
Constantine, Constantinian, 71, 110–13, 117, 124, 128, 135–37
Conybeare, Fred, 114
Corley, K. E., 8, 16
Council
    Fourth Lateran, 138
    of Ancyra, 114, 116
    of Carthage, 119, 120
    of Gangra, 114, 116
    of Trullo, 119, 120
county feast, 145, 146
Cranmer, Thomas, 165
Crossan, John Dominic, 45
Cuming, G. J., 53, 54

thanksgiving, 23, 31, 45, 70, 72, 75, 93,
        115, 158n59, 190n6, 203, 204,
        206n6, 235–47
Thomas, John Christopher, 12, 55–59,
        65, 129, 131–33
Townsend, Michael J., 33
Trajan, Emperor, 20, 21, 73, 74
transubstantiation, 45n38, 138, 139n1

U

unity, 32, 37, 38, 57, 67, 69n97, 70, 83,
        93, 94, 125–27, 137, 139n1, 145,
        150–54, 214, 215, 220, 232, 238,
        240, 244, 245, 253

V

Vanier, Jean, 185
Vedder, Henry C., 144
Visser, Margaret, 14, 15, 98
Volf, Miroslav, 234

W

Wainwright, Geoffrey, 31n4, 50n49,
        244n13
Wells, Samuel, 5, 161, 180, 182, 201
Wesley, John, 158, 159
White, James F., 139, 165
Williams, George H., 141, 144
Wink, Walter, 197, 198
Witherington III, Ben, 8, 33, 35, 116,
        118, 124, 139
women, 10, 11, 16, 35, 36n16, 55,
        65, 72n4, 73, 81, 95–97, 108,
        118n17, 127, 144n18, 155, 157,
        178, 218, 233
Wright, N. T., 226, 243, 245

Y

Yoder, John H., 40, 41, 60, 61, 112, 113,
        136, 170, 172, 173, 193, 229–31